AMERICAN DETECTIVE

AMERICAN DETECTIVE

Behind the Scenes of Famous Criminal Investigations

THOMAS A. REPPETTO

POTOMAC BOOKS | *An imprint of the University of Nebraska Press*

All rights reserved. Potomac Books is an
imprint of the University of Nebraska Press.
Manufactured in the United States of America.

Library of Congress Cataloging-in-Publication Data
Names: Reppetto, Thomas A., author.
Title: American detective: behind the
scenes of famous criminal investigations
/ Thomas A. Reppetto.
Description: Lincoln: Potomac Books, an imprint
of the University of Nebraska Press. [2018] |
Includes bibliographical references and index.
Identifiers: LCCN 2017052153
ISBN 9781640120228 (cloth: alk. paper)
ISBN 9781640120570 (epub)
ISBN 9781640120587 (mobi)
ISBN 9781640120594 (web)
Subjects: LCSH: Criminal investigation—United
States—History—20th century. | Crime—
United States—History—20th century.
Classification: LCC HV8141 .R395 2018 |
DDC 363.250973—dc23 LC record available
at https://lccn.loc.gov/2017052153

Set in Sabon Next by E. Cuddy.
Designed by N. Putens.

To the memory of Arthur Hale Woods, 1870–1942, deputy commissioner of the NYPD in charge of detectives, 1907–9; police commissioner, 1914–17; colonel, U.S. Army, 1918–19. Awarded Distinguished Service Medal (U.S.), Order of St. Michael and St. George (UK), and Chevalier of the Legion of Honor (France). A brilliant police administrator, with an exceptional knowledge of detective work.

Contents

Illustrations

Snapshots from the Lost World of Detectives

San Francisco, October 9, 1926

TERROR IN THE STREETS

In the 1920s automobiles gave criminals a means of striking anywhere in a community and making a quick escape. One police chief who became impressed with this fact was Dan O'Brien of San Francisco. On Saturday, October 9, 1926, shortly before midnight, as O'Brien and his wife were leaving the home of friends, he heard the sound of gunshots around the corner. He sent his wife back into the house and ran to the scene with his driver, Sergeant Neely. There they found a man dying in the street. Just then a sedan raced down the street, and when O'Brien and Neely signaled it to stop, gunfire erupted from the car. The two cops returned fire as it sped past them.

O'Brien had happened into a war that his own army was already fighting. A murderous crime spree by so-called terror bandits had begun a few hours earlier when two men, using a stolen car, robbed a cab driver at gunpoint. A few minutes later another cabbie was robbed. Then the gunmen accosted a doctor as he was about to enter his home. Inspectors (detectives) with shotguns were already cruising through the streets looking for the bandits. Among the inspectors' leaders was a tough ex-marine named Charlie Dullea, who was a lieutenant in charge of the homicide squad.

The robbers were not through for the night. They encountered a man strolling with a woman, her thirteen-year-old daughter, and a female friend. After sticking up the group, the gunmen dragged the mother into the car and drove off. Looking at her under a flashlight, they decided "she ain't young enough" and threw her out of the car.

After midnight the bandits stormed into a pool room and announced a robbery. At 3:30 a.m. they robbed two more men as they entered their house. That was the last job of the night. The robbers got about $400 and assorted pieces of jewelry from the dozen stickups they committed.

At noon on Sunday police officers recovered the stolen auto. There were bloodstains on the upholstery, suggesting that one of the robbers may have been hit in the encounter with the chief. The only description witnesses could give was of two young, white males.

Two days later, at 6:00 p.m. on Monday, the bandits went on another terror spree. They hired a yellow cab driver, shot him fatally, took his cab and his uniform, and threw his body under a viaduct. They then went out with one of them posing as the cab driver. When a bandit asked a man walking on the street what time it was and he pulled out his watch, they shot him fatally. Next they robbed two pedestrians. Then they went to a restaurant where they held up patrons and shot the cook.

Still going, they walked across the street to a filling station where they killed the night watchman and wounded two other men. Next they went to Pier 36 on the waterfront and robbed and pistol whipped a man. Then they drove to a gas station, where they were assaulting and robbing a patron when a police officer drove by. The robbers sped off with the cop in pursuit. The bandits drove the cab into a curb, jumped out, and fled. Somehow they procured another car and drove past a police officer who was waiting for the morgue wagon at the scene of one of their fatal shootings. When he signaled them to stop, they began shooting and the officer returned the fire. The bandits made their getaway and quit for the night.

In just two nights, San Francisco had topped Chicago's reputation for murderous violence. Chief O'Brien ordered the mobilization of the entire police department and radio stations put out a message for all off-duty police officers to report to their commands. There they were assigned to vehicles, some of them the officers' personal cars. Then, supplemented by fire department volunteers and issued one thousand rifles borrowed from the National Guard, a force of two thousand men began patrolling the streets.

The terrorist spree was brought to an end in the old-fashioned way. Det. Sgt. Louis DeMattei and his partner, George Wafer, broke the case after they got word from an informer. On October 18, nine days after the first shooting, detectives picked up a man named Lawrence Weeks, age twenty-two. Under questioning he confessed to twelve holdups on the Saturday night in question but denied he was involved in the Monday-night spree. Weeks named an accomplice, Clarence "Buck" Kelly, twenty-two, as ringleader of the group. Kelly was a street criminal well known to the police. When the cops went to his apartment, he attempted to escape but was hit twice by rifle fire. Though Kelly would never admit his guilt, a search of the premises where he lived turned up part of the dead cab driver's uniform and other evidence.

So outraged were the city's cab drivers over the shootings of their colleagues, they were about to go to the hospital where Kelly was being held and lynch him. To head them off a district police captain assigned twenty-five men to guard the building. Kelly was eventually hanged for murder.

During the two nights of terror it was the detectives who directed police efforts, not the much larger patrol force. The image of detectives that had already begun to form in America was that they were the ones who would lead a city's crime-fighting efforts. Over the next forty-plus years this would be the case in San Francisco under the direction of Charlie Dullea, chief of inspectors and later chief of police, and his successors.

New York City, May 7, 1931

THE GREAT SIEGE

Crime in the Prohibition era, which extended into the early 1930s, is often seen as revolving around gangsters, taking rivals "for a ride," and the introduction of the "Chicago piano" (i.e., the Thompson submachine gun). However, there was more to crime than just mobsters. As in the musical *Chicago*, ordinary people also took up the gun and became temporary sensations under such names as the Bobbed-Haired Bandit or Two Gun Crowley. Francis Crowley of the Bronx was an eighteen-year-old punk, short and slim, who, along with his running mate, Rudolph "Fats" Duringer, carried out a spectacular crime spree in the New York area in 1931. It began in February when Crowley shot two men at an American Legion dance. The next month he wounded a New York Police Department (NYPD) detective who attempted to arrest him. In April Crowley and Duringer were riding in a car with the latter's girlfriend. When she resisted his advances, he shot and killed her.

The hunt for the two fugitives was led by Bronx borough detectives under Insp. Henry Bruckman. The NYPD had been in existence since the middle of the nineteenth century, when the Bronx was sparsely populated and much of it was patrolled by mounted policemen. For a cop in Manhattan to be transferred up to the Bronx was a form of punishment. Rookies often concealed the fact that they could ride a horse because they did not want to be sent to the boondocks. By the mid-twentieth century, though, it was an urban area just like most of the rest of the city. Its detectives were part of the NYPD Detective Bureau, which had been the model for all similar organizations in America since the 1880s.

Bruckman's lead detectives in the hunt for Crowley and Duringer were Dominic Caso and William Mara. During their investigation they learned that the fugitives were running with a girl named Billy Dove, who hung out in upper Manhattan dives. So the detectives went from joint to joint asking about Billy and her boyfriends. In those days the gold shield of a New York detective commanded respect and loosened many tongues. Based on tips from a former girlfriend of Crowley and information from cabdrivers, the detectives went to a five-story imitation French château at 303 West Ninetieth Street, where they were told the fugitives were hiding out. When they showed the building superintendent pictures of Crowley and Duringer, he identified them as Mr. White and Mr. Jones, who were living in apartment ten on the top floor. In fact, he said, the two men were in the apartment at the time.

It might have been wiser for the detectives to call the local precinct and ask that assistance be sent to the scene immediately. However, that would have brought a commanding officer from Manhattan, who would have taken over the case. So, following protocol, the detectives notified their squad lieutenant up in the Bronx, who notified his district detective captain, who informed Inspector Bruckman that the wanted men had been located. Bruckman raced to West Ninetieth Street and West End Avenue with reinforcements. He placed men on the roof of a building on West Ninety-First Street that overlooked apartment ten in the château. From there the cops could heave tear gas grenades into two windows of the apartment. Other detectives went up to the fifth-floor landing. When everything was in place, Detective Caso called out to Crowley, telling him the place was surrounded and that he should surrender. His answer was a burst of machine-gun fire through the door. The battle was on.

Eventually fifteen thousand spectators and the police commissioner himself, Ed Mulrooney, arrived at the scene and watched as officers on the adjoining roof threw gas grenades at apartment ten. They managed to get them inside the apartment twice. Crowley picked the grenades up and threw them out the window. Then the wanted men started shooting at the roof, compelling the detectives on it to take cover. Occasionally Crowley and Duringer would fire their machine gun at the door to hold off any attempt to rush the place. If the cops had followed normal procedure and broken down the door, there would almost certainly have been a few police funerals resulting from the action. The situation was at a standstill, with an army of three hundred of New York's finest held off by two punk gunmen.

Down at headquarters, the teletype in the office of the major case squad, the department's elite detective unit, flashed what was happening at West Ninetieth Street. In the squad room were some of the top detectives on the force. Johnny Cordes was the senior man. He had joined the NYPD in 1915 at the age of twenty-five and had developed a reputation as an expert at tailing criminals. Twice he was severely wounded in gun battles, coming near to death each time. Mayor Jimmy Walker offered to retire him on a full disability pension, but Cordes refused. Twice he won the department's highest medal, a feat never accomplished before or since. Cordes was relatively small for a cop and easygoing. The powerfully built Johnny Broderick had been a city fireman before he joined the department in 1923 at age twenty-three. He had distinguished himself a number of times, including at the Tombs jail (so called because it resembled an Egyptian tomb), where he led the charge against three escaping prisoners who had murdered the warden and a guard. Two of the men committed suicide after Broderick trapped them and the third was shot to death by police. Short, slim Frank Phillips had come on the job in 1926 when he was twenty-two years of age and, after drawing notice as a patrolman, was transferred to the major case squad. In 1928 that was the equivalent of a low minor leaguer going straight to Yankee Stadium. Burly Ray Henshaw was the quiet one of the group, but his record was as good as the others.

The captain of the main office squad granted permission to his four stars to go to the scene of the battle. Probably he thought somebody had to do something up there because nothing seemed to be working. With Broderick at the wheel, the four of them made it up to the scene through five miles of heavy Manhattan traffic in less than ten minutes. They checked in with Inspector Bruckman and asked permission to go up to the fifth-floor landing and see what they could do. Bruckman was already at his wit's end, and he agreed to let them take over. Johnny Broderick led the way, and when he yelled his name through the door, Crowley recognized it and listened. Broderick said, "I'm coming through the door with nothing in my hands" and proceeded to do just that. Both Crowley and Duringer surrendered. The following year they were executed.

Why had Crowley surrendered and why had Broderick taken such a chance? No doubt in the few words that he exchanged with Crowley, Broderick detected in the gunman's voice that he was tired, hurt, and wanted to give up. It was an instinct that a certain kind of detective has and most other people don't. By managing to conclude the battle, he spared the police department, including the commissioner, a great deal of embarrassment. The affair had been the largest siege in the history of the department, and no one had seemed to know how to resolve it. The detective bureau had saved the day for the police department by the action of its most famous members.

Chicago, March 20, 1953

A KILLING AT THE STOCKYARDS

The Union Stockyards on Chicago's southwest side was an old-fashioned slaughterhouse dating from the nineteenth century. It covered nearly a square mile, and thousands of workers spent their time in it butchering cows, pigs, and chickens after driving spikes through their heads or cutting their throats.

The stockyards was the home of giant companies like Armour and Swift as well as lesser-known ones, and each had its own guard force. If the city police were needed in the yards, the Eighteenth District was located near the front entrance on Halsted Street. The back entrances emptied into Ashland Avenue a mile away. The Seventeenth District was only three blocks from one of the back gates. The chief problem for the police was not in the yards but the sleazy saloons on Halsted and Ashland.

At 7:45 a.m. on March 20, 1953, the day shifts in the Eighteenth and Seventeenth Districts (the latter included the writer) stood at roll call. At police headquarters, the detective bureau turned out at 8:30 a.m. with a dozen two- or three-man squads assigned to street duty citywide. Other detectives were working on cases. The detectives regarded themselves as the elite of the police force. Some of the detective cars on the street carried heavy equipment, that is, machine guns, shotguns, rifles, tear gas, and so on, and when a shootout occurred they assumed the role that a SWAT team would today. If it became a siege, they donned their bulletproof vests and moved in to deal with the shooter. The department was not big on negotiating with criminals. The usual way to end a siege was to toss in tear gas. If that didn't work, a team of detectives would storm through the front or back door. To a modern-day policeman it would look like something out of Dodge City or Tombstone, but it was standard operating procedure in most American police departments of that time. In New York City, a policeman would shout to a trapped gunman, "This is Father Murphy, think of your immortal soul." If the shooter did not give up, the cops went in, guns blazing.

There was always a ranking officer available to supervise the detective cars patrolling the city. This day it was the best-known police officer in Chicago, Lt. Frank Pape. He had joined the force in the early thirties and quickly was appointed to the detective bureau. Pape was a good detective and he and his partner, Morris Friedman, made a strong record working out of the robbery detail. In ten years together they had never fired a shot. Then one day, while attempting to execute a robbery warrant from Cleveland, Ohio, they chased a man through downtown Chicago and the man turned around and fired, killing Friedman. After that, Pape began to acquire notches on his gun. All of those he shot were armed, professional criminals. Even though Chicago had a large minority population, none of the people Pape gunned down were nonwhite. In the 1950s Lieutenant Pape and the submachine gun he often carried were well known in Chicago, and the newspapers built him up. On first meeting him, though, people were surprised by his mild looks. Instead of being a huge brute, he was of medium height and weight and did not have the manner of a tough detective. While his name was taken to be Italian, he was actually German and Irish.

Riding in a patrol car on the west end of the Seventeenth District, along with a veteran cop, I listened to radio calls coming in to South Side police units. It was a slow morning. Over at the stockyards, two Libby, McNeill & Libby cannery officials were pushing a pay cart filled with cash. Suddenly, five men with guns surrounded them. The robbers also took three other employees hostage and kept them quiet by hitting them over the head with a lead pipe. Another worker who saw what was happening managed to race up to the next floor and inform the security chief of the company, Theodore Zukowski, of the robbery. Zukowski, though unarmed, was a fearless man and came racing down the stairs toward the pay cart. The leader of the gang was Paul Crump, who had worked at Libby, McNeill & Libby and knew that Zukowski was never armed, but he shot and killed him anyway. The robbers began running out of the building. Outside, a getaway car was parked but the driver panicked and drove off, leaving some of the gang behind to make their way out of the huge complex on foot.

Out of the blue, the police dispatcher came on and announced, "Robbery and a man shot at Libby, McNeill & Libby" and gave the address. All of the cars from the Eighteenth District rushed to the scene. Within a few minutes a call was broadcast—"wanted for murder"—with a description of the holdup men. When the first call had come over, although the Seventeenth District cars were not dispatched, they began to head toward the Ashland exits of the facility. I drove to McDowell Street, a two-block-long road that connected the stockyards to Ashland Avenue. Crump had run down McDowell on foot shortly before my partner and I came racing up the street into the yards. By that time the area was flooded with police. However, all the robbers made their getaway.

The next message broadcast by the dispatcher ordered all detective cars on field duty to proceed to the stockyards and report to Lieutenant Pape. He was going for broke by assembling the cream of the detective bureau and sending them out hunting for the robbers in an attempt to close the case quickly. When they assembled at the scene, Pape issued orders and they began heading out to look for the robbers, including Crump, who had been recognized by one of the employees. It was a memorable sight to see the power of the police department mobilized and on the move. A more prudent supervisor would not have mobilized so many detective bureau units but would have followed standard procedures, working up from the district detectives. However, Pape was a man who acted out of instinct and was very forceful. Soon an army of detectives was combing the South Side. Over the next few days they rounded up all of the holdup men and booked them for murder. At their trials they were convicted, and Crump was sentenced to death, although he was not executed.

In the next few years Pape was at the height of his fame, and it seemed certain he would become chief of detectives. But as the 1960s dawned, the world of policing changed. The old detective bureau was dismantled, and Pape did not find favor with the new leaders of the department. He would never become chief of detectives. In the mid-1960s he was just a patrol captain, while I was in the detective bureau and held a higher rank than he did. Even I thought that was a ludicrous situation.

I would always remember that day in March 1953 when Pape and the bureau swept into the stockyards, took over, and within a couple of days rounded up the gang. If they had not taken action, someone like Crump might have gone down south and disappeared. Seven or eight years could have passed before he would be picked up and his prints matched to those of the wanted man in Chicago.

Unbelievably, nine years after the Zukowski murder journalists made a major effort to get Crump released from prison. They claimed he had the mind of a genius. Prominent writers and civic leaders championed his case. The story they presented of what had happened at Libby, McNeill & Libby was so distorted as to be unrecognizable. They did not even mention that Crump had shot Zukowski, who was unarmed. Then a highly respected federal judge who had prosecuted Crump back in 1953 stepped forward to remind people what the true story was. Crump's sentence was not commuted, but eventually he was released from prison. He never won a Nobel or Pulitzer Prize for any later achievements.

Preface

Strangers Who Walk in an

Atmosphere of Mysterious Greatness

Contrary to conventional wisdom, detectives are the key element in American policing. Undoubtedly, this statement will be disputed by many police administrators and researchers. In recent years it has become almost an article of faith that the patrol force is far more important than detectives. Those who argue otherwise are often dismissed as "buffs" who have seen too many movies and TV shows. Having spent a lifetime in and around police work, I hardly think that title would apply to me. Within police administrative circles detective bureaus are often thought to be vastly overrated and grossly overstaffed, but, because the public is fascinated by the latest front-page murder or million-dollar robbery, they are difficult to rein in.

Patrick V. Murphy, a career New York cop who from 1963 to 1973 headed the police departments of Syracuse, New York; Washington DC; Detroit; and New York City had especially hard words for detectives in his native city. He wrote, "The ambitious ones might be barhopping with reporters, politicians, or judges; shakedown artists, barhopping too, might be 'shopping'; the lazier ones could be glued to a stool ostensibly picking up 'information.'" Of course, Murphy himself never worked as a detective. Instead he spent most of his early career as an instructor in the police academy. The petty chiseling he accused detectives of was not confined to any police unit. It was known in every bureau.

The highly regarded management consulting group known as the Rand Corporation made more fundamental criticisms in less vitriolic terms: "The single most important determinant of whether or not a case will be solved is the information the victim supplies to the immediately responding patrol officers. If the information that uniquely identifies the perpetrator is not presented at the time the crime is reported, the perpetrator by and large will not be subsequently identified. . . . The method by which police and investigators are organized (team policing, specialist versus generalist, uniform patrolman–investigators) cannot be related to variations in crime, arrests and clearance rates." The study led some administrators to argue that half the detective force in any police department could be dispensed with.

The Rand notion that only information from victims or witnesses would lead to an arrest ignored the vast amount of other information detectives received from informers and the general knowledge they acquired from their work. Just because no one witnesses a particular burglary, it does not mean that it cannot be solved. Burglary detectives can sometimes tell from the tool marks on the door what gang pulled the job. Or they can canvas their many informers. They can then start asking questions around the milieu of burglars. They might even be able to set up a trap for the gang that pulled the job. The same is true in other crimes. The murder of union leader Jimmy Hoffa has never been solved officially, but a number of people deemed responsible for it have been punished by being sent to prison on other charges.

On its face, the Rand assertion about detective organization is unsupportable. The way in which an army, business corporation, or government agency is organized is fundamental to its success or failure. After World War I, leaders of the victorious French Army assumed that in any future conflict, defense would prove the key to victory. So they sheltered their troops behind the Maginot Line. In contrast, the Germans envisioned a war of movement and developed mobile forces to carry it out. In 1940

France actually had more and better tanks than the Germans but it used them to support the infantry rather than as a massed attack force. If France had organized a mobile tank army, as a certain Col. Charles de Gaulle had urged in a prewar book, the Allies would have won the war in 1940.

Most murderers, rapists, professional robbers, and burglars are captured by detective follow-up investigations. Police investigators also apprehend less visible criminals such as con artists and members of drug rings. The detective bureau, usually composing around 10–12 percent of a police department, is the only major unit devoted solely to fighting serious crime.

The history of detective work of the present type is not a long one. The London Metropolitan Police, created in 1829, replaced a force of part-time night watchmen hired by the various parishes (local neighborhoods) of the city with a full-time uniformed force. American cities, beginning with New York in 1845, followed suit. Until the late nineteenth century detectives in London or New York were a small adjunct to the main force. Then, in 1878, the London Metropolitan Police created a criminal investigation division (known popularly as Scotland Yard), and two years later Insp. Thomas Byrnes of the New York City Police Department established the modern American detective bureau.

Even before the emergence of powerful police detective bureaus, private detectives, like the Pinkerton Agency, operated nationwide and even internationally. Occasionally a city or state or the national government would hire the Pinkertons. The agency's symbol, an open eye with the slogan "we never sleep," became well known and gave rise to the term *private eye*.

The twentieth century saw the rise in importance of American detectives. From the beginning of the century until as late as the 1970s detective bureaus dominated many American police departments, particularly major ones like New York, Chicago, and San Francisco. The era was the golden age of detectives and every ambitious cop tried to secure an investigative assignment. In some cities a detective post became more desirable than the job of sergeant or lieutenant in the patrol force.

Despite the public's fascination with detectives, most people do not understand how they operate. Contrary to the impression furnished by

TV, Hollywood, or mystery novels, the basis of detective work has not been the intuitive powers of individual investigators. Successful police detectives are individuals who are able to master the systems and methods of criminal investigation utilized by their departments: cultivation of informers, canvassing for witnesses, interrogating suspects, and keeping an eye on known criminals.

Since the 1960s, urban patrol forces have encountered significant hostility in many communities. Simple incidents, like arresting a motorist or dispersing a group of noisy young men, have sparked riots, which in some cases have resulted in a number of deaths. Some police departments have attempted to establish "community policing," where officers seek to emulate the idealized (and often historically unreal) neighborhood beat cop. In that formulation the cop knew, and was known by, everybody and, rather than using enforcement techniques, often engaged in counseling. No doubt some did, but since it took five cops to patrol one foot beat around the clock seven days a week, most beat officers did not live up to that ideal. The new-style community cops generally spend their time attending meetings and filling out reports. In many cities they constitute a sort of showpiece force that exists largely for public relations without having much impact on crime.

Detectives meet less resistance in inner-city areas because the public knows they are there to investigate serious crimes, not to regulate behavior such as loitering, public drinking, and so on. While patrol officers search for criminals in an ad hoc fashion, detectives usually work from a base of previously gathered data and are trained to elicit information without being heavy-handed. As a group, they are more experienced than the young cops who patrol environments they are unfamiliar with and interact with people they find difficult to relate to.

Detectives also benefit from the fact that the public stands in awe of them and sees them as well-above-average cops. Most citizens believe detectives are more skilled and possess higher ranks than ordinary cops. In the NYPD a low-ranking detective outranks a patrol captain at a crime scene because he is thought to be the expert and the captain is not.

Even before detectives became an important part of policing they tended to stand out from their fellow cops. In mid-nineteenth-century London they attracted the attention of the novelist Charles Dickens. The previous image of them had been that of men not very different from criminals. The great French detective chief Eugène François Vidocq, who was in charge of the national detective force (the Sûreté) from 1811 to 1827, hired ex-criminals on the theory that "it takes a crook to catch a crook." Dickens had a different view. He wrote that London detectives "are one and all, respectable-looking men, of perfectly good deportment and unusual intelligence; with nothing lounging or slinking in their manners; with an air of keen observation and quick perceptions when addressed; and generally present faces, more or less marked of habitually leading lives of strong mental excitement."

They were in fact models of the kind of working-class heroes Dickens often wrote about: boys who, despite a deprived background, rose to modest success. In the class-demarcated society of nineteenth-century England, detectives were among the few people who had the authority to pry into the affairs of gentlemen, interrogate them, or place them under arrest. Detective work, with its challenges, offered a much larger field intellectually than walking a beat. Thus it attracted a higher class of officer. Dickens describes his principal hero, Inspector Bucket (based on an actual Scotland Yard detective), as having a "ghostly manner of appearing," and as "a sparkling stranger who walks in an atmosphere of mysterious greatness."

Beyond its importance to public safety, detective work is at the heart of urban life. It tells us what our society is really like. In the late nine-teenth century the NYPD detective bureau of Insp. Thomas Byrnes was the subject of considerable attention from great journalists like Jacob Riis and Lincoln Steffens. Novelist Julian Hawthorne wrote books based on cases "from the notebook of Inspector Byrnes." Steffens and Riis understood that detectives shed light on the urban experience that was coming to dominate American culture. Hawthorne realized that in the late nineteenth century the problems of New England villagers, por-trayed in his father's *House of the Seven Gables*, were less significant than those of city dwellers. In the post–World War II period popular writers like MacKinlay Kantor and Quentin Reynolds explored big-city life by examining the work of New York detectives.

In the present time, books by former Los Angeles Police Department (LAPD) detective Joseph Wambaugh have gone beyond police stories to social commentary that ranks him with such writers as Raymond Chandler, the creator of Philip Marlowe, and Dashiell Hammett, who brought to life detective Sam Spade. Wambaugh's books provide an insightful analysis of American society and the workings of power within it.

The chapters that follow look at American detectives in action from the mid-nineteenth century to the last part of the twentieth. They describe how a police backwater became the most prominent element of big-city forces. The reader will note how this work differs from most detective stories in that it looks at cases not from the perspective of individual detectives but from that of the detective bureau. This is because detectives are not a collection of individuals but products of a system.

In one instance we will analyze the murder of a top Hollywood director, possibly by a major movie star. Though the case was never solved, as late as 1950 old Hollywood-ites may have been trying to point to the killer by sending signals in an Academy Award–nominated picture of that year, *Sunset Boulevard*.

Murder is found in both the highest and lowest elements of society. In the 1920s an Episcopalian priest and his paramour were found murdered in a "lovers' lane" in New Jersey. After an investigation, the minister's blue-blooded family was put on trial for the murder, although they were not convicted. At the other end of the scale, we will explore lowlife in a journey through the skid-row and hobo jungles of Cleveland in the 1930s. Here a "mad butcher" cut off a dozen or more heads in the mid-1930s. The police force, directed by Elliott Ness, could not solve the case. In 1947 the murder and dissection of an obscure girl, labeled the "Black Dahlia," in Los Angeles (never solved) shook the police and the city establishment to their cores. We also look at a series of killings in a medium-size Texas town shortly after World War II. As in Cleveland and LA, the case was never solved.

In highlighting major property crimes we examine three cases. In 1920s Chicago a band of Texas cowboys pulled a train robbery that netted them

$3 million in cash and bonds. The investigation by the Chicago police quickly rounded up the robbers, but further inquiry determined that the crime had been masterminded by an individual above suspicion. In the 1930s an armored-car heist in Brooklyn netted $427,500, the largest cash amount on record up to that time. Though quickly traced to a Hell's Kitchen group, it took four years for the police to finally clear the case with the arrest or death of the participants. Finally we examine the 1950 Brink's holdup in Boston, which was barely solved before the six-year statute of limitation expired. The investigation was constantly hampered by feuding between the FBI and the local police force. In Britain, the secretary of state for home affairs would have quickly resolved a feud between police departments. In the American federal system there is no mechanism for doing the same thing.

In the area of organized crime, we cite the case where a New York detective was sent on a suicide mission and murdered in Sicily. A decade later, another New York detective was sent on a similar mission to Naples, where he barely escaped with his life.

In the political realm, we look at two major events: the 1920 Wall Street bombing in which thirty-eight people were killed and the 1940 New York World's Fair bombing, which killed two detectives and wounded several more and might have led to the death of hundreds of people if the bomb had not been moved outside a building. Neither case has been solved, although historians today generally agree on who set the Wall Street bomb.

Perhaps the most interesting stop we will make is in what was America's most colorful city through most of the twentieth century, San Francisco. Here we will look at bombings, riots, murders, and major heists. For years it was common for the police department to be led by a top detective. Among the detectives profiled herein are private detective chiefs Allan Pinkerton and William Burns, commanders like Thad Brown of Los Angeles, Public Safety Director Elliott Ness of Cleveland, Charles Dullea, captain of inspectors and later chief of police of San Francisco, and America's "top cop," J. Edgar Hoover of the FBI. We will also look at a number of working detectives, including Peter Merylo, who was the lead investigator on the Cleveland butcher case and drew conclusions diametrically opposite to those of Elliott Ness; John St. John of Los Angeles, who was honored by being given detective badge number one; and New York's Frankie Phillips, whose career, including his pursuit of Willie Sutton, made him one of the best-known New York detectives in the mid-twentieth century. In New Jersey we describe West Pointer H. Norman Schwarzkopf, superintendent of the New Jersey State Police, who, although not a detective, played a major role in the Lindbergh case, and in Texas Captain "Lone Wolf" Gonzaullas of the Texas Rangers, who worked on serial killings and other major crimes in his state.

Some detectives were not admirable characters. A rural New Jerseyian, Ellis Parker, chief of detectives of Burlington County, managed to convince many people that he was one of the most brilliant sleuths who ever lived. His interference in the Lindbergh investigation brought his downfall.

By the end of the narrative I expect many people, including individuals with considerable knowledge of the field, to be surprised to have learned things they did not know about detectives. More importantly, I will point out how a restoration of detectives to their primary role might solve many of the current difficulties of American policing.

Acknowledgments

I wish to express my gratitude to the following people and their organizations, who were helpful to me in the writing of this book: Kenneth Johnson, the Library of Congress; Michael Marie Lange, the Bancroft Library, University of California, Berkeley; Christina Stopka, Texas Ranger Hall of Fame and Museum; Sarah Yarrito, Chicago History Museum; Molly Haigh, Library Special Collections, Charles E. Young Research Library, UCLA; Joan Renner, Deranged LA Crimes.com; Brian Meggitt, Cleveland Public Library; Donna L. Stewart, Michael Schwartz Library, Cleveland State University; Linda Wilkins, Federal Bureau of Investigation; Jeff Thomas, San Francisco History Center, San Francisco Public Library; Erica Varela, *Los Angeles Times*; Aaron Schmidt, Boston Public Library; Arthur Pollock, *Boston Herald*; Critical Past LLC; Patrick Frierson, Getty Images; Larry Sullivan, librarian of the John Jay College of Criminal Justice of the City University of New York; Patterson Smith, antiquarian bookseller and publisher; Murray Weiss, CBS News; Raymond J. Kelly, former NYPD commissioner; Robert Schnell; Christa Carnegie; Tom Swanson and Natalie O'Neal, Potomac Books, University of Nebraska Press; other members of the University Nebraska Press: Rosemary Sekora,

Tish Fobben, Sabrina Stellrecht, Rachel Gould, Ann Baker, and last but not least, Joy Margheim.

There are also a number of people who are no longer alive and who, over the years, have influenced my thoughts on the subject matter of this book. There are so many that to list them would require many pages. I am also not sure that all of them would want to be identified. Indeed, some living persons have preferred not to be cited. In any event, my thanks to all of them.

AMERICAN DETECTIVE

1

From the Civil War Era to World War I

The story of American detective work from the mid-nineteenth century to the end of World War I can be told through the work of four men who dominated the law enforcement scene in that era. The first was Allan Pinkerton. Born in Scotland in 1819, he came to the United States in 1847 at the age of twenty-eight, allegedly to avoid arrest for revolutionary activity as a "Chartist." A major working-class revolutionary organization in post-Waterloo Britain, in 1848 the Chartists staged a huge march on London but were met by soldiers, members of the new police force (established in 1829), and special constables made up of gentlemen volunteers. Even the exiled Louis Napoleon, soon to be emperor of France, obtained a police brassard and a club and went on patrol. When the Chartists realized the strength of the government forces, they decided not to create any trouble, and eventually the movement withered away. Throughout Pinkerton's life he told many stories that were of questionable veracity. As his career demonstrated, it was a great advantage for a detective to be able to dissemble convincingly.

Settling down in Illinois, Pinkerton became a barrel maker and, on the side, did minor sleuthing for some of his neighbors who had incurred

losses from thefts or had accepted counterfeit bills. In the 1850s he relo-
cated to Chicago, where he opened his own detective agency, working
for the railroads and other business corporations. Pinkerton was also
active in smuggling runaway slaves to Canada, an interesting fact about
a man who later was widely portrayed as an enemy of the oppressed.

One of Pinkerton's clients was an eminent Illinois lawyer, Abraham
Lincoln. According to legend, in 1861 Pinkerton and his agents escorted
Lincoln to his inauguration in Washington DC. At the time Pinkerton
alleged he had unearthed a plot to assassinate the president-elect in Baltimore, Maryland. The supposed plot resembled actual events that had
occurred in Paris. In 1859 Felice Orsini, an Italian nationalist who was
angry at Napoleon III for not backing Italy's liberation from Austria,
hurled a bomb at the royal carriage outside the Paris Opera House. The
Baltimore plot contained some of the same ingredients, such as the claim
that it was led by an Italian anarchist, Cypriano Ferandini. For generations,
plots were always more believable if a sinister Italian was named as the
leader. One of Pinkerton's top agents, a young widow named Kate Warne,
posed as Lincoln's invalid sister and accompanied him throughout the
trip with her hand on a revolver in her knitting bag. Warne's role in pro-
tecting Lincoln illustrated that Pinkerton's hiring practices were much
more inclusive than those of local police departments. He hired people
regardless of age, race, sex, or politics if he thought they could do the job.
Today most historians question some of Pinkerton's claims about the
Baltimore affair, but at the time it bolstered his reputation enormously.

Another client of Pinkerton's was George B. McClellan, a brilliant
graduate of West Point who was serving as president of a railroad. Shortly
after the Civil War began, McClellan, who was then commanding the
Union army, named Pinkerton chief of the military's Secret Service, not
to be confused with the agency created in 1865 to pursue counterfeiting.
In that capacity Pinkerton posed as Maj. E. J. Allen. While he and his
assistants were competent at gathering information, they were not good
at analysis and constantly overestimated the size of the Confederate
army, thus persuading McClellan not to advance on Richmond. When
McClellan was replaced, Pinkerton left with him. However, the glory

that accompanied him due to his association with President Lincoln and General McClellan (the 1864 Democratic nominee for president) brought many clients to his agency in the postwar era.

The Pinkertons were especially effective because they were able to operate virtually without constraints. Agents pursued western bandits such as Jesse James and other famous desperados of the era. They were also accused of underhanded tactics such as arranging the lynching of the Reno gang in Indiana. Pinkerton was able to get results for companies whose employees had embezzled money and fled to Canada, where there was no extradition treaty. The Pinkertons would simply kidnap the fugitive and take him across the border to the United States.

In 1875 Pinkerton sent an undercover operative, Irish immigrant James McParland, into the Pennsylvania coal fields to spy on a group of Irish miners known as the Molly Maguires. The Mollys were suspected of murdering coal company managers as a form of labor protest. McParland worked his way into their inner circle, and in 1877, based on his testimony, twenty of them were hanged. Union leaders maintained that their men were framed, although the weight of the evidence is on the side of the Pinkertons.

Pinkerton was disabled by a stroke and died in 1884, but the Pinkerton agency carried on under the direction of his sons, William and Robert, who ran it from New York and Chicago, respectively. The most lucrative private detective work came from spying on union organizers on behalf of corporations and breaking strikes. In 1892, when a major strike occurred at the Homestead, Pennsylvania, plant of Andrew Carnegie's U.S. Steel Company, the Pinkertons were engaged to police it. They sent in a number of detectives and uniformed guards. However, in a pitched battle with the workers, the Pinkertons got the worst of it and were compelled to surrender, after which they were brutally beaten by the strikers. A total of thirteen people were killed. The incident at Homestead reverberated throughout the United States, and the mournful dirge "Father was killed by the Pinkerton men" helped to keep the memory alive.

In 1905 there was a rerun of the Molly case featuring the same leading man, James McParland, now the senior Pinkerton manager in the western states. In December 1905 former governor Frank Steuneberg of Idaho opened the front gate of his yard and was blown to pieces by a bomb attached to it. He had been elected governor in 1896 with strong support from the Western Federation of Miners, which included an outlaw labor group called the Industrial Workers of the World (IWW). The union never forgave Steuneberg for calling in the U.S. Army in 1899 after a mine was blown up.

The Pinkertons were engaged to investigate the assassination, with McParland in charge. A suspect, Harry Orchard, was already in custody, and under McParland's interrogation Orchard and an alleged accomplice confessed to being hired by Big Bill Haywood, leader of the IWW, and two of his lieutenants. In typical Pinkerton fashion the three were arrested in Denver by agency operatives and, when extradition could not be secured, they were spirited off to Idaho. At the trial, future U.S. senator William Borah was part of the prosecution and Clarence Darrow led the defense. Darrow largely spent his twelve-hour summation in denouncing the Pinkerton Agency and managed to obtain an acquittal for his clients.

After the agency's defeat in Idaho, the Pinkertons continued pursuing criminals as well as operating in the labor field. Information they supplied led to the killing of Butch Cassidy and the Sundance Kid in Bolivia. But the agency's reputation, which had begun to erode with Homestead, declined further with the defeat in Idaho.

The second great detective of the post–Civil War era was Thomas Byrnes, who had come to America with his Irish immigrant parents and served in the Union army. In 1863 he was accepted into the New York Metropolitan Police, which had been established in 1857 by the Republican-dominated state legislature in place of the Tammany-run New York City Municipal Police. Not until 1870 was the police force returned to municipal control.

Byrnes was a Republican, and it is likely that his rapid ascent to captain, a rank that he attained in 1870, arose from his wartime associations. In 1878 a gang of top heist men, known in those days as "yeggs," robbed the Manhattan Savings Bank at Bleecker Street and Broadway in Manhattan.

It was the largest bank robbery in America up to that time. The total cash and bonds taken amounted to somewhere between $2 and $3 million. However, not all of it could be used because most of the bonds were registered; only about $250,000 of the loot was in negotiable bonds and $12,000 was in cash. Byrnes was the captain of the precinct where the crime occurred, and under his direction, the gang was rounded up.

When big cases are solved there is usually more to it than the official version. Some individuals close to the investigation suggested that a beat policeman named Nugent had served as a lookout for the robbers. Later Nugent engaged in barroom boasting that got back to Byrnes. Another theory was laid out by Julian Hawthorne, who claimed that "Traveling Mike" Grady, a leading fence, was the mastermind, and his lover, a society woman, was also implicated. In those times yeggs who pulled off a big score usually were financed by bankers of the underworld like Grady.

In 1880, because of the accolades he received for breaking the Manhattan bank case, Byrnes was named inspector in charge of the detective bureau. Prior to Byrnes's tenure, detectives were only a small adjunct of the police department. The experiences of William Bell in the 1850s were typical of the work the city's detective force performed. His duties were largely those of a modern-day burglary detective: he inspected the city's pawn shops and familiarized himself with burglars, pickpockets, and petty thieves, men with names like Dick the Blower, Crystal Bill, and One-Eyed Thompson. When he spotted a suspected criminal Bell would "pipe him" (i.e., keep an eye on him to see what he was up to). Sometimes he would frisk him for stolen goods or burglary tools.

Under Byrnes's direction, detectives became a major element of the police department. His men, instead of simply responding to reported crimes, began to gather intelligence on top criminals and to keep regular diaries detailing their work. It was Byrnes who initiated the practice of photographing suspects as a means of identification, and he eventually compiled the portraits and records of seven hundred top criminals. To facilitate criminal identification he published a photo book, *Professional Criminals of America*, which proved an invaluable guide for police departments from Boston to San Francisco.

A large part of Byrnes's success came from the power he was able to accrue, including from the most important interest group in New York, the Wall Street financiers. On the first day of his appointment as commander of the detective bureau, he opened a substation at 17 Wall Street so that the financial community could be served quickly. In return, the stock exchange hooked up a direct telephone line from there to every financial house in the district. Byrnes also drew a "deadline" at Fulton Street, just north of the financial district, and forbade any criminal to cross it. To enforce the rule he posted veteran detectives, such as "Wall Street Johnny" Dunn, who knew many thieves by sight.

Byrnes, in effect, set ground rules for criminals. He required that when any out-of-town yegg came into New York, he had to immediately report to police headquarters or else something unpleasant would happen to him. Byrnes's connections in Wall Street and his obvious success made his operation virtually autonomous. Neither his police superiors nor Tammany leaders could interfere in his work. When politicians tried to help some street tough or even a well-known professional crook who was pulled in by the police, Byrnes would pay no attention to their appeals.

Undoubtedly certain criminals were allowed to work in New York because of their willingness to inform the police about other active criminals. The same system was also used by the intelligence agencies of Europe. Nineteenth-century London was full of anarchists and criminals fleeing from the Continental police. Despite protests from other countries, the British government refused to deport them. One reason for this was that they kept Scotland Yard informed about other anarchists and rogues and agreed not to commit crimes in England. Of course, the general public had no understanding of these practices. In New York detectives were sometimes known as "shadows" because, supposedly, they followed criminals around. It was a useful illusion that Byrnes took care not to dispel. While Pinkerton agents spent much time shadowing criminals, police detectives did not, preferring to rely on informers.

Byrnes's bureau did not have formal specialized units, though he managed to match men's tasks to their skills. Some were good at handling financial crimes. Others, dressed in tuxedos, could pass easily as guests when they provided security at gatherings of the Four Hundred (New York's high society). Certain detectives knew well the gunmen spawned by the street gangs of New York because they had been beat officers in slum neighborhoods such as Five Points or the Bowery. Byrnes's forty headquarters detectives, known as "the immortals," were rated as sergeants, which at the time was a rank just below captain, and were paid a third more than a patrolman's salary. Each precinct captain was allotted four detectives. Attempts to transfer these people to Byrnes's command always failed. Precinct detectives did not receive the rank and pay of a headquarters detective, but some of them were used as collectors by the captains. Byrnes's detectives would frequently receive "rewards" from wealthy people whom they served. However, Byrnes himself was never accused of taking bribes. Instead, he amassed a fortune of $350,000 (or about $7 million in today's money) because of stock tips from his Wall Street friends Jay Gould, Jim Fiske, and Daniel Drew.

While Byrnes had little formal education, he did have a rough grasp of the psychological elements of criminal interrogation. Like the distinguished European criminologists, he understood that a criminal's thoughts would invariably revolve around his crime and, given the opportunity, the criminal would often confess his guilt. So instead of directly questioning a suspect, Byrnes might start off talking about home and mother. The office where he conducted interviews had a thick, soft carpet, and the lower windowpanes were rendered opaque with white paint. Byrnes would sit motionless for long periods of time, with his piercing eyes fixed on a suspect. Other times, he would unnerve a prisoner by showing him around the police "museum" with its pictures of captured criminals and exhibits of their confiscated tools and murder weapons.

Byrnes's detectives were generally successful at apprehending property thieves and killers from the neighborhood gangs because they could tap into their own knowledge and networks of informers. They were less successful at solving "mysterious" murders because these were usually committed by nonprofessional criminals who were often loners or drifters.

In 1886 Jack the Ripper caused a worldwide sensation by murdering five prostitutes in London and evading capture. His notoriety came from the barbarous way in which he cut up his victims. When American reporters queried Byrnes as to whether he would be able to capture the Ripper if he came to New York, he not only said he would but dared Jack to come across the Atlantic.

In 1891 a sixty-year-old woman named Carrie Brown was found sliced up Ripper-style in a dingy, Lower East Side hotel room. Known locally as "Shakespeare" from her habit of spouting poetry from the Bard of Avon, she had once been a respectable woman married to a sea captain in Massachusetts. When he died he left her sufficient funds to live a middle-class life in New York. But gradually her drinking caused her to slip further and further down, and she began to engage in prostitution.

The New York newspapers challenged Byrnes to solve this Ripper-style murder and uphold the honor of American police in general. In the nineteenth century, disparaging remarks about Great Britain were welcomed by all classes of Americans. Writing about the Ripper, the *New York Times* declared, "The London detective force is probably the stupidest in the world." So Byrnes was on the spot to prove America's superiority.

Initially the only clue was that a man named C. Knick had signed the register with Brown when they checked into the hotel. Lower East Side barflies and stool pigeons informed the police that Brown had previously been seen with a man known as Frenchy, but no one seemed to know his last name and descriptions of him varied as to height, weight, language, and so on.

A number of suspects were interviewed, and individuals who fit the various descriptions of the killer were apprehended. None was charged with the murder of "Shakespeare." Finally, Byrnes arrested one Ben-Ali, an Algerian, and booked him for the murder. Most reporters were skeptical because there seemed to be little evidence against him. Nevertheless, the New York courts convicted him. In 1902, after Ali had spent eleven years in prison, the governor of New York pardoned him. Supposedly Byrnes supported the pardon, indicating that he had some doubt whether the prisoner really was guilty.

If anything would move Byrnes to all-out action, it was a threat to a Wall Street tycoon. Russell Sage was a prominent financier and a close friend and professional associate of Byrnes' patron, Jay Gould. Sage hated to spend money and dressed like a tramp. When a little girl in the Midwest wrote asking him to pay for a glass eye to replace the real eye she had lost, he ignored her request until a New York newspaper reporter threatened to blast him in print. Even then, Sage contributed only three dollars and the reporter had to make up the difference.

In December 1891 Sage was conducting business in his office at the Arcade Building on the corner of Rector Street and Broadway when a young man entered and asked to see him. It wasn't easy to be admitted to the inner sanctum of a Wall Street tycoon, but the man claimed to have a letter of introduction from John D. Rockefeller. Sage read the letter. It declared that unless the red-bearded visitor received $1.5 million at once, he would set off a bomb in the briefcase he was carrying. Sage asked the man to wait while he saw off a previous visitor. According to one account, he then pushed the visitor between himself and the bomber. There was an explosion and the bomber, the visitor, and one of Sage's employees were killed.

Byrnes himself quickly arrived at the scene, accompanied by his protégé (and later chief of detectives) Sgt. George McClusky—a man with such a swaggering manner that his colleagues nicknamed him Chesty George. Firemen dug through the debris and unearthed a red-bearded head from within it. Sage's other employees identified the head as the bomber's.

There were few methods available for identification in those days. Fingerprinting was more than a decade off, and "Red Beard" was not listed in the files of professional criminals. So Byrnes put the head on exhibit in the window of a nearby undertaker's parlor, hoping that someone would recognize it. Crowds of curious onlookers filed past to look at "the head in Duffy's window." Because it was on Wall Street, pressure was put on Byrnes to remove the head.

Meanwhile a reporter had picked up a trouser button at the scene and managed to trace it to a tailor shop near Harvard Yard in Cambridge, Massachusetts. Through the tailor he located the parents of the mysterious young man. They admitted that they had received a letter from their son announcing that he would soon come into a large sum of money or be dead. A reporter had accomplished what Byrnes's detectives had not even tried to do.

In building the reputation of the modern detective bureau, Byrnes was helped greatly by the fact that, as public police officers, his men could bring in criminals for questioning any time they wanted, whereas private detectives did not have that authority. He personally provided an essential ingredient of the modern detective bureau, that it was headed by a powerful commander, often with close ties to the newspapers or big business, which made him virtually autonomous. The quid pro quos were that detectives could provide tips to newsmen in an era when crime stories filled the papers or could do discreet favors for business leaders, particularly in matters that the tycoons preferred to keep secret.

In 1892, following a major police scandal, Byrnes was made superintendent of police. In 1895, when Theodore Roosevelt became president of the board of commissioners, he dismissed Byrnes. The detective bureau continued in the same pattern, with Byrnes's trained men playing musical chairs with the top job. Detective work was so complicated that only those who had been taught by the master could command the bureau. The pattern became that if a chief of detectives, like Steve O'Brien or Jim McCafferty, wasn't satisfactory to the commissioner, he was replaced by George McClusky, who was then replaced by another Byrnes alum.

In Chicago and a few other cities, detective commanders often went their own way, defying orders from police chiefs. In other places it would take a generation for the detective bureau to receive virtual autonomy within the department.

William Burns was the early twentieth-century equivalent of Allan Pinkerton. The son of a Columbus, Ohio, tailor (who was also the elected police commissioner of the city), in 1891 he joined the U.S. Secret Service as an assistant operative. His reputation rose like a rocket and he became the most famous detective in America. His investigations brought down the San Francisco city government and sent the mayor to prison. In Oregon, he broke a land fraud ring in a case that led to the indictment of a U.S. senator. In 1909 Burns resigned from the service and opened his own detective agency, which became even more prestigious than Pinkerton's. The symbolic passing of the torch occurred when the American Bankers Association ended its contract with Pinkerton and gave it to the Burns Agency. While Pinkerton was old hat, Burns was fresh and new, as Clarence Darrow, the defense lawyer in Idaho, would learn when he ran up against Burns in the next big case of the era.

On October 1, 1910, amid a citywide struggle between the business community and organized labor, the *Los Angeles Times* building was dynamited, killing twenty-one. Unlike in Northern California, where labor was a valuable commodity and unions flourished, in the barren south, Los Angeles was practically part of the desert and cheap labor was readily available. In 1910 the cost of doing business in Los Angeles was about 40 percent lower than in San Francisco. If the unions imposed San Francisco wages, Los Angeles would not be an economically viable city.

The unions were suspected of dynamiting the *Times* building, owned by their chief antagonist, Gen. Harrison Grey Otis. The investigation was beyond the capability of the city's rudimentary police force, so William Burns was retained to lead the inquiry. At the time, Burns was investigating a series of bombings of construction projects throughout the United States. Among the suspects were Ortie McManigal and Joseph B. McNamara, brother of James McNamara, the secretary treasurer of the Structural Iron Workers. In 1911 Burns, accompanied by a special detail of municipal detectives, arrested Joseph McNamara and McManigal. They were secretly removed to Chicago and held for two weeks in the home of a Chicago officer, as Burns wrote, "to avoid the technicality of a writ of habeas corpus." Burns also had James McNamara seized in Indianapolis and taken to California. Though kidnapping charges were brought against Burns, nothing came of them since he was always careful to have local officers with him, so technically he was not the one making the arrest.

In Los Angeles the general view outside of business circles was that the accused were innocent, and organized labor across the country rallied to their support. They hired as their defense lawyer Clarence Darrow, who had been so successful against Pinkerton in the Idaho bombing.

Darrow's examination of the case convinced him that the McNamaras were guilty and Burns's evidence was too strong to be overcome. Therefore, to save the defendants' lives he had to plead them guilty. The McNamara brothers' conviction landed like a bombshell on organized labor across the country. Several prominent people who had supported their innocence committed suicide. Darrow was charged with attempting to bribe a juror and, in order to have the charges dropped, was required to sign an agreement to never again practice law in California. Burns had completely routed both the union movement in Southern California and the great Clarence Darrow.

Burns went on from triumph to triumph. The *New York Times* declared him to be a "man of genius." Arthur Conan Doyle proclaimed him the "American Sherlock Holmes." World War I brought disaster to Burns because he did some work for the Germans before the United States entered the struggle and also was caught making unlawful entries into a business office to plant a listening device. His enemy, the American Federation of Labor, pressured the New York courts to make him pay a fine.

The last great figure of the pre-1920s law enforcement era was not a swashbuckling detective but a Harvard gentleman. In 1907 the New York police commissioner, Gen. Theodore Bingham, (a former White House military aide to Pres. Theodore Roosevelt), appointed Arthur Woods, *New York Sun* reporter and former Groton School English instructor, to head New York's detective branch. At Groton, Woods had taught Teddy Roosevelt's children, who greatly admired him. This opened a connection with their father.

The appointment of an English instructor to the position once held by Thomas Byrnes was not as ludicrous as it would seem today. The NYPD had grown from four thousand men in Byrnes's time to ten thousand when Woods arrived, and it required men of higher education at the top. This was a credential most career cops lacked, so a number of civilian deputy commissioners were brought in from the law, the military, and other fields. Woods began with a six-week tour of continental Europe, where he studied big-city detectives. Continental investigators (who did not include the British) were miles ahead of Americans. Most of the top officials were university educated and familiar with the sciences, including the use of psychology in criminal investigations. When Woods returned, he introduced European methods to the New York detective bureau by forming special squads such as homicide and establishing a scientific crime detection unit. He avidly supported the use of fingerprinting, which was new to America.

Woods was not an office administrator. He loved to go out with his detectives and get his hands dirty investigating actual cases. The detectives generally liked him. However, in 1909 the mayor dismissed Commissioner Bingham over a case where detectives had allegedly harassed a young street tough named George Duffy. Woods left with him. The case was pushed by a Brooklyn judge named William Gaynor, who was anxious to become mayor. Soon after Gaynor succeeded to the office he was shot by a disgruntled civilian employee, although he survived. Later his administration was overwhelmed by a huge police scandal, and Gaynor dropped dead.

In 1914 Woods was chosen by reform mayor John Purroy Mitchel to be his police commissioner. Usually a society gentleman who was commissioner simply filled space, but Woods was different. Though he would marry into the family of J. P. Morgan Jr., Woods frequently spoke like an old-time detective. Once he declared, "You cannot do detective work in a high hat and kid gloves. We have got to use the methods of the crook and speak the language. There is too much snappy talk about the rights of the crook. He is an outlaw and defies the authorities. Where do his rights come in? If people spent less time talking about the dear criminals and more time helping the police to run them down we would have fewer criminals."

Woods could win the respect of detectives, but as the representative of a reform administration, he could never get similar approval from the rank and file. In 1917 Mayor Mitchel was defeated for reelection, and he and Woods both left to join the army. Mitchel was killed in a plane crash while training as a pilot. Woods returned from the war a colonel.

By 1920 the glory days of the Pinkerton Agency had long passed, Arthur

Woods, though in his prime, would never again hold a law enforcement post, and William Burns would make only a brief, disastrous comeback. The ghost of Tom Byrnes continued to haunt the corridors of the NYPD detective bureau, but no one as powerful as he ever emerged. The real strength of the bureau would be its large number of skilled detectives and the prestige of the body as a whole.

Detective Bureaus Dominate Policing: World War I–1970s

By World War I most sizable urban police departments had detective bureaus. That is, their detective force was not just a collection of individuals but an entity that functioned as the leading crime-fighting element and, in many places, comprised the elite of their departments. Patrol cops who walked beats gave lip service to fighting crime, but their efforts were overwhelmingly devoted to upholding public order. This might involve chasing toughs off the corners, breaking up street or bar fights, and addressing domestic squabbles. Though the patrol force was usually the first to respond to a crime scene, the offenders were most likely long gone when they arrived. It then became the detectives' job to find them. When detectives arrived at the scene of a crime, they usually took charge even if a patrol commander was present.

In addition to investigating crime, detectives gathered criminal intelligence and, in the manner of the British navy in the days of empire, they "showed the flag." Just as Britain's great warships reminded people all over the world of the power of England, detective cars cruised through high-crime areas of the city eyeing the hoodlum types and sometimes stopping to chat with them. By doing so, they reminded criminals of the power of the law. When detective squads drove past corners where thugs hung out, it would be enough to cause the criminals and rowdies to depart. On other occasions, police would line them up, search them, and if one was found with a weapon or stolen goods or fit the description of a wanted man, they would put him under arrest. Suspected criminals then had to appear in the lineup that most police departments ran. In these, detectives and crime victims sat in a darkened space, watching, while prisoners on stage were interrogated. This unnerved criminals because there was always the possibility that some crime victim might pick them out. The so-called experts who saw detectives as simply sleuths missed the point that they were also collectors of criminal intelligence information and, by showing the flag, they kept the criminals off balance.

All detectives had to conform to the culture of the bureau they served in. New detectives generally came from the patrol division, where they had demonstrated an ability to work hard and make arrests. Naturally, in a highly politicized urban environment, some people arrived at the detective bureau due to the fact that they had political influence. However, such men were not welcome and no one wanted to work with (i.e., carry) them. Their best hope was to latch on to some competent detective and function as his Dr. Watson—an amiable partner useful for some tasks but too slow thinking to be a real detective.

Newcomers to the bureau were trained via the apprentice method, working with veteran officers. They were required to learn how to use various data sources within and outside the police department. However, the most valuable information was not written down but possessed by other detectives. If a bureau man wanted information on an active criminal he might get more from his colleagues than from the criminal records section. Newcomers also had to learn bureau style. In many places detectives were expected to dress in classy suits and carry themselves with dignity.

In some cities, like New York, precinct detective squads were also part of the main detective bureau. Some outstanding detectives preferred to stay in a precinct, particularly if it was a glamorous one in Manhattan, Chicago's Near North Side, or Hollywood.

The best detective bureaus were usually run by a swashbuckling chief. In 1920s New York, it was John Coughlin who made his reputation handling big cases. As chief, when he heard shots fired, a not infrequent experience in the gangster area around police headquarters, he would spring from his desk, gun in hand, and lead his men into the streets. A big, burly man who wore a pince-nez, he was a bachelor and lived with his married sister. The police department was his whole life. He could ride down the streets pointing out places where big crimes had occurred or major arrests were made. As a young detective he had been assigned to the Chinatown precinct when tong wars were a feature of life there and occasionally bullets flew through the streets. During most of the Roaring Twenties (1920–28), he was the man who ruled New York City's detectives.

In early 1920s Chicago, "Iron Mike" Hughes, a twice-wounded detective, was chief of the bureau. He left after a Democratic administration replaced the Republicans. When the Republicans came back to city hall, Hughes served as commissioner of police from 1928 to 1930. Though there were other powerful chiefs like William Schoemaker, no one epitomized the spirit of the detective bureau more than the tough-talking Hughes.

Charles Dullea of San Francisco was a two-fisted ex-Marine who headed the detective bureau in his city from 1930 to 1940. Dullea was the man in charge of most major criminal investigations from the late 1920s until his ascension to chief of police. Sometimes he had to overcome crooked politicians or his own superiors to get the job done.

Several factors combined to ensure that the detectives would become the most powerful unit in American policing. One was the emergence of large-scale ownership of private automobiles. At the beginning of the century, there were only a handful of cars in the United States, and they were usually rich men's toys. By 1920 there were 7.5 million cars on the streets. Before the First World War, most crime was perpetrated in or adjacent to the offenders' neighborhood, where they were known to local police. Automobiles allowed criminals to journey to places far from their own areas. Keeping track of them throughout the city became a job for headquarters detectives.

Around 1910, gangsters from New York's Lower East Side slum districts began to operate in the Broadway Theater District and the socially elite Upper East Side. Tammany Hall's czar of organized crime, Sen. "Big Tim" Sullivan, began to worry that with criminals branching out he would lose control of them. Sullivan could not stop them from operating outside of their neighborhoods, but he could deliver them a crippling blow. He rammed through a law that made it illegal to carry an unlicensed firearm. The Sullivan Act (passed in 1911 and still in effect in New York) provided for a sentence of up to seven years in prison. At the time, there was virtually no limit on police authority to search an individual. If a cop frisked a man and found a gun on him, a court could not throw the case out for lack of probable cause because the legal rule was that the criminal must not go free just because the constable had blundered. This gave detectives a powerful weapon against anybody they deemed suspicious.

The 1920s brought Prohibition to the country, which strengthened the power of criminal gangs manyfold. A neighborhood gang that became big-time bootleggers could no longer be controlled by precinct cops. Only the virtually autonomous headquarters detectives under a swash-buckling chief were able to arrest them.

Another factor in the rise of detectives was the growing circulation of sensational newspapers, particularly those known as tabloids, a format that most blue-collar readers could comfortably peruse while riding to work via public transportation. Broadsheets, by contrast, generally envisioned their readership as middle class or above, people who would examine the paper in a leisurely manner at the breakfast table. The tabloid *New York Daily News*, founded in 1919, would eventually have a weekend circulation of four million.

Nothing was off limits to the tabloids. A *Daily News* photographer once sneaked a camera into the Sing Sing death house and secretly photographed the electrocution of murderer Ruth Schneider. A Chicago reporter put a stethoscope up to the wall of a grand jury room, where proceedings are, by law, secret. When the reporter learned who was indicted, he immediately called his paper, and it got out an extra in time to hand copies to some of the jury members as they came out of the criminal court building.

Crime stories were the lifeblood of the tabloids, and detectives possessed the information required by reporters. A detective commander could give out news tips to papers that favored the police department and withhold them from those that didn't. A city editor in a big town usually had two top police reporters, one at headquarters and one he kept in the office. If a negative police story by the office man appeared in the paper, the headquarters man would commiserate with the police brass and curse his colleague. It was the newspaper version of the police's "good cop/bad cop" routine.

Individual detectives benefited from maintaining a close friendship with reporters. Johnny Broderick, a famous New York detective, was known for his aggressive behavior, even demanding that criminals tip their hats to him. Those who were slow to comply usually found themselves upside down in a garbage can. One night at a Madison Square Garden championship prize fight, Broderick noticed two tough-looking characters hanging around and assumed they were gangsters. When they failed to remove their hats, he almost removed their heads. It turned out they were businessmen from out of town, and Broderick's job hung by a thread. Luckily for Johnny, his friends in the newsrooms managed to save him. Broderick was immortalized in the 1936 movie *Bullets or Ballots*, with Edward G. Robinson playing him on screen.

In the Southwest, where the traditions of the frontier remained, detective work often revolved around manhunts that ended up with the wanted man (or in Bonnie Parker's case, woman) being riddled with bullets. Some lawmen in that area had as many as two dozen notches on their guns.

Within headquarters detective bureaus, each special squad had its own persona. Homicide men were methodical, possessed above average knowledge of forensic science, and were adept at testifying in court, where they would be worked over by top lawyers. The robbery detectives were often blood-and-guts types with a notch or two on their service weapons. Their cousins the burglary detectives investigated crimes that were usually without witnesses. So, unlike robbery detectives, they had no suspects to pursue. Instead they spent time following known burglars and identifying possible offenders by their method of operation. In both units, and all other property crime squads, informers were a vital necessity. The problem with stool pigeons was that a detective sometimes got into trouble by averting his gaze when an informer committed crimes, and then if the informer was caught, by trying to keep him out of jail in order to continue using him.

When the "dragnet" was thrown out—that is, a roundup of all known hoodlums after a front-page crime—it was usually the headquarters robbery and burglary detectives who knew where most of the top thieves could be found. Lesser squads, like stolen autos or cartage (theft from boxcars or the hijacking of trucks), were meant to service the automobile insurance industry, the railroads, and trucking companies. Some detectives preferred to work in narrow fields, such as stolen autos. This was partly because there were never any big cases that brought heat to the unit. Also, having mastered the intricacies of the craft, it was less likely that they would be pushed out when some big shakeup came. In contrast, a front-page murder or big-time heist that remained unsolved might cause some detectives to be sent out to patrol in uniform alongside a cemetery. After doing penance, they would usually make their way back into what New York detectives called (plain) "clothes" and Chicago detectives referred to as "soft" (clothes).

Certain squads did not belong to the detective bureau per se but represented various special departmental interests. Chicago's antigangster squad, with the quaint name of Scotland Yard, reported directly to the commissioner. Chicago's youth-gang-control squad came under a deputy commissioner for staff service. In the middle part of the twentieth century it was headed by a saintly police commander who believed wholeheartedly in the tenets of liberal ideology, such as the necessity of providing more welfare and actively combating racial discrimination—strong sentiments for the 1950s. Though his cops did not always agree with him, they loved the guy, and so they managed to handle tough youth gangs without the excessive use of force. This brought them a great deal of praise from the social work community, not usually fans of policing. The commissioner thought the squad was a waste of manpower, but Mayor Richard J. Daley liked it because it gathered compliments from people who were normally cop critics. The unit's commanding officer's untouchable status was heightened by the fact that he was a legendary sports hero and a model Catholic layman.

A headquarters detective unit that was somewhat detached from the others was the bunco squad, which operated against fraudsters who worked the "big con" (large-loss swindles). Well-dressed, smooth and polished con men frequented the best restaurants and hotels, traveling from city to city, working their scams. A bunco officer was equally well dressed and frequented the best restaurants and other establishments where the con artists gathered. When a particular city was holding a major convention or other event likely to attract bunco men from all over the country, bunco officers would call on other big-city fraud detectives to come to their town to point out con men. San Francisco, Chicago, and New York were such great convention cities that their bunco commanders routinely requested help from out-of-town detectives.

As a residue of the anarchist, sabotage, and espionage era that ended after World War I, some departments had squads such as Chicago's security unit or New York's BOSSI (Bureau of Special Service Investigations). Every city had a bomb squad. Often members of these units would undergo special training in detecting secret writing and other tricks of terrorists. Some detectives would try to conceal the fact that, thanks to their immigrant parents, they were fluent in a foreign language or had been intelligence officers in the armed forces, in order to avoid assignment to security units. The work often involved boring surveillance and listening to dull speeches in a Balkan language. The security unit's work carried detectives into close cooperation with military intelligence and the FBI. In certain cities ethnic rivalries had to be carefully monitored. For example, where there were large Serbian and Croatian populations, the two traditional enemies were often at loggerheads. Some Croatians had been allies of the Germans during World War II. And some Serbians, though loyal Americans, continued to obey the dictates of the Serbian Orthodox Church, which was controlled by the Communist Party in Yugoslavia. Thus the long, dull speeches could sometimes turn into inflammatory material that would get the police department and the FBI moving. Yet such cases drew little attention from the American press.

The bomb squad was always made up of volunteers and usually its members were related to each other, because anyone dismantling an explosive device wanted to be sure that the person he was working with was a careful individual who followed directions precisely.

In the era between the two world wars, police departments were smaller than today, and the detective forces usually averaged 10 to 12 percent of the total size of the department. Most cities had about two police officers per thousand residents, although in eastern cities, where the cops had always performed administrative functions—in Boston they took a census—the ratio of police to population was higher. New York City, with nineteen thousand officers in the 1930s, had more police than marines in the U.S. Marine Corps, whose commandant had worldwide responsibilities. Chicago, with the addition of the Park District police, had a little over seven thousand. (The great architect Daniel Burnham, famous for his statement "make no small plans," had made the Chicago parks a sacred object. So the parks had their own police force identical to the city cops. In 1958 the two forces merged.) As one moved farther west, police ranks became thinner. In 1937 Los Angeles had only about twenty-seven hundred officers, San Francisco, thirteen hundred.

One surprising fact about the interwar era was that crime was low during both Prohibition and the Depression. Chicago averaged about two hundred murders a year. If it could drop to such a figure today, the city fathers (and mothers) would declare a month-long civic holiday. A city like Detroit, long written off as the murder capital of the country, was reporting about seventy murders annually in the 1930s, and San Francisco, around thirty. New York murders were in the three hundred range, minuscule compared to the 2,245 logged in 1990. The lower case-loads permitted more time for detectives to investigate crimes.

Detective bureaus often had their own rank structure. San Francisco detectives were rated as inspectors and received a higher salary than a sergeant. A first-grade New York detective had the same pay and prestige as a San Francisco inspector. Some Los Angeles or New York detective captains only held a civil service rating of patrolman or sergeant. Still, the public and other cops treated them as though their ranks were substantive. A detective "in charge" of a Chicago detective bureau roving squad might only be a patrolman, but he often operated as though he were a lieutenant. Hoodlums who might glare at a patrol car doffed their hats for a detective bureau squad car.

Finally, there were men in the bureau who specialized in tracking down extremely violent criminals. They were essentially man hunters, not investigators, and they usually got their quarry, dead or alive. Often these men were known throughout the department by nicknames such as Machine Gun Joe or Two Gun Pete. Detectives assigned to check out a gangster hangout for someone wanted for murder would not hesitate to walk in with Thompson submachine guns in their hands.

In most police forces only experienced detectives were chosen for command posts in the bureau. In some cities, such as San Francisco, there was a tendency to elevate the chief of detectives to head of the police force. Often this was a bad move because detective bureau chiefs were known not as good administrators but rather as strong leaders, who went out in the field with their troops. The active detective, upon becoming chief, usually would not be as interested in the myriad of administrative problems crossing his desk as he would be in the latest front-page murder.

Not all big-city detective forces were first rate. In Philadelphia in the 1930s, a ring of poisoners among Italian Americans carried out over a hundred murders and were not discovered by the police. Not until 1938, when U.S. Secret Service agents investigating a counterfeiting operation learned of the plot and informed the local prosecutor, was action taken. As a result, the two ringleaders were executed, and fourteen other members of the gang were given life sentences. About the same time, Washington DC was experiencing a number of murders that police were unable to solve. Finally, the U.S. Congress, which controlled the district (and was itself responsible for a great deal of police inefficiency), ordered the Metropolitan Police Department to appoint detective captains with extensive experience in criminal investigation from outside the force.

In the succeeding chapters we will study detective bureaus, embryonic or fully formed, in New York, New Jersey, Los Angeles, Chicago, Cleveland, San Francisco, Boston, and Dallas, as well as the FBI and the Texas Rangers. These were the men who, between the world wars and for fifteen to twenty-five years after, dominated American police departments.

2

Italian Squads

The Cops Replace the Private Eyes

On the night of March 12, 1909, New York City police headquarters at Centre and Broome in lower Manhattan was quiet. The tradition in the NYPD was that it hummed during the day when the commissioner was present and slowed down after he left. In the early morning hours there was virtually no one around with any authority.

Suddenly the desk officer on duty received a call from a reporter asking for confirmation that Lt. Joe Petrosino, head of the Italian squad, had been murdered in Sicily. The officer had no information to that effect, but it alarmed him, especially when the reporter told him the story had already appeared in a European newspaper and had been cabled to the United States. Shortly afterward, the American consul in Palermo, Sicily, confirmed that Petrosino had been killed. The next day panic swept the headquarters brass, who had sent their star detective into the lair of the Italian Mafia despite many warnings of the danger involved.

The police commissioner, Brig. Gen. Theodore Bingham, had previously been White House aide to Pres. Theodore Roosevelt. His army career ended when he lost a leg in an accident. An unimportant figure in Washington, where he was popularly referred to as "the White House butler," he was given the commissioner's job in 1906. Usually civilian police commissioners (there were no career cops appointed until 1918) simply presided over the department while the brass ran it. However, generals are usually a bad choice as a figurehead because they are used to controlling things in a czar-like fashion. They also tend to blurt out wild statements. Politicians are reluctant to tangle with the generals they have appointed for fear that the public will side with the man with the medals on his chest.

In 1909 Bingham got into trouble by describing Italians and Jews as "a riffraff of desperate scoundrels, ex-convicts, and jailbirds." When a storm erupted, the commissioner issued a formal apology, but his heart wasn't in it, and he cast about for a way to save face by amassing evidence of foreign-born criminality. A recently enacted federal law allowed for deportation, within three years of arrival, of any alien found to have concealed a criminal record. So Lieutenant Petrosino was sent to Italy to investigate the background of Italian criminals in America with a view toward deporting them. It was thought he might also be able to extradite some fugitives wanted in New York. Now Petrosino was dead and the responsibility was on Bingham, the man who had conceived the plan, so his staff scrambled about for an alibi.

Police detective work, as opposed to that of private eyes, always involved a heavy infusion of politics, which only a strong detective chief, like Thomas Byrnes of New York or Herman Schuettler in Chicago, could resist. In contrast, the Pinkertons were controlled by the brothers Robert and William and, as in any business, the paramount concern was the bottom line. As Josiah Flynt, a chronicler of turn-of-the-century criminals, observed, "The police hire men because of their political affiliations. The privates because of their ability to get something done."

One place where local police found it difficult to operate more effectively than the Pinkertons was the investigation of foreign organized criminal societies. The difference was illustrated by the way their Italian squad leaders operated. Frank Dimaio of the Pinkerton Agency was rarely seen publicly, and few people even knew what he looked like. Joe Petrosino was a celebrity interviewed by the press and often in the company of people like opera star Enrico Caruso. The Pinkertons liked to operate undercover, particularly in spying on labor organizations, but also in other cases. The municipal police felt that officers who went undercover might become corrupted, and so they used civilian informers as spies. The problem with the latter was that they were unreliable.

In the late nineteenth and early twentieth centuries, criminal secret societies were a relatively new phenomenon in America. The first to attract widespread attention had been the Irish "Molly Maguires" in the 1870s. The Pinkertons not only destroyed their organization but left twenty Mollies dangling from ropes. Detective McParland's success demonstrated how to deal with ethnic conspiracies—have a man of the same nationality as the gang penetrate their organization. Operating within, he would gather evidence to obtain criminal convictions at a trial.

Significant numbers of Italians began to arrive in the United States late in the nineteenth century. Most were from the depressed southern portion of the new Kingdom of Italy. Among them were men who had belonged, or claimed to have belonged, to societies like the Sicilian Mafia, the Neapolitan Camorra, or the Calabrian Fibbia. Italians had a history in Europe as plotters and assassins. This was natural because before 1860 Italy was not free but controlled by a number of outsiders, such as Spanish Bourbons and Austrian Habsburgs. After the kingdom was established in 1861, the northerners from the House of Savoy turned out to be as hard on southern Italians as any foreign ruler. The secret societies in the south provided resistance to northern control. However, ruthless crackdowns by police and troops, which killed many of the alleged "bandits," sent others to the United States.

One fault of the American police in dealing with the newcomers was that they did not learn from their failures. In 1888 an Italian was stabbed to death in New York City by a counterfeiter named Carlo Quartararo. Chief Inspector Byrnes told the *New York Times* the Sicilians were "banded together in a secret society known as 'the Mafia.' . . . Murder with some of them is simply a pastime." Carlo fled the United States but his brother Vincenzo, who had been his accomplice, was charged with murder. However, New York State was unable to convict him. An angry Byrnes then announced, "Let them kill each other." This was a typical reaction of American police. They did not understand the Italian secret societies and they had no interest in learning.

Beware the Raven

Frank Dimaio left an insurance job in Philadelphia in the 1880s to join the local Pinkerton office. Fluent in several languages, he was ideal for undercover work among other Italians.

Dimaio's tales of his adventures are like Allan Pinkerton's accounts of his activities—often exaggerated. When I did research in the Pinkerton archives for a book on the American Mafia the material available came from a series of 1940s magazine articles for which the Pinkertons had supplied information. Reading them, it was clear that Dimaio was not a one-man gang. His work benefited from that of many other detectives in the agency. However, a writer cannot introduce ten characters into an article when the adventures of one, usually the leader, can tell the story. However embellished Dimaio's accounts were, they checked with known facts and were essentially true.

In 1890 local mafiosos murdered New Orleans police chief David Hennessey. The whole affair was murky. New Orleans was a wild town. After the Civil War it was policed by blacks who were members of the occupation force. The Union commander Gen. Ben Butler, a Yankee lawyer, had publicly declared that any Southern belle who disrespected a Union soldier would be treated like a woman of the town (a prostitute). Thus by the time the occupation ended, New Orleanians did not hold the police in high regard, and young men often tested their muscles against cops. When Hennessey was a detective he had been fired for his part in the murder of his superior, the chief of detectives. As chief of police he was accused of favoring one faction of Italians over another. One evening Hennessey was shot-gunned to death while walking home. Nineteen Italians were arrested for the crime, though in the end there was sufficient evidence to bring only nine to trial.

Dimaio was planted among a group of Italian suspects being held in the local jail. There he assumed the name of Ruggerio, a well-known counterfeiter who was in an Italian prison at the time. Carrying $6,000 in high-quality phony money sewn into the lining of his coat, he had gone to a small Louisiana town where, by prearrangement, he was seized by Secret Service men. When they delivered Dimaio to the New Orleans jail, they warned the guards that they had had to fight a gun battle to overcome this desperado. The Italian inmates were wary just the same. A jail clerk had tipped them to a mysterious prisoner who might be an informer, and when Dimaio was put in a cell block with eight of the suspects, they eyed him suspiciously.

Finally, Dimaio managed to win the confidence of the mafiosos. Instead of cozying up to his fellow prisoners, he treated them with the scorn of a high-level criminal for small-time punks mixed up in a murder. Like any good detective investigating a crime with multiple suspects, he was looking for the weakest link. His eyes soon fell on one of the suspected trigger men, Emanuele Polizzi, who worked hard to ingratiate himself with Dimaio. At first the detective ignored him, though eventually they became friendly.

The prison conditions took their toll on Dimaio, whose weight dropped from 185 pounds to 140. Alerted to his condition by a lawyer that his agency had secretly retained for him, William Pinkerton sent word that it was time to have Dimaio released on bail. The detective refused. The frightened Polizzi had at last begun to talk about the Hennessey assassination and how the gang had drawn straws to determine who would do the actual shooting (a familiar detail in murders allegedly involving Italian secret societies). Dimaio covertly wrote down everything Polizzi said on scraps of paper and got him to make his mark on them. Finally, satisfied that he had enough, Dimaio contacted his lawyer to bail him out.

The trial itself lasted two weeks, with the prosecution presenting sixty-seven witnesses. Polizzi's supposed jailhouse confession was not introduced in evidence—although the information it contained provided useful leads, it was not thought to be legally sound. When the jury finally reached a verdict, six of the defendants were acquitted outright. As for the three others, the jury could not decide. The crowd outside the courthouse was stunned. Then came shouts that the jurors were bribed. The New Orleans newspaper the *Picayune* described the verdict as one that "astonished every person." Later an official federal investigation would find that the evidence in the trial was far less compelling than people believed.

W. S. Parkerson, an attorney close to New Orleans mayor Joseph Shakespeare, took charge of a citizen rally, delivering a fiery oration. "When courts fail," he declared, "the people must act. . . . Our chief of police is assassinated in our very midst by the Mafia society and its assassins again turned loose on the community. . . . Are you going to let it continue?" His audience roared, "No! No! Bring on the dagos!" Parkerson led the way to the jail where the six acquitted defendants were still locked up pending the adjudication of some lesser charges. By the time they arrived the crowd numbered six thousand.

Outside the jail, the mob began pounding on the doors, which had been locked by the sheriff's deputies. "We want the dagos," people shouted, while others called out mockingly to the prisoners inside. The mob entered the building and quickly proceeded to the women's quarters after a female inmate pointed out that some of the prisoners were hiding there. Polizzi was one of the first caught, taken outside, hung from a lamppost, and blasted with rifle fire. A second prisoner soon followed. Cornered in a courtyard, a half a dozen others dropped to their knees and begged for mercy. They were all shot dead.

For a time the Italian government threatened to go to war with the United States, but it settled for payment of a few thousand dollars for each dead Italian who was actually a citizen of that country. No charges were brought against anyone for the lynching. A Genovese family named Reppetto, who had been living in the city since the 1860s, like all Northerners disliked the Southern bandits. In 1890, when the Southerners began to institute their reign of terror, the Reppettos and a number of their relatives departed for Chicago, abandoning any connection with the South and their background as seafaring people.

New Orleans was only the beginning for Dimaio, who went on with his undercover work, especially in the mid-American industrial belt.

He wandered through the Italian colonies of cities like Chicago and Pittsburgh dressed in the garb of the typical Italian laborer. The reports he produced inspired Joe Petrosino to declare that Dimaio was the most knowledgeable man in America about the Mafia.

When an undercover detective is used frequently, word begins to get around about him in the underworld. Gangsters whispered about the mysterious man in Columbus, Ohio, who arrived in their circle shortly before a police crackdown and disappeared afterward. As the word was passed, confederates in other cities recalled a similar individual whose sudden appearance and equally sudden disappearance seemed to coincide with law enforcement drives. The underworld even gave him a nickname, The Raven, as in Edgar Allen Poe's poem.

In 1905 a state game warden was murdered in Pennsylvania and the Pinkerton agency was retained to investigate the case. Dimaio and his squad began their assignment by assuming false identities. They went to Ellis Island, where they blended in with other immigrants and were eventually hired by a group of contractors from the Pennsylvania limestone quarries and taken to Hillsville. The town was known locally as Hellsville because it was dominated by Italians who extorted money from the locals. Posing as hard-drinking tough guys, the Pinkerton detectives worked their way into the mainstream of the local Italian gangs.

In July 1907 a plan was laid to arrest the Hillsville extortionists in one fell swoop. On payday a Pinkerton agent assumed the role of paymaster. As a suspect came to the window to get his wages, he was told that his pay envelope was short a dollar and he was asked to step into a back office where it would be made up. As each man entered, he found a detective pointing a gun at him while another handcuffed him. After eleven men who had gone into the office did not come out, an Italian woman who was part of the gang sounded an alarm, and the remaining suspects bolted from the line. Suddenly, the engineer in a freight locomotive idling on nearby tracks moved his train forward and frantically blew the whistle. The doors of several boxcars opened and disgorged police, who proceeded to complete the roundup. Thirty-five of the men arrested were convicted and sentenced to terms of three to ten years. The killer of the game warden was hanged. The case was eventually written up by Arthur Conan Doyle as a Sherlock Holmes mystery entitled *The Valley of Fear*.

Of course there was another side to the Hillsville story. The union leaders claimed that the convicted men were not mafiosos but just workingmen who opposed management policy. The murder of the game warden had occurred not because of Mafia issues but because he had killed an Italian's dog.

Dimaio lived into his nineties and, as late as the 1957 Appalachian conference of the American Mafia, provided valuable information on the Mafia to reporters.

The Hero of Little Italy

Joe Petrosino was born in 1860 near Salerno in southern Italy and arrived in New York with his family at the age of thirteen. At eighteen, he became a "white wing," or city street sweeper, and quickly rose to a foreman's job. In 1879 the famous police inspector Alexander "Clubber" Williams took charge of the sanitation department, where the graft was exceptionally good. Petrosino, who had come to admire cops while shining shoes outside police headquarters, managed to impress him with his drill-sergeant style of bossing his crew around. Like Williams, the powerfully built Petrosino took no back talk. When Williams returned to precinct duty, he used the young Italian as an informer, and in 1883 he had him appointed to the regular force, even though Petrosino was three inches below the required height of five foot, seven inches.

His superiors always liked Petrosino, who was hard working and deferential. With his swarthy complexion and broken English, he was not overly popular with his mostly Irish colleagues in the Lower East Side precinct to which he was first assigned. As Italian crime grew, however, Petrosino began coming to the attention of the top brass. In 1890 the department made him a detective, principally to investigate crimes involving his countrymen. His knowledge of the language and culture gave him an advantage over the mostly Irish and German detectives. Many of them did not understand, for example, that Italians preferred to live among their own *paisanos*—people from their town or section of Italy. Thus if a suspect was from Calabria, the place to look for him was among other Calabrians. Sometimes men from particular villages all lived in the same building.

Petrosino became feared among Italian criminals and, since his name was close to the word for parsley in Neapolitan dialect, when he prowled an area some hoodlums would shout out, "Parsley, see the nice parsley."

In 1895 reformer Theodore Roosevelt, as president of the board of police commissioners, named Petrosino a detective sergeant with a roving commission to investigate Italian crime. In 1905 Commissioner William McAdoo formed an Italian squad with five detectives working under Petrosino.

Petrosino would sometimes wander about disguised as an Italian laborer just off the boat, but he did not go undercover in a Mafia gang. Municipal police did not do that. He received medals from the Italian government for capturing fugitives wanted in Italy and was constantly praised by the New York press, which he courted assiduously.

In 1903 a U.S. Secret Service operative was following a suspect in New York's Little Italy. The man was unknown to the service, and they dubbed him "the newcomer." The federal man, Larry Richey (né Ricci), was only eighteen but already a veteran investigator. As a thirteen-year-old boy living in Philadelphia, he had served as an aide to William Burns in breaking a counterfeiting ring run by politically powerful individuals. He would later become a star of the service. While Petrosino was plodding and inarticulate, the American-born Richey was bright, glib, and ambitious. In 1901 Richey's mother secured her sixteen-year-old son an appointment as a full-fledged Secret Service operative. Shortly afterward, he Americanized his name. A quarter of a century later, he would be the principal secretary (in modern parlance, the chief of staff) to Pres. Herbert Hoover. For nearly half a century he served Hoover in a number of capacities.

Although Richey left his papers to the Herbert Hoover Library in West Branch, Iowa, they do not contain much mention of his career as a Secret Service man. If a scholar could obtain any notebooks or similar documents that Richey maintained throughout his career, he would have a priceless guide to fifty years of high politics in the United States. For example, it was Richey who recommended J. Edgar Hoover for the directorship of the FBI. Once, as a journalist, he pursued a federal judge notorious for raping hotel maids. When the judge heard Richey was on his case, he resigned from the bench.

On that day in Little Italy in 1903 Richey heard that the New York police had been called to a location where a body was found in a barrel. He contacted the NYPD, and together they identified the corpse as the man Richey was investigating. Bill Flynn, chief of the New York Secret Service (who would later be deputy commissioner over NYPD detectives, then chief of the Secret Service, and finally director of the [federal] Bureau of Investigation), took over the government's investigation. Now three of the greatest detectives in America, Flynn, Petrosino, and Richey, formed the triumvirate that worked on the so-called barrel murder case.

The chief of the NYPD detectives at that time was Thomas Byrnes's protégé "Chesty George" McClusky, who wanted to make sure that the NYPD, and not William Flynn, controlled the case. So McClusky ordered his men to round up a couple of dozen members of the Lupo-Morello gang, the first prominent Mafia family to operate in New York City. Petrosino went to visit the victim's brother in Buffalo and learned that the dead man carried a certain watch on his person. The police linked the watch to a one-dollar pawn ticket for a wristwatch that they found on one of the Lupo-Morello gang members, Thomas Petto, age twenty-four. McClusky then staged what would today be called a perp walk. He marched the gang members from headquarters, through Little Italy, to the courthouse, allegedly on the grounds that patrol wagons did not arrive in time to fetch them. It was in fact the old Roman parade of the captives before the crowd. Supposedly some Italians attempted to liberate the prisoners, and the police met them with heavy force. Administering a public beating to the mafiosos was a way to demonstrate to other Italians how impotent the gang really was. The idea probably originated with Petrosino, who was the expert on Italian affairs. Petto was indicted for murder, but he managed to beat the rap. Afterward he settled in Pittston, Pennsylvania, but was murdered by an assassin sent from New York.

Describing the work of Petrosino's Italian squad, the *New York Times* declared, "When murder and blackmail are in the air and the men folks are white faced but searing and the women folks are saying litanies to the Blessed Mother that their dark-haired cherub children may be safe from the Black Hand kidnappers [although it was a popular reference to the Mafia, this term actually referred to a method of extortion in which individuals received letters with black hands in the margin, demanding money or else], a telephone call comes to police headquarters in Mulberry Street for Petrosino, and all Little Italy looks to the Italian detective for protection." Compared to Dimaio's undercover investigations, Petrosino's were amateur hour. But the Pinkerton agents were "private" eyes. The NYPD was open to press scrutiny, and many of its actions were meant to be political or to protect the reputation of the mayor and the police commissioner.

It was natural for Petrosino to go to Italy in 1909, but it was a huge mistake. He had left his homeland as a boy and knew little of that country's corrupt politics. Friends warned him that "south of Rome everyone is Mafia." Even the prime minister had Mafia connections. Petrosino departed carrying a list of two thousand names. Though his trip was supposed to be secret and he traveled under the name Guglielmo Desimone, many people recognized him. Police Commissioner Bingham even mentioned Petrosino's trip to the press.

Social class was important in Europe. Italian police officials were educated gentleman of high standing, and they did not look favorably on a simple peasant representing his country on so vital a mission. The investigation should have been carried out by the U.S. State Department in consultation with a European-educated police official like the patrician Deputy Commissioner Woods. If Woods had come over, the Italian police would have taken steps to ensure that a Harvard gentleman and an intimate of Pres. Theodore Roosevelt was not murdered on their soil.

Petrosino went to Sicily, the stronghold of the Mafia, and began to nose around. At around 9:00 p.m. on March 12, he was murdered while waiting for a trolley car near a statue of Garibaldi in downtown Palermo. According to the American consul, four shots were fired, three of them striking the unarmed detective. Petrosino had actually left his gun back at the hotel.

The killing might have been contracted in America, as some people would claim. More likely, it was to avenge the effrontery of Petrosino walking into the Mafia's headquarters city. It is certain it could never have been carried out without the approval of the local Mafia leader, Don Vito Cascio Ferro, who years later claimed credit for it.

In the aftermath Bingham began to dissemble. He stated that detectives were on their way to continue Petrosino's investigation, knowing full well that the Italian government would not allow a New York detective to go into Sicily. He claimed Petrosino himself had conceived the plan, although the detective was ill at the time and, for the first occasion in his career, he was somewhat reluctant to take an assignment. One story that circulated claimed Petrosino was working as an advance man for President Roosevelt, who had just finished his term in the White House and was going to travel in Europe. Of course it was false. Petrosino was given a virtual state funeral, but the Italian squad was abolished. Bingham himself was soon out the door at police headquarters.

Richard Enright, the first career cop to serve as police commissioner (1918–25), characterized the individuals who served in commissioner ranks from 1901 to 1914. According to Enright,

> During the last 13 years, nine Commissioners have come and gone, with an average service of a little more than one year. With them have come and gone some 33 Deputy Commissioners, and all the fads and fancies mixed with ideas, good and bad, that mortal man has ever dreamed of. Everything has been tried upon the police dog.
>
> Some have been lawyers, some have been Judges, some have been railway men, some have been schoolmasters, some have been book-keepers, some have been bartenders, some have been plumbers, some have been milliners, and some have had no visible means of support. We have had everything but a clam digger and an undertaker.

Of course, a lot of those gentlemen's families were among the leading citizens of New York.

Big Mike

In the 1970s *New York Times* reporter and best-selling author Robert Daley would spend a year as commissioner of public information of the NYPD. Like any good journalist, Daley set out to make himself familiar with the history of the organization he was working for. To his surprise, he discovered that the police department did not care a whit about its history. Nobody ever felt that anything could be learned from it. All problems were addressed as if it were the first time they had occurred.

This is not the view of the military. What happened in World War I and II is still studied in staff colleges, and Vietnam is almost as contentious an issue in the Pentagon as it was during the war that ended forty years ago. Once, when I questioned police recruits at an academy graduation, I asked them if they knew who Lewis Valentine was, and none could answer affirmatively. At the time he had been the longest-serving commissioner of police in New York City, holding the office from 1934 to 1945. Any West Pointer who could not identify Douglas MacArthur or Dwight Eisenhower, contemporaries of Valentine, would never have made it to graduation.

No more clear example of the police department's institutional amnesia can be found than in an incident in the career of Mike Fiaschetti, the eventual successor to Petrosino as head of the reinstituted Italian squad. In 1914 a reform administration took over city hall and installed Arthur Woods as police commissioner. Woods revived the Italian squad under the leadership of the Roman-born Detective Fiaschetti, who grew up in Massachusetts. When Fiaschetti was appointed to the NYPD in 1908 at age twenty-two, he had been quickly chosen by Petrosino to work on the Italian squad. After Petrosino's death, when the squad was abolished, its members went back to precincts but they were sometimes called upon when there was an upsurge of Italian crime.

In 1918 the Tammany administration's police commissioner, Richard Enright, increased the Italian squad to 150 members. Fiaschetti was made an acting captain and put in charge. His fame as an expert on Italian crime spread, and the city of Akron, Ohio, soon asked that he be lent to them to help locate a group of New York gunmen who had killed four of their police officers. Fiaschetti picked up two of the suspects, transported them to Ohio, and obtained confessions from others. A local Italian brothel keeper had paid the gunmen $150 each for the murders. Fiaschetti remained in Ohio to continue his investigation and, because of his work, a number of men received life sentences.

It was the kind of investigation that once had been undertaken by private eyes, but now cops were more likely to be called in to handle the matter. In his new position, Big Mike was the king of Little Italy, entitled to the best seat in any Italian restaurant and, the most prized, a complimentary box at the Metropolitan Opera.

In 1920 an Italian gunman named Papaccio shot at another man on a Lower East Side street, killing two innocent women. Fiaschetti found that the killer had fled back to Naples. So Commissioner Enright ordered him to go there to apprehend the fugitive, taking along the records of some other Italian gangsters who had fled to Italy and picking them up too. The move sounded like a rerun of the Petrosino mission, which had ended so badly just eleven years earlier. To "assist" Fiaschetti, the mayor's brother-in-law, Det. Sgt. Irving O'Hara, was sent along. O'Hara was not bashful about throwing the mayor's name around. When Mayor John Hylan's first police commissioner took office on January 1, 1918, the detective sergeant was full of advice for him. The commissioner, Frederick Bugher, was a Prussian sort who constantly clicked his heels and saluted. He had previously been one of the gentlemen deputy commissioners of the department and had no interest in his subordinate's views. So after just twenty-nine days in office Commissioner Bugher was called into the mayor's office, where Hylan yelled at him, "You're fired!" All Bugher could do was click his heels and withdraw.

The Italian police picked up Papaccio before the New York detectives landed but refused to extradite him because he was not a U.S. citizen. Fiaschetti then requested that thirty-four other fugitives be picked up. O'Hara returned to New York, but Fiaschetti remained in Italy.

At first he accompanied the Italian police on a series of raids. Then he decided to go undercover in Naples, headquarters of the Camorra. Being Roman born, he would stand out there, so he went to the capital of Italy and adopted the guise of a criminal fugitive. There he persuaded the locals to arrange his passage to America, which meant having to go to Naples to board a ship. He was given a torn five-lire note, and the other half was mailed to a Camorra leader in Naples as a means of identification.

Fiaschetti had not been in Naples long when he was arrested by detectives with whom he had previously gone on raids. At first they did not recognize him, and when they frisked him they found two automatic pistols and a stiletto. Finally, as they were handcuffing him, he cried, "It's me, Fiaschetti." Word reverberated throughout the Italian police, all of whom were aware of Petrosino's ill-fated trip to Sicily. Now another American detective was about to get himself killed and cause a lot of problems for the Italian government. From then on, the Italian police assigned detectives to follow Fiaschetti, but they couldn't keep up with him. Eventually he made contact with the "oyster woman," a gray-haired lady who was active in the Camorra. When Fiaschetti gave her the torn five-lire note, she handed him the other half and welcomed him. He then became an honored guest in Naples. Like Petrosino, Fiaschetti reveled in danger and intrigue, but it was a good way to get killed. Finally Fiaschetti went to a meeting of Camorra leaders where it was announced that the leader of the New York Italian squad, Fiaschetti, was traveling around Italy in disguise. The Camorras thereupon vowed to "hunt this policeman by the blood of the Madonna." Fiaschetti decided it was time to depart for New York.

Back in America, Fiaschetti led his squad in a drive against Italian criminals in New York and other cities. Once he assigned detectives to accompany an informer to Grand Central Station to trap a Mafia emissary. The lead detective, a Genovese named Reppetto (no relation to the author), posed as a traveler at the station, and when the Mafia emissary, Stefano Magaddino, approached the informer, Reppetto arrested him. At headquarters, the thirty-year-old Magaddino knocked the eighty-seven-year-old informer down, and Fiaschetti and Reppetto had to teach Magaddino the error of his ways. Magaddino would later become head of the organized crime family in Buffalo and one of the ruling members of the national Mafia commission. His experience with Fiaschetti and Reppetto might have influenced him to go to Buffalo and stay there.

Fiaschetti was becoming a problem for his superiors because he talked too much and too indiscreetly. So in 1920 the commissioner merged the Italian and the bomb squads. Fiaschetti was reduced to his substantive rank of sergeant and subordinated to an Irish lieutenant. Next came an incident where an Italian American lawyer connected with Tammany tried to force his way into Fiaschetti's office when the detective was conducting an interrogation. Fiaschetti threatened to throw him out, to which the lawyer said, "You wouldn't dare." Fiaschetti dared, and as a result was transferred from the detective bureau to the district attorney's office. In 1924 he was pressured into early retirement. Not until 1934, when Fiorello LaGuardia became mayor, did Fiaschetti come back as deputy commissioner of the city's Department of Markets, with the mission of cleaning up the produce rackets.

During LaGuardia's administration many Italian American detectives were used in drives against top gangsters. For some reason, no officer of Italian ethnicity has ever been chosen to be commissioner of the NYPD, though the post has been occupied by Irish, Scandinavians, WASPs, Jews, and blacks. In the wider world, any time an Italian would appear to be moving up, the cry of Mafia would be raised. In many cases it did not matter if the person was a northerner, who by definition would never have been allowed into a southern secret society.

The fundamental mistake the American police made in dealing with Italian organized crime from 1890 to 1920 was to assume it was just a series of quarrels among unimportant foreign immigrants. In the 1940s, when Frank Costello owned Tammany Hall and the Mafia influence extended through state, local, and even federal government, Italian organized crime was finally taken seriously. By that time, however, the Mafia was so powerful it would take forty years for the federal government to defeat them.

3

Murder in Hollywood and the Real Los Angeles Detective Bureau

It was fitting that the first sensational murder in the era of detective dominance occurred in Hollywood, California, and not surprising that nearly a century later we still don't know "who done it." Murder mysteries in movie land were always hard to solve. Its inhabitants were trained to assume false personas and spin lies. Half of them were using names that were not on their birth certificates. In addition, the industry jealously guarded its secrets.

In 1922 the city of Los Angeles was a thriving boomtown with a population of over half a million. Two decades earlier it had one-fifth that number. The causes of its growth were the sunny climate that attracted the old, the ill, and the stereotypical Iowa farmer fleeing winter's blasts; a hard-driving group of entrepreneurs who accumulated wealth through land speculation; and the fortuitous arrival of a great national industry.

Around the same period as the 1910 *Times* bombing, New York nickelodeon operators were looking for a place with sunshine year-round, which would permit outdoor shooting, and that would provide legal shelter from the Edison trust, whose lawyers and goon squads constantly went after filmmakers for infringement of patent. Moving three thousand miles from New York put moviemakers in a locale where the sun shone most of the time and the state courts took a different view of the law than those back east. When the moviemakers arrived they settled in a Los Angeles orange grove called Hollywood.

By the time of the First World War, films were America's fourth-largest industry, and Hollywood was the home of America's only true royalty—movie stars like Mary Pickford, Douglas Fairbanks, and Charlie Chaplin. The United States had never before had royalty. The Astors and Vanderbilts of New York, the Biddles of Philadelphia, and the Cabots and Lowells of Boston were lords and ladies among their own circle. But the average American knew or cared little about them.

In contrast, the whole nation went to the movies regularly to follow the doings of Mary, Doug, and Charlie as if they were members of their own family. Everybody was familiar with the official life stories of the beautiful young women who had come to Los Angeles from mid-America (or in Pickford's case, Canada) and were paragons of maidenly virtue. The male stars were all war heroes, champion athletes, or Western lawmen. The truth was that most of the girls had been involved with men and drugs while the men were like cowboy superstar Tom Mix, who often had trouble remembering in what towns he had supposedly served as marshal or what wars he had fought in. Even Pickford, "America's sweetheart," dumped her husband to marry Fairbanks.

If Hollywood was dreamland, then the city of Los Angeles was all too real, an example of the corruption and inefficiency that characterized many municipalities at the time. The business community was the strongest bloc, but there were others. There were the Protestant ministers who served the vast flock of migrants from mid-America who poured into the city. The Protestantism of California was not the kind taught in Ivy League divinity schools but rather the hellfire and damnation variety that arose out of the camp meetings and revivals of nineteenth-century mid-America. The ministers took a dim view of movies, which frequently portrayed half-naked women.

In a dark corner of the political structure were the gangsters who controlled the city's gambling, prostitution, and bootlegging as well as the police department. The reality of Los Angeles policing was demonstrated by a popular detective, Capt. Guy McAfee, who was well known for warning gamblers of raids by calling them on the telephone and whistling "Listen to the Mocking Bird." McAfee eventually became tired of simply accepting bribes from the gamblers and instead became a major player himself. On the plus side, the climate and glamour of Hollywood and the rapid expansion of the city, where a fortune could be made in land speculation, convinced many people that Los Angeles was a desirable place to live. It did not take a seer to forecast that someday the City of Angels would be a great world metropolis.

On the morning of February 22, 1922, Henry Peavey, a colored (the polite term then) servant entered the bungalow of his employer, William Desmond Taylor, in Alvarado Court, an upscale residential community favored by members of Hollywood's elite. Peavey's regular schedule was to arrive at around 7:30 a.m. to start grooming his boss for work as a top director at Hollywood's leading movie studio, Famous Players–Lasky. The studio had been founded by the pioneer moguls of Hollywood, Adolph Zukor, Samuel Goldwyn, Jesse Lasky, and Cecil B. DeMille. Later known as Paramount, it would be a top power in the industry until the studio era ended fifty years later.

As Peavey entered the bungalow, he noticed Taylor, fully dressed, lying on the floor face up with blood on his shirt. He was obviously dead. Peavey began shouting, "Mr. Taylor's dead. Help! Help! Mr. Taylor's dead."

Residents of the court flocked to the scene, where some started collecting souvenirs and trampling over possible evidence. A few called their friends to tell them the news. The most important call went to the manager of Famous Players, Charles Eyton, who headed for Taylor's home and dispatched a crew of employees to search the house and remove any papers they found. Shortly after 8:00 a.m., Det. Thomas Ziegler of the LAPD, alerted by the housing complex manager, arrived at the scene. Ziegler, a heavyset man in his sixties, had been a cop for thirty years, starting when the job was little more than a small-town constable's position. A local doctor also turned up and began examining the victim's body. Since Taylor was wearing an expensive diamond ring on his finger and had seventy-nine dollars in his wallet, he probably had not been attacked by robbers. The doctor concluded Taylor had died of a stomach hemorrhage.

Eyton was about to have the body removed from the scene, but one of the bystanders, an actor himself, argued that it should be left until a coroner could examine it. When the deputy coroner arrived and turned the body over, he found a bullet wound in Taylor's back. Though only a trained male nurse, the coroner had prevented the case from being literally buried. The "doctor" disappeared. Soon more detectives arrived and ordered everyone out of the house.

In 1922 Hollywood was already reeling from major scandals and its future was in jeopardy. In one instance, a beautiful young star named Olive Thomas was found dead of a drug overdose. A virile young leading man named Wallace Reid allowed his body to become wasted from excessive use of drugs and, at the time of Taylor's murder, was known to be dying. Superstar comedian Roscoe "Fatty" Arbuckle had been arrested in San Francisco for allegedly murdering a young actress named Virginia Rappe in an orgy at a local hotel. One account had Arbuckle trying to penetrate her private parts with a broken Champagne bottle. Unfortunately for Arbuckle, Los Angeles influence did not extend to the Bay Area, and the local district attorney was turning the case into a national sensation.

By the beginning of the twenties, clergymen and society leaders were beginning to question the impact of Hollywood on the country. Cecil B. DeMille, who usually struck a high moral pose, was regularly turning out sex orgies disguised as biblical dramas. Among Hollywood's most severe critics was the Catholic Church, America's largest religious institution. Unlike the Protestants, Catholics spoke with one voice. If its millions of members were told by their bishops to stop attending movies, the church would present serious financial problems for the industry. What the protesters were really aiming for was censorship of Hollywood, in which case DeMille's biblical spectacles would be reduced to real religious tracts and there would be plenty of empty seats in the theaters.

Like many Hollywoodites, Taylor was not the man he appeared to be. He had been born William Cunningham Deane-Tanner, a member of an Anglo-Irish gentry family. While pursuing a career as an actor on the Broadway stage, he married a chorus girl who was the daughter of a wealthy Wall Street broker. In 1908, at the age of thirty-six, he deserted his wife and daughter, went to Hollywood, and changed his name. Not until 1912, when his wife saw him acting in a movie, did his family learn his whereabouts.

The LAPD, which was charged with solving Taylor's murder, did not have the kind of power possessed by cops in New York, Chicago, or San Francisco. Los Angeles had become a big city too recently for the police department to have developed any kind of traditions or system. Police chiefs were fired frequently. Police officers in other cities were usually local boys or immigrants from Ireland with relatives in politics and on the police force. In Los Angeles, virtually all cops came from somewhere else, particularly the South. Immigrants from Ireland went to San Francisco. A patrolman's salary of one hundred dollars a month looked attractive to a young man from Tennessee, but less so when he found out the cost of living on the coast. The detective bureau, such as it was, had no institutional memory or long-established working procedures. It was simply a collection of individuals. Within the leadership of the LAPD, a number of men held the rank of brevet or acting captain or lieutenant. Even some civilians were given badges and operated as though they were real cops. Finally, there was no powerful chief of detectives like Thomas Byrnes of New York.

The most successful police officer was a Texan named Jim Davis, who had arrived in Los Angeles in 1911 when he was twenty-two years old, fresh from the army, and within a month was hired by the LAPD. At that time there were no entrance exams, and maybe the fact that he had been a soldier in the Philippines indicated that he could work in a disciplined organization and knew how to use firearms. Davis was lucky to arrive when the force was being doubled from 250 to 500 officers. After three days being paired with a veteran cop, he was sent out alone on the streets to maintain order. While patrolling his beat, young Davis became friendly with a married woman and was soon called in by Chief Charles Sebastian, who fired him. That sort of thing was common in Los Angeles. Sebastian himself was charged with being too fond of the ladies. To meet the criticism, he staged a fake attempt on his life and won so much public sympathy that he was elected mayor. When a newspaper finally revealed that the murder plot was false, the tall, handsome Missourian left town. In Davis's case, Sebastian later allowed him to come back on the force. Soon he was working on the vice squad, where the earnings were a lot higher than a hundred dollars a month. Later Davis would serve two nonconsecutive terms as chief of police, where his principal accomplishment was giving pistol demonstrations that included having a cigarette shot out of his mouth.

In the Taylor case the police had a cast of suspects worthy of any Hollywood crime drama. The coroner's inquest ruled that death had occurred about 7:50 the previous evening. Around that time superstar Mabel Normand, who had often teamed with Fatty Arbuckle, came to Taylor's home, ostensibly to borrow a book. Normand, the on-and-off girlfriend of Mac Sennett, the producer of the Keystone comedies, was also a drug addict who lived a wild lifestyle. Upon banning her films, the state of Ohio declared that she always seemed to be involved in shootings. In addition to the Taylor incident, her chauffeur had once shot a man with Normand's gun. One theory in the Taylor murder was that he had been killed by a drug dealer whom he had threatened to expose as Normand's supplier.

Another movie star involved in the case was blonde Mary Miles Minter, officially eighteen though actually twenty, who was being built up by the studio as a rival to Pickford. Minter had been a stage child in New York and was brought to California by her mother, Charlotte Shelby. When the murder weapon was declared to be a .32-caliber pistol, suspicion fell on Shelby, who owned such a gun. Later it was revealed she had a family member deliver it to relatives in Louisiana with instructions to dispose of it in a swamp. Charlotte Shelby's motive was thought to be fear that she would lose control of her meal ticket, her daughter Mary, or because she herself cared for Taylor. The fact that Taylor was bisexual did not seem to discourage his female admirers.

The movie industry wanted the murderer to be some petty criminal, like a robber or a disgruntled ex-employee such as a valet named Edward Sands, who had been previously discharged from Taylor's service for theft. The press, led by the Hearst papers, wanted it to be a woman because that was better for circulation. If it turned out to be a star, like Minter or

Normand, newspaper sales would go through the ceiling. Hearst's ace reporter, Adela Rogers St. John, pushed a story about Minter's intimate garments being found in Taylor's bed. She even reported that the two women had a physical clash when Minter showed up at the same time as Normand on the night of Taylor's death.

The direction of the investigation fell to the local district attorney, an office usually held by a hack politician. The incumbent at the time was Thomas Woolwine, a man with his eye on winning the governorship later in 1922. He decided to appoint as chief investigator LAPD detective sergeant Edward King, age forty-six, who had been a cop since 1906. A jockey-sized man, he was an expert motorcyclist. King brought along his partner, Jesse Winn. While King was one of the shortest cops on the force, Winn was one of the tallest. They made an odd-looking pair riding around on their motorcycles. Only in small towns did detectives ride motorcycles, but usually there they also did double duty as traffic cops and funeral escorts. King swore that he would maintain absolute loyalty to the district attorney. To bolster King's position in the police hierarchy, Woolwine had him promoted to lieutenant immediately. It was a clever move by the DA. He already had his own detective squad, called "district men," who maintained a considerable distance from the LA police. District men could always be identified by their more expensive suits. By putting an LAPD officer in charge, Woolwine hoped to head off some of the obstruction and criticism that would come from the city police, and his own detectives would be respectful toward King as a Woolwine appointee.

The city police broke into different camps regarding the murderer. Some officers felt sure it was Charlotte Shelby. Others pointed to Henry Peavey, who had recently been arrested for making improper advances to men in a Los Angeles park. The narcotics squad looked at the drug dealers mixed up with Normand, and still other detectives focused on Sands, the valet who had been seen hanging around the area not long before the murder. Capt. David Adams, who forced his way into the case, insisted that Sands was guilty. One of Taylor's neighbors who had arrived at the director's home shortly after the murder claimed that a man brushed past her. However, she later thought it might be a woman disguised as a man. This pointed to Charlotte Shelby. Certain detectives got so frustrated that they asked to be taken off the case.

When Lieutenant King began zeroing in on Shelby, District Attorney Woolwine shocked him by revealing that he had a personal relationship with her and was convinced that she had nothing to do with the murder. In essence, the man who was in overall charge of the investigation was functioning as a lawyer for the chief suspect. Later that year Woolwine was badly beaten in the governor's race and lost interest in the investigation.

As is still common in Hollywood cases, the press decided to solve it themselves. Reporter Florabel Muir, a power in Los Angeles for the next thirty years, believed that Peavey was the murderer. So she decided to take advantage of a stereotype associated with African Americans and trick him into a confession. In movies, blacks were often portrayed as frightened of ghosts. So with the help of two confederates, Frank Carson and Al Weinshank (the latter a Chicago hoodlum who in 1929 perished in the St. Valentine's Day Massacre) Muir offered Peavey ten dollars if he would identify Taylor's grave in Hollywood Park Cemetery. When Muir and Carson drove Peavey to the site, Weinshank was waiting. Dressed in a white sheet, he declared, "I am the ghost of William Desmond Taylor. You murdered me. Confess, Peavey!" Since Weinshank spoke with the accent of a Chicago gangster, whereas Taylor's speech was that of an English aristocrat, Peavey laughed out loud.

A number of detectives later reported that they were told, or at least it was intimated to them, that they should not probe too deeply into the Taylor case. When two Chicago journalists were sent out to Los Angeles to report about the crime, they learned quickly that it was bad business to write a detrimental story about the movies, as "the boys might cut your throat." Undersheriff Eugene Biscailuz, later the longtime sheriff and a powerful political figure, took the two reporters to his office and informed them that they were in physical danger. He was alleged to have said, "The industry has been hurt. Stars have been ruined. The stockholders have lost millions of dollars. A lot of people are out of jobs and incensed enough to take a shot at you."

Gradually the Taylor case faded from the scene. In the 1940s a woman named Margaret Gibson, who had been an actress and moved in the circle of Taylor and his friends, supposedly confessed on her deathbed that she was the killer. Deathbed confessions are generally worthless, except in movies, and Gibson's was ignored.

For years some Hollywood people tried to solve the crime. King Vidor, a top director, thought he had the answer, and he later tried to make a movie about it but failed to get financial backing. Some people believed it was because the powers in Hollywood still did not want the true story told. As noted earlier, the 1950 Hollywood classic *Sunset Boulevard*, starring former silent star Gloria Swanson, may hold a clue to the murder that occurred twenty-eight years earlier. In the film, Swanson was given the name Norma Desmond, an approximation of Mabel Normand's last name and William Desmond Taylor's middle name. Her character shoots and kills William Holden because her love for him is unrequited. At the time, many people in the movie industry who had been around at the time of the Taylor case were still working. Was the film's "Norma" an effort to offer a clue to the killer? In Hollywood anything was possible.

Mabel Normand died of a drug overdose at age thirty-seven. Mary Minter was let go by her studio but lived on for many years; however, she never shed any light on the case. Minter broke away from Charlotte Shelby, who was always the leading suspect. For some years, mother and daughter kept apart, but they eventually reconciled.

Hollywood cover-ups, or alleged cover-ups, would continue as part of the normal business routine. In 1932 the industry was stunned when the reigning sex goddess, Jean Harlow, twenty-one, married Paul Bern (né Paul Levy), a forty-three-year-old mousey but cultured European. He hardly resembled the men Harlow made love to on the screen, such as the rugged Clark Gable. The marriage lasted just two months, ending when Paul Bern put a bullet through his head. In the best Hollywood fashion, the butler found the corpse and notified the studio first. The bosses of MGM, Louis B. Mayer and Irving Thalberg, rushed to the scene. Only later did anyone think to call the police. Instead, they held what many called a "scenario conference" over the corpse. Allegedly, they found a letter from Bern to Harlow saying, "Dearest Dear, Unfortunately this is the only way to make good the frightful wrong I have done you, and to wipe out my abject humiliation. I love you. You understand that last night was only a comedy."

However, the handwriting was not Bern's. After two hours the police were summoned to the scene. They did virtually no forensic work and accepted the scenario MGM had prepared. Hollywood's ultimate response to the incident was to make a movie about it starring Jean Harlow.

Just three years later, on the morning of December 16, 1935, a colored maid named Mae Whitehead went to the home of movie star Thelma Todd to wake her up and get her ready for the day. She was unable to find her employer in the apartment she maintained atop a business that she was part owner of, Thelma Todd's Sidewalk Café, a place patronized by elite Angelenos. Whitehead then looked in the garage and saw Todd slumped over the wheel of her Lincoln Phaeton. At first she thought the star was sleeping. When she could not wake her mistress, she went to the café and got an employee to accompany her back to the garage. The employee told Whitehead to fetch the café manager, who called the police. When LAPD officers arrived on the scene, other than a little blood around Todd's mouth, they claimed there were no signs of violence. There were two and a half gallons of gas left in the Lincoln's tank and the ignition was on, but the battery was completely discharged. Apparently, Todd had died of asphyxiation.

The twenty-nine-year-old Todd had come to Hollywood from Massachusetts when she was only twenty years old. At first, her good looks earned her the name the "ice-cream blonde." After a few years in Hollywood, though, her wild lifestyle was such that the nickname was changed to Hot Toddy. When talkies arrived, she went to work for Hal Roach, the king of comedy.

In 1932 Todd married Hollywood talent agent Pat DiCicco, who was known to be connected with Hollywood mob figures. During the Depression the studios cut wages and, to help break employee strikes, Mafia muscle was brought in. When the strikers were beaten off, the employers could not get rid of the mob. After Todd and DiCicco were divorced in 1934, she took up with a director named Roland West, who was co-owner of Todd's roadhouse and maintained an apartment next to hers. West, who was married, did not live with his wife, a minor actress.

Todd had attended a party the night before her death at the Cocoanut Grove, where she had an angry confrontation with DiCicco, who was there with movie star Margaret Lindsay. Detectives concluded Todd had sought shelter in the Lincoln because West, angry that she had stayed out late at the party, arranged to have the door to her apartment locked. Todd had to get out of the cold by sleeping in the car. The fact that Todd was still wearing $20,000 worth of jewelry when she died made robbery an unlikely motive for her death.

By the mid-1930s, the public was down on Hollywood in the same way it had been at the time of the William Desmond Taylor murder. Famous director Busby Berkeley was on trial for being the driver in an automobile accident in which two people were killed and five seriously injured. Allegedly, Berkeley was intoxicated at the time. He was not the only Hollywood person who ran over people. Clark Gable did it, but the LA authorities could not indict the king of Hollywood.

The Los Angeles Police Department of 1935 was no different than the one in 1922. Scores of officers held acting captain and lieutenant ranks, corruption was rampant, and the police were inefficient. It was later alleged that three detectives from Sheriff Eugene Biscailuz's county police force came to Hal Roach and told him Roland West had admitted killing Thelma Todd. They asked his opinion of what should be done. Biscailuz was the movie industry's man in Los Angeles and the detectives likely persuaded Roach to agree that West should not be arrested.

There were rumors that Todd had dated New York mob boss "Lucky" Luciano, and when he wanted to put a casino in her roadhouse, she refused. Eventually, it became the conventional wisdom that she had been murdered on Luciano's orders. A coroner's jury ruled the death was accidental with the possibility of suicide, though no suicide note was found. Once again it was thought that Hollywood had reached into the police department and had the investigation closed because it did not wish to have one of its stars known to have been murdered by a Mafia kingpin, for fear it would open the industry to more criticism. At the time, Luciano was positively identified as being in an Arkansas jail, where he was hiding out from Special Prosecutor Tom Dewey back in Manhattan.

A few years later, mob influence was exposed in Hollywood and even Twentieth Century head Joe Schenck had to go to jail for a while until he turned government witness. Schenck, who was the brother of Nick, who ran Lowe's Inc., which controlled MGM, was probably the most powerful man in Hollywood. He was also the power behind Sheriff Biscailuz. Despite many charges and scandals involving the sheriff's office, Biscailuz remained on the job until his voluntary retirement in 1958, just as the studio system he had served so well was beginning to collapse.

In 1923 August Vollmer was appointed chief of police. He had held a similar job in the university town of Berkeley, California. There he had achieved a national reputation as an efficient police administrator and a well-known advocate of law enforcement reform. The tall, handsome, and divorced Vollmer soon ran into the typical kind of trouble that Los Angeles celebrities did. He was accused by a woman of breaking his promise of marriage, and she allegedly attempted suicide over him. Political opponents charged that Vollmer's appointment was illegal because he had not taken an entrance exam, so he had to sit for the patrolman test. With his one-year appointment coming to an end, the local newspapers predicted the beginning of September would see the end of August. Soon he was back in Berkeley. Like any LA chief, the only way Vollmer could have survived was to make "arrangements" with the people who ran the vice and gambling in the city.

"Red" Hynes, the Real Chief of Detectives

In 1930, at a Congressional hearing on radical influence in the United States, one witness produced such extensive files and gave such knowledgeable testimony that he quickly became rated as the top security policeman in the country. He was Capt. William "Red" Hynes of the LAPD. Born in 1897 in St. Louis, he had joined the army in 1914, where he spent the next seven years working as an undercover investigator spying on the Industrial Workers of the World (IWW) and other leftist organizations along the Pacific coast. As a result of Hynes's effort, whole groups of individuals were sent to jail. One federal official credited him with doing "more than any other person to help the government in their operation against the IWW throughout the nation" and for breaking up the organization in Southern California.

In 1921 Hynes joined the LAPD and was assigned to the Red Squad. Such units already existed elsewhere. In Chicago it was known as the security unit and commanded by Lt. Make Mills (the Americanization of a Polish name). Mills claimed to have served as an officer in the Russian czar's army, and from 1896 to 1947 he ran the Chicago security unit, which doubled as the bomb squad. In New York there were various names for the antiradical squad, but the one that eventually emerged was the Bureau of Special Service Investigations (BOSSI). Neither Mills nor his opposite number in New York had a fraction of the power that Hynes possessed in LA. Still, big-city police always cracked down hard on radicals whenever they raised their heads. Sometimes a "radical" was defined simply as a man who opposed the mayor. Though often accused of being a Communist, New York's Fiorello La Guardia established a special squad of detectives to spy on the Reds. The only one to complain was J. Edgar Hoover, who did not want the competition.

In 1927 Hynes was appointed acting captain, a position that carried no extra pay but allowed him to make a great deal of money as a private consultant for the business community. Businessmen furnished him and his squad with offices in a commercial building. The symbolism was telling. Hynes did not work for the LAPD, he worked for private interests. So totally obsessed with his mission was Hynes that even his nickname did not come from the color of his hair (which was brown) but from his fanatical efforts against the Communists he saw under many Los Angeles beds.

Like any detective commander, Hynes understood the importance of amassing voluminous records on the people who were his targets. He seized various documents and prepared long reports on different organizations. One factor to his advantage was that reform organizations were easy to penetrate. All that was necessary was a display of ideological fervor. Only the actual Russian Communists, who had learned from their time under the czar, screened potential members carefully. Reformers also had a tendency to fight among themselves and to turn petty slights into grudges. Such individuals were easy to recruit as police informers. Hynes compiled dossiers on leftist organizations in Los Angeles and maintained a network of spies within them. One woman, a reformer on the board of every radical group in the city, was later revealed to be working for Hynes. It was simple for her to take the attendance list at various meetings and send it to the police. Detectives then knew whom to watch. If it was a marginal member of a leftist group, the detectives made a call on the individual's employer and warned them about the dangerous tendencies of one of their workers. This was usually enough to cause the individual to drop out of leftist activities. Hynes also maintained a very close relationships with military and naval intelligence. While most Americans were unaware of it, agents of these organizations spied on American radical groups, kept an eye on possible Japanese spies, and burglarized Communist Party offices. Many of the men who supplied the military with information were former officers who held key positions in civilian life and were far above the usual police informant type.

Hynes's squad didn't just serve as detectives but acted as shock troops against the various Red demonstrations, and they did not hesitate to use rough tactics. They often broke up Communist meetings with tear gas. Sometimes they were called in by leftists, such as Upton Sinclair, whom they had once refused to allow to read the Declaration of Independence in public, to protect them from a rival group. When protesters gathered for demonstrations in the street, Hynes's detectives, bolstered by American Legionnaires, were present to engage in a tactic called "shove day." They would bump up against the various demonstrators until they finally shoved them off the streets. Naturally, complaints were made about the squad by the ACLU leaders who often had their heads broken at such events. However, the support for the squad by powerful leaders of Los Angeles like Harry Chandler, publisher of the *Los Angeles Times*, meant nothing could be done to stop its activities.

Even jurisdictional boundaries did not limit Hynes. His squad frequently went into other cities, like Ventura, and broke up Communist meetings. On one occasion they were evicted from a leftist meeting by the Pasadena police.

In retrospect, the Red Squad met the definition of an outstanding detective bureau. It had an enormous amount of information available to it, its men were good at what they did, and it was headed by a dynamic commander who, because of his support from the business community, did not have to answer to his superiors in the police department. Hynes was Thomas Byrnes reincarnated. In Los Angeles, where cops stopped all automobiles at 3:00 p.m. on Good Friday so the drivers had time to contemplate the life of Christ, the automobile-loving public did not protest. Thus most Angelenos were hardly likely to be concerned about Hynes's tactics against some left-wing radicals.

Another man who used a special intelligence squad was Mayor Frank Shaw, who was elected in 1933. He centralized gambling and other payoffs in his office, where his brother Joe was the collector. His squad also spied on enemies of the mayor. While Hynes's and Shaw's squads rampaged, Chief Davis occupied himself by participating in shooting matches, though he did establish "bum blockades" by stationing Los Angeles cops at the state lines to turn back transients.

In the 1930s, the police reform forces were led by Clifford Clinton, the son of missionaries in China, who was the owner of two popular restaurants. During the Depression he did not charge people for their meal if they could not afford it. He was constantly being sued as a form of harassment. Hollywood had plenty of trick motorcycle riders and stuntmen and most of them, over the years, seem to end up on the hood or under the wheels of Clinton's car, or they slipped on the floor of his restaurant. Of course, this was mild compared to what could have been done, and the boys in Mayor Shaw's squad would argue that they were just "funning" him. When none of that worked, they set off a bomb outside Clinton's house. Clinton then made the mistake that many reformers do: he fought fire with fire. He hired a shady private investigator named Harry Raymond, a former Los Angeles cop and San Diego police chief. Raymond was straight out of a Dashiell Hammett story featuring a rogue private eye of the type played on the screen by Humphrey Bogart. Apparently Clinton and other reformers adhered to the philosophy of Vidocq, that "it takes a crook to catch a crook."

On January 16, 1938, Raymond opened the hood of his car and a bomb exploded, giving him twelve dozen shrapnel wounds, but he survived. Subsequently Mayor Shaw was recalled in a special election and replaced by a straight-laced judge, Fletcher Bowron. The intelligence squad was disbanded and the captain who headed it was sent to prison for his role in the bombing. As part of the cleanup, Hynes's Red Squad was abolished, though he had nothing to do with the Raymond incident. The mayor reduced him to the civil service rank of patrolman and sent him out to pound a quiet beat on the West Side.

The key to understanding Los Angeles detective operations is to recognize that criminal investigation was not the most important function. Instead, LA sleuths had to concentrate on controlling radicals and to play ball with the press and the city's elite groups. In the 1920s and 1930s intelligence work was more important than solving murders and robberies. In the 1940s and 1950s law enforcement was devoted to keeping eastern gangsters out of the city. Between Red Squads, gangster squads, and intelligence squads, collecting information for the chief of police became the most important detective task.

Often this led to false information being circulated that would cause Hollywood to make mistakes. In the 1940s the movie moguls believed that federal narcotics officers were going to arrest America's sweetheart, Judy Garland, for extensive drug use. The information was wrong. The feds had no intention of doing such an unpopular thing, but the studio did not know this. Federal arrests, unlike local ones, could not be fixed. So Hollywood found a patsy, Robert Mitchum, who had served time on a Georgia chain gang and was hard for studio brass to handle. When Mitchum was set up and busted for drug use at a party by state detectives, it looked as if his career was over because that had been the traditional pattern for previous Hollywood bad boys. But the cool guy who puffed a joint appealed to a new generation of filmgoers and, instead of ending his career, the arrest made him a big star.

4

The Hall-Mills Murders

Seven months after the murder of William Desmond Taylor, an even more sensational killing occurred three thousand miles away in New Jersey. On the morning of September 16, 1922, Lt. Thomas Dwyer of the New Brunswick Police Department received a phone call about bodies in De Russey's Lane, two miles away at the far end of town. He immediately dispatched Ofc. Edward Garrigan to the scene. Since there were no police cars in the department, Garrigan hitched a ride from a motorist. En route they picked up Patrolman James Curran, who was walking a beat. When the officers arrived, there was a crowd gathered. A couple walking through the lane had found two dead bodies and ran to the house of a neighbor, who called the police. Some people were already helping themselves to souvenirs and to crab apples from the trees that overlooked the lane. When detectives arrived and completed their preliminary investigation, it was clear to them that the scene had been staged. Both bodies were lying on their backs, shot in their heads with a nearby .32-caliber pistol, the man once and the woman three times. The bodies had been positioned side by side after death, and the man's Panama hat was placed over his face with his calling card at his feet. Torn-up love letters were placed between the bodies. The woman's throat had been sliced open.

The dead man was identified as Edward Wheeler Hall, forty-one, an Episcopal minister at St. John's Church in New Brunswick. The woman was determined to be Eleanor Reinhardt Mills, thirty-four, a choir singer at the church. The couple were married, but not to each other. Mrs. Hall (née Francis Noel Stevens) was reputedly a very wealthy woman because she was related to the family that owned the Johnson & Johnson medical bandage company. Mills's husband was a church sexton (janitor) who also worked at a local elementary school in the same capacity.

Before the investigation could get fully underway, some time was spent arguing as to which county the bodies were in. The crime had been reported to New Brunswick in Middlesex County but some police argued that it actually occurred in Franklin Township, part of Somerset County. Finally it was decided that Somerset, the seat of which was Somerville, had jurisdiction, and its county detectives took over the investigation. During the progress of the case prosecutors and detectives from four other New Jersey counties would become involved.

New Jersey was a hybrid state. The northern portion was largely an extension of New York City; the southern portion was a satellite of Philadelphia. While the cities in the state had had regular police forces since the nineteenth century, rural law enforcement was a patchwork of sheriffs and other members of the local courthouse crowd until well into the twentieth century. This meant that many places were very poorly policed. However, the system held up reasonably well until the automobile age, when cars began bringing urban criminals into small-town America.

The Middlesex and Somerset County detectives who were the investigators in the early stages of the Hall-Mills case were appointed by their county prosecutor, and most had learned their trade on the job. George Totten of Somerset had held his post for twenty-eight years. Another veteran, Ferdinand "Ferd" David of Middlesex, declared, "This case is a cinch." Four years later it no longer looked that way.

None of the cops who arrived were skilled in forensics. No one thought to secure the crime scene or photograph and fingerprint the bodies.

Patrolman Garrigan, of New Brunswick, allowed a reporter to handle Reverend Hall's calling card, which was later found to contain a number of prints. The police also did not maintain any chain of evidence on possession of the card.

None of the county detective forces numbered more than a handful of men. There was no such thing as a detective bureau. These existed only in cities like Newark and Jersey City.

The year before the Hall-Mills murder, a threat to the county courthouse crowd arose with the formation of the New Jersey State Police. It was modeled after similar forces founded in New York and Michigan in 1917 and Pennsylvania in 1905. Its troopers enlisted for two years and, if they absented themselves without permission, they could be prosecuted for desertion. Troopers were required to live in a barracks and could not marry during their first enlistment.

The troopers were the American equivalent of the Royal Irish Constabulary, the French Gendarmerie, and the Italian Carabinieri. All three were half military and half police. Americans had never embraced this form of policing, and the Pennsylvania troopers, who frequently clashed with labor unions, were nicknamed the Cossacks (though the real Russian Cossacks were not police at all but a fearsome body of warriors who served the czar).

The founder of the New Jersey force, Col. H. Norman Schwarzkopf, was a resident of Newark and a graduate of West Point who had fought in France in World War I. Seeing no future in the tiny peacetime army, he sought the top job in the new constabulary. It was thought that the first superintendent would be chosen by New Jersey's powerful political czar, Frank Hague. However, Gov. Irving Edwards listened not to his patron but to his son, who had fought overseas with Schwarzkopf. The West Pointer put his men through a rigorous boot camp, where they were taught the basic principles of law enforcement. Then they were assigned to patrol the state (by motorcycle in the built-up north and on horseback in the still-rural south). Though Schwarzkopf's troopers were a hand-picked body of men, they were not well trained as criminal investigators. Thus when they were confronted with serious crimes they were ill prepared to deal with them.

Many people forecast trouble for the troopers from Frank Hague, who was simultaneously the boss of Hudson County, mayor of Jersey City, and czar of the state's politics, no matter what party was in power. Hague had started his career as public safety commissioner in Jersey City. As mayor he used his police to run a virtual dictatorship. Civil libertarians who came into Hague's town to protest his actions would be greeted with a marching American Legion band that would follow them around and play so loudly that the protesters could not be heard. On occasion, cops would simply pick up the interlopers, take them to the waterfront, and put them on a ferry to New York City. A police lieutenant sat in the office of Western Union reading all telegrams that came into the city. During Franklin Roosevelt's administration, the postmaster general of the United States wanted Hague arrested for opening mail. Roosevelt had no intention of doing that to the man who had delivered previously Republican New Jersey to the New Deal. So he simply sent a messenger to tell Hague to cease the practice. Every Hudson County cop owed his appointment or promotion to Hague, and there was no countervailing force. Anybody who opposed the mayor would be summarily fired. He became known nationally from a statement he once made when an official denied his request, declaring that it was against the law. Hague replied, "I am the law."

Hague made sure his police in Jersey City were efficient. He would sometimes put in a call and wait around to see how long took for officers to arrive. If they were too slow, Hague would boot them in the rear. To many people's surprise, his cops and the state police troopers got along well. Schwarzkopf was smart enough to stay out of city affairs and therefore had no clashes with the various New Jersey bosses. In Hague's view, the spit-and-polish troopers in their French blue and gold uniforms looked impressive patrolling the highways. This included the main road between New York and Washington, the busiest thoroughfare in the country. They were a good advertisement for Hague's New Jersey.

Somerset County, where the Hall-Mills murder would be tried, was one of those areas where the local gentry was very influential, and DA Azariah Beekman was not eager to bring a criminal case.

Many people had long suspected that Reverend Hall and Mrs. Mills were carrying on a love affair. In any such situation a spouse would be considered as the possible murderer. Eleanor's husband, James Mills, appeared to be one of life's losers. He made thirty-eight dollars a week and gave everyone the impression that he was a beaten man. He might have had the motive to kill, but he did not seem like an individual who would be up to it.

Francis Hall was seven years older than her husband. A decade earlier, he had come to St. John's Church in New Brunswick from Brooklyn. Though Hall had no doctorate and St. John's was not the leading church in town, it was still a desirable position in an era when Episcopalians were ranked as the most prestigious denomination in America. So the marriage raised the social status of both parties. Living with the Halls was Francis's brother Willie Stevens, a dimwitted individual who never held a job and spent most of his time hanging out in the local fire station. Willie had been born in the South and possessed what some people believed were African American features. Another brother, Henry Stevens, lived in nearby Lavallette. The most successful of the family was Francis Hall's first cousin Henry de la Bruyere Carpender of New Brunswick, a stockbroker in New York City.

County detectives turned up an eccentric farmer who was known by the name of Jane Gibson, although she also had others. Gibson owned a hog farm adjacent to De Russey's Lane. On the night of the fifteenth she claimed to have heard a noise near the road, where thieves had recently been stealing her corn. According to her, she saddled up her mule, Jenny, and rode to the scene. There she heard and witnessed two men and two women struggling in the lane. Suddenly a gun was discharged, causing one of the women to call out, "Oh, Henry." Then three more shots were fired. So Gibson got back on Jenny and left the scene, telling no one what she had seen. In the end, the case seemed to boil down to the "Pig Woman" versus a society family.

Like the courthouse crowd anywhere in America, one talent New Jersey's members had was a nose for politics. They knew that the leading citizens of the county sympathized with Francis Hall, and since prosecutors were elected to office and detectives appointed, they did not want to risk their jobs. Had the case occurred in a place like New York City, where there was a regular detective bureau and public sentiment would probably have been against the Stevens/Hall family, it would have been a different story. Yet the detectives could not ignore the fact that the arrangement of the bodies, with the love letters displayed, suggested that the crime had been committed not by a robber or casual passerby but by someone who wanted to show the close relationship between the two victims. Despite the expectations of some detectives, the family did not crack under interrogation. Though, given their social rank, they were not questioned too harshly.

As the investigation in Somerset County dragged along, public criticism forced the governor to appoint a special counsel, a former prosecutor in Essex County, the center of which was New Jersey's biggest city, Newark. He brought a detective staff with him, but again, they did not move too vigorously. No matter where the special prosecutor was from, the case would have to be heard by a jury from Somerset County, and in the end, no charges were brought. This pleased most Somerset voters but did not sit well with the state's newspaper readers, particularly those who subscribed to New York City papers.

The New York tabloids were deeply dissatisfied by the outcome of the case. They had been hoping for a lengthy murder trial involving socialites. Their readers liked crime, scandal, and sport, not stories out of Washington or Wall Street. The *Daily News* even developed a name for their typical reader, directing their reporters to "tell it to Sweeny." Sweeny was envisioned as a burly, blue-collar Irish American who read the paper while he rode the subway or had a brief lunch out of a bucket. Two other tabloids in New York, the *Mirror* and the *Evening Journal*, both owned by William Randolph Hearst, competed vigorously with the *Daily News*.

Broadsheet newspapers were read by the upper middle class, who did care about things like the tariff and what was happening in European banking circles. Sometimes these readers would steal a look at a story on the latest sex scandal, but most such news was generally played down in "respectable" papers like the *New York Times* or the *Herald Tribune*.

The tabloids had been checkmated, but all was not lost. New Jersey law enforcement would be made to do its job. Whatever the power of the local gentry in some rural county, it was assumed it would not be sufficient to stand against the mighty New York newspapers, then at the height of their power. Philip Payne, editor of Hearst's *Daily Mirror*, began an investigation of the matter. When tabloids went after someone they did not worry too much about ethical rules. Because of constant stories that appeared in the *Daily Mirror* and other papers, in 1926 the New Jersey governor appointed a special prosecutor to reexamine the Hall-Mills murders. Hudson County senator Alexander Simpson was a much tougher individual than the previous prosecutors. He was not impressed when the Stevens' defense lawyers told him that their clients could not have committed the murder because they were a fine Christian family. He sarcastically exclaimed, "I suppose only Mohammedans commit murder."

The appointment of Simpson meant that the investigation was transferred from the hicks to the city slickers. Simpson tapped a number of figures from Hudson County to go along with him, including Capt. Harry Walsh of the Jersey City police, who was later chief of detectives and then chief of police of the city. Simpson also brought with him Patrick Hayes, the chief of police of Hoboken, Hudson County's second-largest city. These were Frank Hague's people, but their influence did not extend to Somerset County. The New Jersey State Police, now grown old enough to play with the big boys, assigned Capt. John Lamb, who had worked on the case in 1922 as a sergeant.

The feeling among the Hudson County crew was that the Somerset team had not conducted a thorough investigation and that the Stevens family could not stand up to vigorous interrogation. So on July 28, 1926, Francis Hall was arrested at her home by a contingent of officers, including Captain Lamb and Captain Walsh. Captain Lamb also secured warrants for Willy Stevens and Henry Carpender, the cousin who was a stockbroker. The fourth man charged was Francis Hall's other brother, Henry Stevens.

Detectives are a tough lot, and so are some of the characters they run up against. But the police succumb easily to stereotypes, such as the one that says rich people are not strong enough to withstand the kind of grilling the police can administer. Detectives do not know enough about upper-class life to recognize that many people who have gotten on top have done so, and stayed there, because they are a pretty tough lot themselves. In 1922, during the original investigation, if cops had picked out the weakest links in the Stevens family and suddenly confronted and grilled them, they might've gotten some kind of confession. But now, with the constant retelling of the story, the family was not likely to change what they had previously said.

When the cast was assembled, Simpson faced an uphill battle. Henry Carpender could produce many witnesses to testify that, at the time of the murders, he was blue fishing in front of his house miles away. The state did catch one break. A vestryman named Ralph Gorsline and another young choir singer had denied in 1922 that they were anywhere near the scene of the murder. In 1926 they admitted they were and had heard shots, but beyond that they did not provide much information.

Once again, the state had to rely on the Pig Woman, Jane Gibson. It was too bad that someone like Thomas Edison, the noted New Jersey scientist, was not walking down De Russey's Lane at the time of the killing. Though when the high-priced defense lawyers got through cross-examining him, they probably would have cast doubt on whether he had invented the lightbulb. But reputable witnesses usually are not roaming around lovers' lanes at midnight. Finally, Gibson was brought in on a stretcher to testify, and the court was notified that she had very little time to live (in fact, she would live another four years).

The main problem facing the defense team was to discredit Gibson. This was largely accomplished by pointing out that she had told several versions of the event and her own life history. At the very least, her personality was unique. However, the testimony she presented was logical in that she lived adjacent to the scene of the crime, and because she owned a farm, it was hard for the Stevens lawyers to paint her as a complete idiot.

The state was also compelled to use witnesses such as a state police deserter who had worked on the case in the first investigation and claimed that he had been bribed by a detective for the defense to leave New

Jersey. The former trooper was brought in from prison, handcuffed to a military policeman, and on the stand he had to admit to deserting not only from the state police but also from the U.S. Army and the U.S. Navy. Such an individual did not seem to the jury like a man who had a great deal of respect for the truth, even under oath.

In the end, the Somerset jury arrived at the verdict they had wished to arrive at in the first place: not guilty for all the defendants.

The Hall-Mills case involved more than a criminal investigation. Blue-bloods, such as Francis Hall's family, had suffered a lowering of status because of the First World War and the events of the Jazz Age that followed. Their claim to leadership in America was in jeopardy. The Great Depression and World War II would put the finishing touches on the power of the old WASP aristocracy. By the 1960s they couldn't even control the great universities that their families had supported for years. Indeed, they could not manage their own children.

In the 1920s there was a strong feeling that the upper classes should stick together. If in 1926 an Episcopal minister was found to have behaved like a New York playboy and his relatives were vicious murderers, it would undercut the claimed moral superiority of their entire social class. So there was a drawing together of the gentry on the side of the Stevens family. A typical response from upper-class individuals was written by Frederick Lewis Allen in his well-known book *Only Yesterday*. Allen was a Harvard educated Boston Brahmin who could trace his lineage to seven Plymouth Colony settlers. After having devoted a whole three pages to the Hall-Mills case, he concluded that the reputation of the Stevens family had been butchered to make a Roman holiday of the first magnitude for newspaper readers. What he failed to explain was who might have killed the two victims in De Russey's Lane. Nor did his sympathy extend to an ordinary person like Eleanor Mills.

Over the years, various writers would attempt to offer alternative explanations for the case. William Kunstler, the famous radical defense lawyer of the 1960s, wrote a book declaring that the Ku Klux Klan had murdered the victims. Some of us recall that Kunstler was a man who could pull rabbits out of a hat. When a rabbi who was an outspoken supporter of Israel was shot dead while making a speech in a New York hotel room, Kunstler, acting as defense attorney for the gunman, was able to obtain an acquittal, even though the jury found him guilty of possessing the murder weapon.

Until some researcher can place a suspect like a hooded Klansman in De Russey's Lane at the time of the killing, I will continue to draw the obvious conclusion that some member(s) of the Stevens family murdered Reverend Hall and Eleanor Mills.

The "World's Greatest Detective"

In the law enforcement world, there are always men who earned a reputation as outstanding detectives simply by proclaiming themselves as such. Ask anyone who the greatest lawmen of the Old West were, and they are likely to say Wyatt Earp and Bat Masterson. Their legends are largely based on the men's own telling of the time when they were marshals in Western cow towns. Many years later, and a long way from the West, they were able to make claims without fear of contradiction.

Wyatt Earp lived in Hollywood from 1910 to 1929, where he served as an advisor to many filmmakers. This permitted him to spin his yarns for movie writers. In 1903 Bat Masterson, a journalist by trade, went to New York City, the media capital of the nation. He worked as a sports reporter and editor until his death in 1921. Many a night he could be found in a Broadway bar relating tales of the Old West. The men's success was based on two news mottos: "never let the truth get in the way of a good story" and "if the truth clashes with the legend, print the legend." Reporters would argue that they were not historians; their job was to present interesting stories. Filmmakers would point out that their movies were meant to be dramas and the truth was reserved for documentaries.

Similarly, today some reputable news organizations will bring on TV a law enforcement officer described as a great expert, although he may never have passed beyond the lowest grade of investigator in his own agency. If the story is about terrorism, he will suddenly become an expert in that field. After all, the media needs guests quickly when a story is breaking, and the self-promoters have established an act that works well on TV. They talk tough and are willing to express extreme views without qualification. Nuances are out.

Bernard Kerik never rose beyond third-grade detective in the NYPD. When Rudy Giuliani was running for mayor, Kerik volunteered to be his chauffeur and bodyguard. Eventually, the mayor named him police commissioner. With that title, he was assumed to be an expert on law enforcement. After the September 11, 2001, attacks on the World Trade Center, where Kerik largely served as Giuliani's bodyguard rather than the commander of the police on the scene, Kerik presented himself as an expert on international terrorism. In truth, he had never worked that beat in the police department and never rose beyond the rank of sergeant while serving in the army. So convincing was Kerik that President George W. Bush nominated him to be secretary of homeland security of the United States. Kerik's high visibility led some people to look more closely at his career, and eventually he ended up being sent to a federal penitentiary for tax fraud and lying to officials.

Another man who managed to be regarded as a top sleuth for forty years beginning in the 1890s was a New Jersey county chief of detectives named Ellis Parker, who persuaded New York authors and others that he was the best detective in the world. Many of them knew better, but he was always good for a story. One writer claimed that Parker was more efficient than either Scotland Yard or the French Sûreté, though he never made it clear how a man with two or three assistants in a rural county in New Jersey could outdo the national police forces of two great world empires.

Parker was born in 1871 and in his youth was a popular fiddler at country dances. One night, after someone stole his horse and buggy at one of the affairs, Parker investigated for days and eventually apprehended the offender. In 1893, when the Burlington County detective post opened, it was given to Parker, in part due to memories of the buggy theft case. According to his own reckoning, he successfully solved twenty thousand cases over the years. Few were murders or armed robberies. In the early days, most cases involved horse stealing, and in the later years it was bootlegging. Part of Parker's popularity came from the fact that he had a certain type of persona that Americans liked—the rural sage who outwitted the city slickers. This was the essence of some of Will Rogers's movies. The stories confirmed the belief of many Americans that the fast-disappearing, small-town life was a superior mode of living.

Most of Parker's celebrated cases were routine matters that any other county detective in New Jersey could have handled. In 1922 Ocean County borrowed Parker to work on the murder of a man found in bed, shot in the head. According to the victim's wife, two burglars awakened her while her husband was still asleep and took her into the kitchen of the apartment, where one intruder tied her up. Suddenly, a shot rang out from the bedroom. It was the kind of story that detectives often hear when one spouse is killed in the presence of the other and there are no witnesses. So Parker assigned a detective to tail the woman, Ivey Giberson. Over a few days the detective followed her to an outside shed. Then he got a warrant and searched it. Under a pile of debris, he found the murder weapon with Giberson's fingerprints on it and recent love letters to her from another man. She was convicted and received a life sentence. Any rookie detective could have accomplished the same thing.

In another instance, when a man sitting in his chair in his living room was shot, it was determined that the fatal bullet came from outside. It turned out that the man owned part of a circus along with his wife's brother. The brother-in-law and the wife inherited his share of the business. Eventually, under questioning, the wife broke down, confessed, and implicated her brother in the murder. Both were given life sentences. Parker received much of the credit because he had become well known and had a close relationship with many reporters.

Not all events that occurred in Burlington County were as favorable to Parker. In 1916 A. D. Rider, a wealthy cranberry farmer, was returning from town after picking up his payroll, accompanied by his daughter, his brother, and a hired man. En route, they were ambushed by ten men, who began shooting. Rider's brother was killed and he and his daughter were wounded, but the assailants were driven off by the armed hired man. After receiving treatment, the Riders returned to the scene of the crime, where they found the sheriff, the coroner, and Ellis Parker gathered around, but no pursuit was being organized. In fact, Parker left the scene to go to the Mount Holly Fair, explaining that there were "a lot of fakirs" there and he had to watch them. The bandits were eventually tracked down and arrested by the Philadelphia police.

Parker was the most vociferous opponent of the creation of the New Jersey State Police in 1921. While he did not think there was any necessity for the unit, he felt that if one were to be created, he was the right man to head it. When the Hall-Mills case broke, he believed that he should be in charge of the investigation. However, the leaders of the state of New Jersey saw him as essentially a braggart and a self-promoter.

There was one point in the Hall-Mills case when Parker might have solved it simply because of his own personality. The Stevens family were not professional criminals. If, in the 1922 investigation, Parker had confronted one of them out of the blue, it's possible he might have gotten some damaging admissions. His basic interrogation tactic was to appear sympathetic to the victim and persuade him or her to tell him what he or she knew. The question was, which one of the four members of the Stevens family should be the one suddenly confronted? The brother Henry and cousin Henry were both successful professional men and would likely not have fallen for anything Parker said. Willie, who was considered simpleminded, would be the likely choice to interrogate. However, during the later stage of the investigation, Willie sometimes shocked investigators by his ability to recall facts and to speak as a rational human being. For example, when one of the investigators mentioned Reverend Hall had a doctorate, Willie politely corrected him by telling him that he held no such degree.

Probably the best choice would have been Francis Hall. Had Parker suddenly appeared and behaved in a kindly and sympathetic manner, it is possible that he would have elicited incriminating statements from her. However, the danger would have been that if she did not break down and instead complained that Parker had browbeaten her, the cops would have been in for terrific criticism. That alone might have ruined any possibility of convicting the family for murder.

Parker continued to brood over being upstaged by the state police.

Eventually he would worm his way into the crime of the century and in so doing prove that he was not a world-class detective, just a con artist.

The Power of the Press

Hall-Mills has come to mark a watershed in the way the press covered crime. Before 1922 most newspapers were reticent about how they approached the subject. Afterward, anything went. Of course, since the turn of the century, the Hearst newspapers in various cities had followed a sensational approach. Thus it was not surprising that they went all-out in the Hall-Mills case. As one analysis of the case notes, "When Adolph S. Ochs, publisher of the *Times*, was asked [by a tabloid editor] why his newspaper was devoting as much space as the *Daily News* to the Hall-Mills case, he replied, 'when the *Daily News* prints it, it is sex; when *we* print it, it is sociology.'" Of course, sociology also sold a great many copies of the paper. After 1922 many news organizations followed Hearst's approach. Even in New York, Hearst was often outdone by the *New York Daily News*.

Most front-page cases were not as sensational as Hall-Mills. The murder of the famous architect Stanford White by Pittsburgh millionaire Harry K. Thaw in 1906 attracted attention but was not a mystery. Thaw shot White to death in a theater on the roof of Madison Square Garden because he believed that White had abused Thaw's wife, Evelyn Nesbit, in the days when she was single. Thaw did not seek to flee but rather held his gun up in the air and handed it to a city fireman who was the first official to arrive on the scene. The interest in the case came after the murder, when there was a major campaign to diminish the reputation of Stanford White, who previously had been a very popular figure. Thaw fought to avoid incarceration, claiming that the district attorney was persecuting him because of the influence of White's friends.

In other cases, it was not the victim but the issues involved that drew attention. In 1913 the murder of a young girl named Mary Phagan in Atlanta, Georgia, attracted widespread attention because the man accused of doing it was her teacher Leo Frank, a Jew. Though a jury found Frank guilty, there was a feeling that the conviction was due to prejudice against him. After the governor commuted his death sentence, vigilantes invaded the jail where Frank was held and hanged him. So powerful was the impact of the case that it led to both the revival of the Ku Klux Klan and the establishment of the Anti-Defamation League.

The 1924 Leopold and Loeb case in Chicago, where two wealthy "geniuses" murdered a young boy, attracted attention because of the barbarity of the crime, the status of the killers, and the fact that the publicity-seeking Clarence Darrow was a lawyer for the defendants (see chapter 5).

While New York tabloids received credit for the sensational style that became common in the 1920s, it was Chicago where the practice reached its height and pervaded every aspect of criminal investigation. The 1928 play *The Front Page*, written by two Chicago reporters, Charles MacArthur and Ben Hecht, characterized crime journalism at the time. The feelings of the criminals, the reporters, their families, or anyone else were secondary to getting "the scoop." And this attitude characterized all the papers, including those that were not tabloids, as possessing the same desire.

The leading newspaper in Chicago, the broadsheet *Tribune*, was the respectable voice of midwestern Republicanism and the most powerful paper in the region. It was understood in Chicago city government that the appointment of a chief of detectives must be cleared with the *Tribune* publisher, Col. Robert McCormick, to ensure that the police would continue to favor the *Tribune*. The only time this did not happen was when Colonel McCormick and Mayor William Hale Thompson were at war with each other and each traveled around with bodyguards because he feared the other was going to assassinate him.

After 1931 a Democratic administration took control of Chicago, but the influence of the Republican McCormick remained high. So close were the new mayor, Edward Kelly, and the colonel that in the 1920s, when Kelly was indicted for misconduct while working at the Sanitary District, McCormick stormed into the grand jury room and tore up the indictments.

Tribune reporters carried great weight with the police, and many would not hesitate to go into a police station and, without asking permission, open the files and study the reports. One *Tribune* reporter, Jake Lingle, became the confidant of Comm. William Russell. In 1930, when Lingle was shot and killed while walking on the street in downtown Chicago, the case revealed many of the relationships between the press, the police, and the criminals, and it cost Russell his job. Eventually a St. Louis gangster was convicted of killing Lingle, though he received the exceptionally short sentence of fourteen years. But nobody really believed that he was the murderer. Instead, the conviction was seen as an effort to protect the honor of the *Tribune*. Despite the revelations of the Lingle case, the *Tribune* would continue to occupy the most prestigious media position in the Midwest.

Most big-city detective bureaus investigated crime with one eye on the press, and it was common for them to be pressured to provide inside information to reporters. Given the fact that sensational cases did not happen regularly, both police and reporters sometimes cooperated to inflate public interest in a particular crime, as the 1975 musical *Chicago* illustrates. In the musical, an ordinary woman who kills her boyfriend becomes a temporary celebrity through the manipulations of reporters and her attorney. After a while, when another girl killer arrives in the jail, the first one is ignored.

The summit of crime reporting in America came in 1942, when movie star Errol Flynn was charged with the statutory rape of two girls. The whole country followed the story closely. Flynn was not only a major star but a man with a reputation for getting into various difficulties, especially with the ladies. Whether on screen or in real life (and it made little difference to him), he was either brawling or wenching. The so-called rape victims, although worldly wise and adult appearing, were dressed up like milkmaids at the trial. However, with a top-notch lawyer and public sympathy, Flynn was acquitted. The shadow of the case hung over him the rest of his life, however, and a popular saying, "in like Flynn," reminded people of the affair.

With the right lawyer, the right defendant, and the right amount of money, the same thing happened in many cities around the United States. The only place where a prominent defendant would likely be brought down was New York City, where the New York County district attorney, whether Tom Dewey, Frank Hogan, or Robert Morgenthau, had a competent staff and was a no-nonsense individual. In any city, one thing the detectives knew was that press coverage would always be the unknown factor in a big criminal case. Therefore, there would always be two trials, one on the law and the other on public opinion, and most of the time the latter would prevail.

5

The Big Squads Roll

The Chicago Detective Bureau

The Chicago Police Department always had a reputation as a rough-and-ready bunch. Maybe that was because they policed a very rough-and-ready city that sometimes reminded people of the Wild West. Surprisingly, it was an image many Chicagoans rather liked. It was the town that Carl Sandburg described as "stormy, husky, brawling, city of the big shoulders."

In 1929 as many locals were as thrilled by the St. Valentine's Day Massacre as were outraged by it. The case was never officially solved, though it was generally believed that Al Capone's gangsters, in company with a hired gun from the St. Louis Egan Rats, had done the shooting. Capone himself beat two of the shooters to death, and the Egan Rat was given life for killing a policeman in Michigan. In 1937 the city witnessed a less well-known massacre. At the time, labor unions across the country were using a new tactic, the sit-down strike, in which workers would occupy a plant and remain until the employer settled with them or police or national guardsmen ejected them. When the tactic was tried in Detroit by the United Auto Workers, Michigan governor (later Supreme Court justice) Frank Murphy refused to send in troops, and the strikers won. In May 1937 Chicago workers were on strike against the Republic Steel Company, whose president, Tom Girdler, was an outspoken antilabor figure.

In May 1937 two thousand strikers marched to the Republic plant on the city's far southeast side. Their leaders were apparently not aware that for many years there had been an understanding between the Democratic political machine and the Republican business community that cops would protect property, and unions would not be allowed a free hand to engage in violence. This despite the fact that at the time every local labor leader could call the mayor on his private line and the Kelly-Nash machine was a bulwark of FDR's New Deal.

A number of officers were assembled under an old-time captain, Jim Mooney, who had been chief of detectives twenty years earlier. When the workers marched and refused to halt, Mooney ordered his men to fire tear gas. However, as the strikers arrived at the police line some officers began to fire their revolvers. Ten strikers were killed, forty wounded, and scores more injured by clubs in a police charge. There was no prosecution or any disciplinary action undertaken against the cops. The city administration had sent them there to stop the march by whatever means necessary, and they did, so the local political machine and the New Deal government it supported could hardly punish them for it.

In Chicago it was always wise to plan for the worst because that was often what happened. Violent strikes, race riots, bombings, and blood in the streets were constant occurrences. In 1968, when the Democratic National Convention was held in Chicago at a time of great national turmoil, it was obvious no officials had ever opened a history book about the city. After it was over, Chicagoans simply shrugged and said, "Well, no one got killed."

A Chicago detective bureau modeled after New York's was in existence by 1900. Whoever commanded it, the real boss was Hermann Schuettler, the city's most famous detective, who made his name by capturing some of the anarchists convicted of killing eight policemen with a bomb at the Haymarket riot in 1886. By the turn of the century Schuettler held an assistant superintendent rank, and he became superintendent in 1917.

Any time crime appeared to be getting out of hand, Schuettler and his Flying Squad took charge of the situation.

Though the detective bureau assumed a distinct organizational form and subculture, most investigations were still left to detectives at the local patrol district, who reported to the station captain. Headquarters detectives handled the big cases and tracked major criminals. Their boss, the chief of detectives, reported directly to the superintendent (chief or commissioner) of police.

District detectives usually knew who not to "pinch" and what joints to leave alone. Bureau detectives moved about anywhere they chose and arrested anyone they wanted. When the bureau men entered some mob hangout, the place usually fell quiet, and the only sound that could be heard came from pistols being dropped to the floor and kicked away from their possessors.

Chiefs of detectives were so powerful that if they happened to be sent to prison, it did not mean much. "Cap'n Jack" Halpin, who held the job just before the First World War, was sent to Joliet Penitentiary for corruption. His stay was not particularly onerous since the warden of the prison was the brother of a well-known detective, Chief Matt Zimmer. After a few months the courts decided that Cap'n Jack should be released.

The station detectives were selected by the district captain (often on the advice of a politician). Though the practice was forbidden, most district detective squads had a "bull dick" who bossed the others. In some instances, when a captain was transferred out, the bull went with him to his new command. In others, the bull stayed through several changes of captains and was so powerful that he often told his ostensible superior what to do. Of course, the bull was expected to take very good care of the captain, who could plan on playing golf and having lunch and drinks with his friends every afternoon. In addition, when the captain retired he did not have to go on welfare. In the 1940s an IRS official estimated forty (out of seventy) police captains were millionaires, even though their salary was around $6,000 a year.

In 1901 President McKinley was assassinated in Buffalo, New York, by a self-proclaimed anarchist named Leon Czolgosz, who said he had been influenced by the "Red Queen" Emma Goldman. Goldman was summarily picked up by Chicago detectives. Despite an order from the superintendent of police to release her, they continued to hold her because Schuettler and the detectives had maintained a grudge against the anarchists since the Haymarket bombing. Finally, Red Emma was let out, but every time she came to Chicago she was hauled in for questioning. That the detective bureau could defy orders from the superintendent of police showed how powerful it had become by 1900.

In the bureau a recommendation from a politician was always helpful to an aspiring detective, but unless the chief of detectives went along, or the applicant's sponsor was the Cardinal Archbishop (and he did not recommend detectives), the individual could not get in the unit.

By the 1920s the bureau had settled down to a regular routine. Roll call, held at 8:30 a.m., was presided over by a ranking officer. After listening to instructions, the men went to their units, such as robbery or homicide, or began patrolling particular zones of the city. Bureau cars rolled the streets at night so that there was constant coverage. Until the 1930s, each car had a crew of four or five men under a squad leader, who himself was rarely more than a sergeant. His seat alongside the driver, known as the "in charge" seat, was sacrosanct. The bureau squads were equipped with rifles, shotguns, and from 1927, machine guns. Everybody recognized that when men in a Cadillac touring car came by, it was a "big squad" (as opposed to the smaller district patrol cars). Each team was expected to pick up known hoodlums and suspicious characters and hold them for the thrice-weekly show ups. If a big squad rode past a corner where rowdies, crooks, and thugs hung out, all eyes watched the car to see if it would make a U-turn and come back. If it did, the street characters would dive over fences, run down alleys, and otherwise make themselves scarce. Sometimes, to speed them on their way, the detectives would fire a couple of shots in the air.

Once, a county judge ordered bureau squads into nearby Cicero to suppress violence by the Capone gang, which was killing people during an election war. When the Chicago detectives arrived on the scene, they killed Capone's brother. Another time a noted hoodlum was shot dead while under arrest in a bureau car. He had allegedly tried to snatch a policeman's gun, but the legend was that the hoodlum was killed because he used a vicious term linking the officer and his mother in an impropriety.

The most notable detective chief of the 1920s, the legendary "Iron Mike" Hughes, when accused of mistreating criminals would always say, "What am I supposed to do, kiss 'em?" Of course, a lot of that was tough talk. Most professional criminals had a lawyer available twenty-four hours a day, so if his client were arrested, he would immediately "spring" him on a writ of habeas corpus. When the criminal went before the court that issued the writ, it was not a good idea for him to be covered with bruises because the judge might get upset. In my youth I knew many persons picked up by the bureau who emerged from captivity looking none the worse for wear. There is no doubt that, on occasion, some roughhousing occurred on the upper floors at 1121 State Street, the detective bureau section of police headquarters, but I believe it was only a small fraction of what people thought it was.

It has been my experience that people relate stories they have heard as though they personally experienced or witnessed them. Some war veterans succumb to that practice. Detectives are known to magnify their role in certain investigations, even ones that they had nothing to do with. Journalists who go to the scene of a plane crash usually find people who say they saw the whole thing but, in fact, did not. Young men from rough neighborhoods would recall how cops used nightsticks on their posteriors. This rarely happened, because their families and the local politicians would never have allowed that kind of practice to go on. While growing up in the tough Stockyards District, I was never struck by an officer, even though on occasion I probably deserved it. Of course, I never made the mistake of striking a police officer either.

Chicago did have one wild night of the year, when all restrictions were off, and that was Halloween. Everybody, high and low, seemed to go wild, committing vandalism and rioting in the streets. There were also a number of shootings, not by police but by irate citizens whose property had been harmed. My theory about this phenomenon (for what it is worth) is that it stems from medieval Europe, which celebrated

Walpurgisnacht, the night when witches rode on broomsticks and ghosts walked. (See also the section in chapter 6 on nationality murders.) One argument supporting the thesis that it was a phenomenon imported from Europe is that the black population of Chicago engaged in no such conduct on Halloween night; they just threw parties and showed off their costumes.

One allegation that had some truth to it is that the Chicago police played fast and loose with the rules of criminal law. Until the 1950s, Illinois was the only state in the union that followed the federal exclusionary rule, which forbid the introduction at trial of unlawfully seized evidence. Defense lawyers used to say, "Your Honor, I realize this is the Windy City, but in every gun case that comes before this court the officer testifies that he saw the defendant's coat blow open and therefore the weapon was in plain sight." Criminals, and their lawyers too, were not bound by the literal truth, and trials often turned into swearing matches, with the cops swearing that he did and the defendant swearing that he did not. Criminal hearings at the lower level were very informal and rules of evidence were generally ignored, since there was rarely a jury impaneled. The judge knew how to separate the wheat from the chaff in both sides' story.

The reputation of the detective bureau was firmly cemented in 1924. The Taylor case in Los Angeles had ended in police failure, and Hall-Mills in New Jersey did the same. Meanwhile, in Chicago a multimillion-dollar train robbery and the investigation of a murder that to this day still catches the imagination of Hollywood were both solved by the bureau.

The Newton brothers of Uvalde County, Texas, were typical of the Western gangs that had existed for over fifty years. Between 1919 and 1924, they were reported to have robbed as many as eighty-seven banks. It was confirmed that they had held up six trains. Early in the century the Newtons were petty thieves, though one, Willis, had begun to move up to the big time. In 1914 he and an accomplice held up a Southern Pacific Railroad train and took $4,700 at gunpoint from the passengers. In 1916 Willis joined a gang that robbed a bank in Oklahoma of over $10,000 and escaped on horseback. In 1917 he was sent to prison for burglary. Later he formed his own group, including his brothers Dock, Joe, and Jess, along with an outsider, a top safecracker named Brent Glasscock. The crew began robbing banks in Texas and the surrounding southwestern states. They also switched their modus operandi considerably. Instead of storming into a bank in daylight, they would break in at night and blow the safe, thereby avoiding any contact with the public or law enforcement.

In July 1923 the good old boys made a bad mistake when they attacked bank messengers in Toronto, Canada. The victims refused to surrender the money they were carrying and a shootout ensued, leading to the wounding of two messengers. The gang escaped with $84,000 Canadian. This should have taught them to stay in the Southwest, which they knew well. However, they developed a liking for nightlife in places like Chicago and Kansas City, which, at the time, were two of the hottest towns in America.

The Newtons were country boys and did not know that Chicago was full of small-time operators who talked big. They fell in with some minor hoodlums, bootleggers, and corrupt politicians, and out of this friendship evolved a plan to carry out a major train robbery. Chicago was not like Texas, a place where train robbery was a local sport. In the railroad capital of the United States, any interference with the railroads was always taken seriously. During the great strikes of 1877 and 1894, the U.S. Army was dispatched to the city to prevent the stoppage of trains. Twenty people were killed in 1877, thirteen in 1894.

In Chicago, only the wildest of the wild local hoodlums attempted train robberies. It was usually their downfall because the federal government would capture them and give them long sentences in prison. However, both the Texas cowboys and the big-talking Chicagoans became convinced it would be easy to pull off a railroad heist.

The train selected was number fifty-seven on the Chicago, Milwaukee, and St. Paul line, which carried large sums of money. On the night of June 12, 1924, Willis and Jess secretly boarded the train in Chicago and began crawling over the tops of the cars to the engineer's cab, where they stuck guns on him and his fireman. They ordered them to stop at

Rondout Junction, a switching center thirty-two miles northwest of Chicago. Other members of the gang were waiting there to carry out the robbery. However, the nervous engineer stopped the train several car lengths too far ahead and then had to back up, which caused some of the gang to leave their assigned positions. In a big robbery in which each participant has a specialized role, any departure from the plan is likely to bring disaster, and Rondout was no exception. When crew members in the last car ran forward to see why the train had stopped, the gang took them prisoners. Then they attacked the mail car, in which eighteen armed postal clerks were sorting the mail. Willis called on the clerks to come out, and when they refused, he threw tear gas into the car. Some passengers looking on screamed that the robbers were murdering the clerks. The gas warfare of World War I, which had ended six years earlier, had left a vivid impression on its generation. So the passengers might have rushed the robbers if the clerks had not tumbled out, coughing and choking.

Meanwhile, Glasscock spotted what appeared to be an armed postal worker coming along the side of the train. He opened fire and hit the man several times. When the gas cleared from the mail car, the gang, which included some of the individuals they had joined up with in Chicago, began taking selected mail sacks. Suddenly, the brothers noticed that Dock was missing. They ran back along the tracks and found that he was the man Glasscock had shot and severely wounded. The gang helped him to a getaway car.

Taking sixty-four mail sacks, the robbers left the scene shortly after 10:00 p.m., and by midnight the local sheriff's office, U.S. postal inspectors, railroad detectives, and Chicago police detectives were tramping over the scene. Given the circumstances of the crime, the postal inspectors had jurisdiction, the know-how, and the national contacts to investigate the heist, and the Chicago cops had the manpower and local contacts to scour the metropolitan area. The postal inspectors were led by the chief of the Chicago office, William Fahy, a man who was regarded as a brilliant sleuth with an outstanding record of breaking big cases. Recently, he had solved a $780,000 mail robbery that occurred at a railroad station in downtown Chicago. The Chicago police crew was led by Dep. Chief of Dets. William Schoemaker.

At the scene of the robbery, searchers found a .44-caliber revolver with the serial numbers filed off, a bottle of nitroglycerin, and gas masks. The nitro would have been used to blast open the mail car, if necessary. The loss was initially set at $1.5 million in wartime liberty and commercial bonds plus $100,000 in jewelry and cash. A later calculation found that nearly $3 million had been taken. The bonds were of a type easy to cash. The day after the robbery, local police in Joliet, Illinois, a southwestern suburb of Chicago, found the getaway cars. One contained $100,000 in cash that had been taken in the robbery. The license plates had been stolen.

From the outset, postal inspectors, including some who were brought from other parts of the country, suspected that Rondout could be an inside job. Otherwise, how did the robbers know how much money was on the train and which mail sacks to take?

Old Shoes, as the cops called the deputy chief, was an island of integrity in a sea of corruption. Some cops attributed his stance to the fact that his daughter had once been lured into working in a bordello in Chicago's red-light district. Later Shoes would mentor a young prohibition agent named Eliot Ness and watch the federal man's back. Schoemaker's detectives began shaking up the underworld.

They went to a pool room on Roosevelt Road where the Dion O'Banion gang hung out. O'Banion and his boys were stone-cold killers. When one of their beer trucks was seized by a detective squad and was being held until a payoff could be delivered to the scene, O'Banion told the driver of the vehicle that instead he would send a hit squad to kill the cops. Police wiretappers monitored the conversation and immediately sent a heavy-weapons squad to support their colleagues. It was one of those brief periods when O'Banion was on good terms with the Italians led by Johnny Torrio. So the driver, not thinking too much of O'Banion's plan, called Torrio for a second opinion. Torrio, always a diplomat, immediately canceled the order for the hit squad and dispatched a payoff to where the truck was being held. Eventually, Torrio had O'Banion killed, and in turn, O'Banion's men severely wounded Torrio.

Most Chicago cops would never have gone into one of O'Banion's headquarters, but Schoemaker and his right-hand man, Sgt. Fred Tapscott (occasional bodyguard for heavyweight champion Jack Dempsey), began grilling the boys. Shortly afterward, Schoemaker received a tip that some of the people involved in the train robbery were in a house on Chicago's West Side. It is possible the information came from O'Banion because the gangster felt the robbers had gotten out of line. So instead of killing them, he allowed the police to capture them and send them to prison. Perhaps O'Banion just wanted Schoemaker off his back.

The chief and his men went to a house on Washtenaw, a grimy side street, and stormed in. There they found two men and a woman standing over the bed of a man swathed in bandages. Schoemaker recognized one of the men as Walter McComb, a well-known bootlegger. The other man gave his name as John Wade (though he was actually Joe Newton) and introduced the woman as his wife. The wounded man identified himself as John Wayne (the future movie star was only seventeen years old at the time, so it was not meant as a joke). He claimed to have been shot by a stickup man and then changed his story to say it was an angry girlfriend. In fact, the man was Dock, though the police did not know it at the time. They sent him to the hospital at the Bridewell jail and took the two men and the woman to an outlying police station, where they could be secretly questioned. However, the Chicago press corps had many contacts, and they soon learned where the suspects were being held and flocked to the scene.

Back at the house on Washtenaw, two more people arrived. Sergeant Tapscott, who had been left behind with a few detectives, grabbed them and began questioning them. Although he did not admit it at the time, one of the men was Willis Newton himself. As the sun was rising, another man appeared at the house and was taken into custody. This one was Jim Murray, a Chicago bootlegger and minor politician. Outside, newsboys were shouting extras that some of the Rondout robbers had been picked up. One of the suspects became confused and finally admitted he was Willis Newton and that "John Wayne" was his brother Dock. A search of Willis revealed that he was carrying a $1,000 bill and a $500 bill taken in the robbery.

It was not unknown for criminals to buy their way out of a pinch, so Willis offered Schoemaker $20,000 if he would release them. He took the chief to a bank, where he withdrew the money from a safe-deposit box; after examining it, Schoemaker informed Willis that he was under arrest for the Rondout robbery.

Only one Newton brother was still missing. Jess had been sent to bury some of the money in the Southwest, but he later claimed he forgot where he put it. He then fled into Mexico. On the Fourth of July, he was inveigled into entering a race where the contestants would ride horses from Mexico into Texas. Jess finished first, and when he arrived in the Lone Star State he was congratulated by Harrison Hamer, sponsor of the event. Hamer was one of four brothers who were Texas Rangers, and he informed Jess that the first prize was a trip to jail. Another Hamer brother, Captain Frank, later led the force that killed Bonnie and Clyde.

The case was not over as far as the U.S. government was concerned. As might be expected in Chicago, troops were summoned. The postmaster general sent marines to ride mail trains with orders to "kill all marauders on sight." Marines were always the force used against criminals because, under federal law, the army could not be deployed to assist civil law enforcement. The restrictions did not apply to the marines because they were part of the navy. However, the money had not yet been found, and the postal authorities in Washington still believed that someone in their organization had tipped off the robbers. It was evident that the Newtons were not smart enough to conceive of a job like Rondout, and the local crooks would have refused to carry it out as too risky unless they had assurance that someone inside would set it up. The postal authorities combed the records to see who knew of the movement of the money.

Chicago cops always mistrusted Chief Postal Investigator Fahy. He was a drinker and ladies' man whose lifestyle could not be supported on a government paycheck. On the night of the robbery, when he got word of it at 10:00 p.m., he was still in the main post office in Chicago, as if he were waiting for the call. When he arrived at the scene in a limousine with an African American chauffeur, Fahy was obviously drunk.

Fahy made the mistake of carrying on a love affair with the wife of a man whom he had sent to jail. Based on information she gave and admissions from some of the politically connected Chicago group that broke down, investigators learned that the mastermind of the robbery was Fahy. As Joe Newton said, "You can't lose when you've got a real-life cop bossin' the job."

The lawyers for the Newton boys managed to project an image of them as charming "good old boys," and they received relatively light sentences. Fahy served a lengthy prison sentence, and when he was released, he went to work for a municipal investigation agency that did not have police authority or carry guns. Those who worked with him at that time remember that he was an extremely polite, quiet individual.

The Leopold and Loeb Case

Nathan Leopold and Richard "Dickey" Loeb were brilliant young men who were fast friends; indeed, they were lovers. When they became famous in 1924, Leopold was nineteen and Loeb eighteen. Leopold had already graduated from the prestigious University of Chicago, a few blocks from his home in the upscale Hyde Park district, and was enrolled at the university's law school. Loeb had graduated from the University of Michigan at age eighteen and in the fall would join Leopold at the law school. Both boys' families were extremely wealthy and socially prominent.

The two believed themselves to be Nietzschean supermen who were above the ordinary rules of society. To test their ability to flout the law, they began committing minor thefts and arsons for thrills. Then they decided to up the stakes by committing a murder, planning to disguise it as a kidnapping for ransom. They spent seven months plotting such factors as choosing a weapon and disposing of the body. The modus operandi they decided to adopt was to lure a young boy from a wealthy family into their car, kill him, bury him in a remote spot, and then demand ransom from his family.

On May 24, 1924, the pair rented a car under an assumed name and cruised around near a prep school that Loeb had attended. They had no particular victim in mind, but they finally chose fourteen-year-old

Bobby Franks, son of a Chicago millionaire. Franks had played tennis at the Loeb family mansion, and Dickey Loeb, who was his second cousin, told people he didn't like the kid.

When Leopold and Loeb approached Franks walking on the street, he was at first hesitant to get into the car. They finally talked him into it, claiming they wanted to discuss something about a tennis racket. In the car, one of them (probably Loeb) hit him over the head with a chisel, pulled him into the backseat, and put his body under a blanket. They headed for an area on the far south side known as Wolf Lake. The killers waited until nightfall, then poured acid on the body to frustrate identification, and buried Franks there.

Back in Hyde Park, Loeb, using a false name, called Mrs. Franks to tell her that Bobby had been kidnapped. The two also sent a ransom note to the victim's family. The next day, they called the Franks' house and told them to place the ransom money in a bag and leave it at a nearby drugstore. However, the family member who answered the phone did not write down the address of the store. In the meantime, a man walking in the Wolf Lake area found the body and notified the police. Detectives searched the area where the corpse was found, and one of them discovered a pair of eyeglasses near the body. The glasses had an unusual hinge mechanism. A check of optical stores in Chicago found that only three people had purchased such glasses, one of whom was Nathan Leopold. When detectives questioned him, he told them he had probably lost them while birdwatching the previous week. Detectives asked Leopold to demonstrate how his glasses would have fallen from his pocket. He suggested he had tripped on a tree root and placed the glasses in his jacket pocket to demonstrate. Though he threw himself on the ground several times, each time the glasses remained in place.

Leopold, in accounting for his time when Bobby Franks disappeared, stated that he and Loeb had been driving around in Leopold's automobile, and they had picked up two girls whose names they could not remember. Any detective looking at these two would realize they were not the type to run around picking up girls. Surprisingly, Leopold's family was not alarmed when their son was held by the police, and they sent their chauffeur to the police station to drop off some pajamas and toiletries in case the police were going to hold him overnight. Leopold's father was a highly respected lawyer and should have gotten an attorney to spring a writ. The families also had the resources to spirit the boys out of the country, but they did not consider it. In the meantime, the chauffeur, trying to be helpful, insisted the boys could not have been involved in the murder because he was repairing Leopold's car at the time of the killing. So much for their alibi.

The case solved, the state's attorney, Republican Robert Crowe, an ambitious Yale graduate, jumped into it with both feet. Given his rank, the police deferred to him. The first thing he did was to house the suspects in a hotel rather than a jail cell and question them vigorously.

Surprisingly, brilliant individuals are often the first to crack when being interrogated. Apparently, Leopold and Loeb had not read the work of the great Austrian criminologist Hans Gross, who taught police that a criminal's thoughts constantly revolve around his crime and he is always very close to blurting out his guilt. Crowe and his assistants obtained confessions from both boys.

With the city outraged and defendants who were Jewish, homosexuals (the newspapers could communicate that in euphemisms that their readers would readily understand), and rich men's sons, there would be great pressure on the criminal justice system to find the boys guilty and hang them. So the family hired Clarence Darrow, probably the most famous lawyer in America. Darrow cultivated a great reputation as a fighter for the underdog, but in truth he took more cases from rich people and corrupt politicians than any other groups. In 1915 he had defended the crooked chief of police of Chicago and got him off at trial. Darrow's method when he had obviously guilty clients was to try to persuade the jury to go against popular opinion. This time, though, no jury would have let them off. So Darrow elected not to request a jury trial.

The judge in the case, John Caverly, was a First Ward jurist, which meant he owed his position on the bench to the most corrupt political organization in Chicago. Normally, such a judge could be persuaded to see the case the way the defense lawyers did, particularly if a great deal of money was involved. However, the public would never accept anything short of execution. Darrow's task was to give Caverly enough justification to impose a sentence other than hanging. So he approached the trial as a sort of play. He would appear in a battered coat pretending to be a very humble individual. However, he was skilled at writing, directing, and starring in the dramas that he put on for judges and juries. Everybody expected that Darrow would try an insanity plea, but that had been used so many times in criminal cases it would probably not work with the public. Darrow pled the boys guilty and admitted that they should never be allowed to be free again, but then he launched into a long social-psychological discussion and called for mercy. The cops saw it all as a bunch of high-flown nonsense. After all, the two defendants were not products of a poverty-stricken background but were among the most privileged in American society. Judge Caverly handed down life sentences. Darrow had done his job because many people accepted the verdict.

Darrow was expecting a large sum from the defendants' families, at least $100,000. For several months he heard nothing, and then he approached Mr. Loeb, who responded that any lawyer would have been glad to take the case for the publicity value. Finally, Loeb gave $30,000 to Darrow, so that, counting the retainer, his total package reached $40,000. It was the equivalent of approximately a half million today, but since Loeb was worth about a quarter of a billion in today's money, it was a modest fee for saving the life of his son.

Dickey Loeb was murdered by a fellow convict in 1936. In the 1940s a public relations campaign was instituted to earn a parole for Leopold. The theory was that society needed his brilliant mind to make great scientific discoveries. He was released in 1958 and lived quietly until his death in 1971; however, he was never nominated for a Nobel Prize.

In the end, the cops from the Chicago school of hard knocks were able to get the best of brilliant young men from one of the world's leading universities. In truth, it had not been a hard case to solve. The difficult part was the prosecution. In a time when the death penalty was commonly given to ordinary murderers, anything less than that could be seen as failure. Thus, for many people, the Leopold and Loeb decision was a defeat for justice. Once again, Darrow had proven that the law was just a game in which victory belonged to the most successful manipulator.

The detective bureau continued its leading role in the police department. It was so powerful that it could veto a choice for police commissioner. In 1935 Capt. Dan "Tubbo" Gilbert, the chief investigator for the state's attorney, was made chief of the uniformed police. This meant he would control all thirty-nine district stations, including their detective squads. Gilbert was known as America's richest cop, and he had taken the job anticipating his succession to the commissionership. Because of the opposition of the detective bureau and others, he lasted just sixty days and went back to the state's attorney's office. Gilbert was reputedly not only a corrupt cop but also a member of the ruling group of organized crime known in Chicago as the syndicate and popularly in the country as the Mafia.

Chicago produced a plethora of colorful criminals to keep the detective bureau in the headlines. "Midget," or as the media would call him today, "Vertically Challenged," Fernekes was a daring robber who led the cops on many chases. When detectives finally caught him, he was sitting quietly in a public library reading a book—on how to make a bomb.

Eventually, Chicago gangsters cut down on the use of machine guns, but cops did not. The problem was many of the detective squads worked better in a commando role than as criminal investigators.

When faced with high-profile investigations, the detective bureau sometimes failed, and in so doing, brought down the bureau's hierarchy. Chicago's Near North Side, adjacent to the ultra-wealthy Gold Coast, was the habitat of Chicago's top society figures. Its fashionable Drake Hotel was the place where the annual coming-out party for the city's debutantes was held. In contrast, the west end of the district was exactly the reverse, built around the dives of North Clark Street. Both areas were encompassed by the thirty-fifth police district, known as East Chicago (the street the station was located on), the premier district in the police department.

When a big case such as a front-page murder occurred, in most districts the detective bureau had no trouble taking charge and elbowing the district detectives out. Not in the thirty-fifth. If the captain of the district wanted his station detectives to take over the case, he usually had enough power to arrange it. The bifurcated detective system and the investigative tactics that had developed early in the century were to come crashing down in 1944, when a murder occurred in the Drake Hotel.

On January 19, 1944, police were summoned to room 834 in the hotel, were a woman had just been shot. The badly wounded victim was Mrs. Frank Starr Williams, fifty-eight, formerly Adele Born. Her first husband was a multimillionaire and her current one had been a U.S. diplomat stationed in Tokyo just before Pearl Harbor.

According to Adele Williams's daughter, Mrs. Patricia Goodbody, she and her mother had entered the room shortly after 6:00 p.m., and the daughter had gone in to use the bathroom. Suddenly, she thought she heard a noise and called out to her mother. About that time a woman in a black Persian lamb coat came running out from hiding and shot at both women, hitting Williams.

Lt. James Quinn, in charge of the Thirty-Fifth District detectives, rushed to the scene. Simultaneously, as was procedure, the detective homicide squad, led by Lt. Phil Brietzke, responded. The homicide squad served under Chief of Dets. John L. Sullivan, a powerful figure in the police department and widely touted to become the next police commissioner when the elderly incumbent, Jim Allman, retired.

Williams, seriously wounded, was removed to St. Luke's Hospital. During his investigation, Lieutenant Quinn began to doubt the story of the daughter, Patricia Goodbody. He believed that the mother and daughter had gotten into an argument in the room and that in a struggle for the gun the daughter had shot her mother. Goodbody denied it and was outraged when Lieutenant Quinn asked her to take a paraffin test to see if she had recently fired a gun. The lieutenant was on dangerous ground; he was not questioning a prostitute in a Clark Street dive a few blocks away but a member of the city's elite who was wealthy in her own right and whose father and stepfather were both rich and influential.

When the sergeant who headed the robbery squad in the detective bureau entered the hotel, he noticed a woman at the key desk whom he knew as Ellen Bennett (plus many aliases), who had been previously arrested for robbery. Strangely, an alternate key for room 834 was missing and did not appear for many hours. Bennett also had a sister, Anna Minick, who had a criminal record as a hotel burglar.

Initially the murder weapon, a .38-caliber, five-shot Iver Johnson revolver, also could not be found. When detectives finally located it on a fourth-floor landing, it was broken, as though it had been hurled there, and bore no fingerprints. Eventually, the weapon was found to have been owned by Ellen Bennett, who had received it a few years earlier from her brother, a Chicago police officer.

Williams died a few hours after being shot. Detectives, though, were at an impasse. The Thirty-Fifth District crew believed that she had been shot by her daughter, Patricia Goodbody. The detective bureau, which normally would have run the investigation, looked to the Bennett-Minick sisters as the killers. The case became an embarrassment to the police department because the army of reporters covering it highlighted the contrasting theories on the front pages of the city's newspapers. So Commissioner Allman assigned his top aide, Capt. "Mickey" Naughton, a man of sterling integrity who commanded the commissioner's confidential squad known as Scotland Yard, to take charge. In addition to the police, the Cook County state's attorney and the coroner were involved, and they too had their theories of what might have occurred.

Eventually, Commissioner Allman moved the captain of the Thirty-Fifth District out and gave the detective bureau the lead in the investigation. However, when the case was not solved, Sullivan was dismissed as chief of detectives, ending any hopes he had of becoming police commissioner.

Both Goodbody and her sister Ellen Born passed lie detector tests, as did the sisters Bennett and Minick. This stymied the investigation. Chicago was the home base of top lie detector experts like Leonard Keeler, and local authorities placed great stock in the machine. Personally, I never had much faith in it. Some people were easily able to "beat the box."

The case was never solved, although for a time, bored reporters circulated the notion that Williams had been so hostile to the Japanese in Tokyo that perhaps the emperor's secret agents had killed her. When reporters have to write about a case every day and there is nothing new, they commonly invent little fantasies.

Chief Sullivan was succeeded by another strong figure in the bureau, Walter Storms. But soon he would encounter his own difficulties. Immediately following World War II, a series of murders occurred around Chicago. One was a famous case where the killer murdered a WAVE and wrote with her lipstick, "Catch me before I kill more." Another of his victims was a six-year-old girl named Suzanne Degnan. Some of the best detectives in the force worked on the case, and they arrested a man who was the janitor of the apartment building where young Suzanne's body was found in the basement. One of the aces of the bureau was interviewed on the radio and declared, "I'll stake my thirty years as a detective that this is the man." The department had already hauled in a couple of individuals who were innocent and had to be released. It turned out this was another example. The janitor was eventually found to have had nothing to do with the murder, and he sued the police department, claiming he was beaten.

The fallout from the case necessitated Chief Storm's stepping down, and he was succeeded by Tim O'Connor, himself later police commissioner. For the next fifteen years the bureau was commanded by O'Connor or one of his top assistants. These men, steeped in the traditions of the 1920s, continued to operate as though nothing had changed. The postwar era required more subtle methods of policing, but any suggestion of revamping the detective bureau was rejected. Then, in 1960, the old bureau would disappear virtually overnight.

6

Eliot Ness Pursues the Butcher, the
Ups and Downs of Dr. Sam, and Lone
Wolf Gonzaullas Stalks the Phantom

The Mad Butcher

In the 1930s a series of murders occurred in Cleveland, Ohio, that should have been solved. Despite four years of intensive police work, they were not, and to this day no one has been able to determine who the killer was. At the time, Cleveland was one of the most important cities in the United States. It ranked seventh in population and third in the number of major corporations headquartered there. Only New York and Chicago had more. Its elite were among the business leaders of America. Of course, most Clevelanders were blue-collar people, many of them immigrants who had come to the city because of the number of manufacturing jobs available there. In short, it was nothing like the Cleveland of today. Its population now reduced by half, it is not even among the twenty-five largest U.S. cities, and its importance in the country is far less.

During many periods of its existence, the city had been governed by reformers. In the 1920s, however, Prohibition brought bootlegging gangs to political power and corruption to city hall. In 1935, amid a Democratic tidal wave in America, Clevelanders elected as mayor Harold Hitz Burton, a Republican lawyer prominent in veterans' affairs. Burton would later be elected to the U.S. Senate and then would be named an associate justice of the U.S. Supreme Court by Pres. Harry Truman, a Democrat with whom he had served in the Senate. As mayor, he selected for his director of public safety Eliot Ness, a Treasury agent who had built a small reputation fighting organized crime in Chicago. Ness's mandate was to clean up corruption in the police department. Little did he know when he took the job that his principal task would be to catch a serial killer.

In the 1930s the phenomenon of serial killers was often not recognized, and investigations of such events usually failed to unmask them. This is despite the fact that the 1886 Jack the Ripper murders in London were probably the most studied criminal events in the Anglo-American world.

September 5 is usually still summerlike in northern Ohio, but in Cleveland on that day in 1934, the skies were gray and overcast. Euclid Beach, which fronted Lake Erie on the city's far east side, was practically deserted. A twenty-one-year-old carpenter was walking along the shore looking for any items the tide had washed in when he spotted something sticking out of the sand. It was covered by driftwood, so he walked over to see what it was. When he pulled the wood off, he discovered it was part of a human body. The carpenter notified the police. At the morgue, Coroner Arthur Pearse identified the part as the lower part of a female body that had been severed at the waist and the knees. He determined that the victim had been dead six months and in the water for about four.

The next day, after a story appeared in the newspapers, a man in North Perry, Ohio, thirty miles north of Euclid Beach, called Cleveland police to inform them that two weeks earlier he had found what he believed was part of a human body on the shore close to his home. However, a local sheriff's deputy had theorized that the remains were those of an animal and suggested he bury them. After reading the story, though, he thought maybe it was a human. A squad of Cleveland detectives, including homicide specialist Emil Musil, went to North Perry, where they located the site of a makeshift grave and unearthed what proved to be the upper part of a woman's torso, minus the head and arms. It turned out to match the Euclid Beach corpse. The coroner reported that the dismemberment was done skillfully, with a razor-sharp, butcher type of knife. The only mistake the killer had made was in removing the right arm: he missed the joint and had to hack through the shoulder blade. The coroner also noted that the victim's skin was discolored and eventually concluded that a chemical preservative had been applied, accounting for an unusual tinge of the flesh.

Despite the stories in the newspaper, no one came forward to identify the body, nor were there any listings in the police's missing-persons files. The identity of the victim, whom the detectives labeled the Lady of the Lake, was never determined. They decided that the body could have come into Ohio from some distant area, such as a Canadian river flowing into the Great Lakes. The case was filed as "cause unknown, probable homicide." Later, when similar murders occurred, there was an argument over whether the body in the lake should have been victim number one. The authorities settled for calling it victim zero. The reason for playing down the case was the usual one. The police and the city fathers did not want to alarm the community.

A year passed by, and on September 22, 1935, the Eucharistic Congress met in Cleveland. This was a huge Catholic event held periodically in some American city. The city administration went all out to present a good face. New York's Cardinal Patrick Hayes, the most powerful figure in American Catholicism, accompanied by the papal legate (the representative of the pope in America), presided over the opening ceremonies at St. John's Cathedral in downtown Cleveland.

Just west of downtown was the heart of Cleveland's industrial area, known as the flats, a basin sixty feet below ground level, carved out by the Cuyahoga River, which contained row after row of factories. Between the railroad yards that serviced the city and the industrial section was a hobo jungle (gathering place) known as Kingsbury Run. At night the area was pitch-black. In daylight it was a place even police did not want to go into. For practical purposes, the principal law enforcement in the area was provided by railroads such as the Erie and the Nickel Plate. Its officers attempted to stop the hobos from jumping onto trains under the cover of darkness. During the Depression, hopping a train was a leading means of travel for thousands of people who were out of work.

The only Clevelanders who entered Kingsbury Run, and then only in the daytime, were young boys who could not resist the railroad yards. Some would even try to imitate the hobos and jump aboard slow-moving freight trains. Railroad cops used clubs on the hobos and shot the boys in the rear end with pepper-spray guns.

On the afternoon of September 23 two boys, age sixteen and twelve, raced down Jackass Hill. The sixteen-year-old arrived at the bottom first and spotted something in the bushes. It turned out to be a headless body. Both boys ran back up the hill and told the first adult they saw, who in turn notified the railroad police.

When a sergeant and patrolman from the Erie arrived at the foot of Jackass Hill, they noted that the victim was naked, except for his socks, and had been castrated. The cops began searching around and about thirty feet away the patrolman yelled out that he had found another headless body. Obviously, this was a case for the city police, and top detectives and commanders arrived from headquarters. Among them was homicide detective Musil and his partner, Orly May. They noted that there was no blood on the first victim's body, suggesting he had been washed with some substance and brought to the area. The second victim was more decomposed. Apparently, the men had been killed elsewhere and at different times.

Finding a dead body in a hobo jungle was not particularly unusual. However, detectives are invariably individuals with a professionally developed sixth sense. May said to his colleagues, "I've got a bad feeling about this case." Soon, all of Cleveland would have a bad feeling.

The two victims were listed as John Doe 1 and John Doe 2. Fingerprints disclosed that number one was Edward Andrassy, a twenty-eight-year-old resident of the near west side who hung out in the third police precinct, popularly known as the Roaring Third, because of its sleazy nightlife. Kingsbury Run was part of the precinct. Andrassy had been picked up frequently for being disorderly or for small-time gambling. If he had been shot in a bar or on the street, there would have been no surprise. But he did not seem the type to hang out in a hobo jungle and end up with his head cut off. It had been reported that he once shot an Italian man, but Andrassy's mutilations did not seem to follow the Mafia pattern. One detective speculated that he might have been part of a homosexual love triangle. The condition of the body was such that a precise time of death could not be calculated, though Coroner Pearse estimated he had been dead for about two days. The second victim was never identified.

Shortly after the Kingsbury Run victims were found, Eliot Ness arrived to take over as safety director in charge of the police and fire departments. He had not been the first choice for the job. The local head of the FBI refused it, as did the local U.S. attorney. Joseph Keenan, a prominent lawyer who later led the prosecution of Japanese war criminals, recommended Ness, who was then heading a five-man Treasury Department alcohol-tax enforcement unit (ATU) in Cleveland.

Ness had made his reputation leading a squad of Prohibition agents in Chicago, and he was especially good at getting publicity for the raids he made. A 1950s book vastly overrated his work in Chicago. The television series and movies that followed converted him into a mythical character who fought machine-gun battles with the Mafia and rolled around on rooftops battling mob kingpins.

Despite having earned a degree in business from the University of Chicago, Ness was one of those people who did not like office work, so he managed to get an appointment with the Prohibition Bureau. When the "noble experiment" ended, he sought a job in the FBI. J. Edgar Hoover, who had no use for Ness's publicity-seeking activities, refused. Ness ended up as a Treasury agent in the South, where the local still operators were known to "bounce a rifle ball off'n a revenoer's head." Law enforcement in the southern hills was a job for local men, who went by names like Cap'n Dan or Cap'n Jim and could handle a pack of bloodhounds. So Ness had to settle for an obscure post in Cleveland.

While the reaction of Cleveland cops to the appointment of Ness has not been recorded, it can easily be guessed. In the 1920s Harvard Law School dean Roscoe Pound and Prof. Felix Frankfurter had been brought to Cleveland to study crime and the justice system. They concluded that a basic cause of crime was the pressures of urban industrial life on a justice system ill equipped to deal with them. The police must have been impressed by the finding that a city with thousands of industrial workers, drawn from all parts of the world, was not as peaceful as a rural village.

The Cleveland detective bureau was comparable to the ones in other big cities, though less powerful than those in New York or Chicago. It was conventionally organized into squads and was commanded by an inspector. The chief of police during the Butcher investigation, George Matowicz, always wore his uniform at crime scenes, as if to say, I am not going to personally play detective. The stars of the bureau who "caught" most of the big cases were usually homicide men. By the end of the investigation of the Butcher murders, one detective, Peter Merylo, seemed to be more powerful in the case than the city safety director, the chief of police, or the commander of detectives.

In 1928 Cleveland detectives had won accolades for a raid on the first-known summit conference of the American Mafia, which was held at the local Statler Hotel. Detectives went to the room where the mobsters were meeting and told the manager to unlock the door, after which he could step aside. When he complied, they shoved him through the door as a shield against the gangsters' bullets. Mob leaders from all over the United States were arrested. As it turned out, they were not planning any murders but discussing the price of corn sugar, an important ingredient in the manufacture of liquor, a large supply of which was produced in Cleveland.

An additional resource was the railroad police, who played a larger than normal role in the Kingsbury Run killings. Many of the murder scenes were on their turf. Railroad police were not rent-a-cops but were hired by an industry that had traditionally been the most powerful in the United States. Criminals feared railroad cops, whether uniformed or detectives, because they were not political hires and were always backed up by their employers.

The word from Chicago to the Cleveland Police Department was that Ness, who was not a real cop, would spend his time going after crooked officers. Some accounts have claimed that he was largely an office administrator who concentrated on police corruption and had little to do with the investigation of what became known as "the Butcher murders." To imagine that a man as energetic and publicity conscious as Ness would sit at his desk while his police department handled the largest murder investigation in the United States defies logic. In addition to being a corruption fighter, he would end up essentially as the chief homicide investigator, a position he was not qualified for.

Ness also acquired a staff of well-educated non-cops to assist him in his investigations of the police and law enforcement matters in general. They were young men who, in the postwar world, would become agency heads, judges, and so on, but their qualifications for catching the Butcher were minimal.

Ness received his baptism by fire in the Butcher murder investigations in January 1936 when a body was found in the Roaring Third. A woman told a butcher that someone had left a basket sitting in a nearby alley. When the butcher went out to see what it contained, he found half of a woman's torso in the basket. The victim's fingerprints disclosed that she was a forty-one-year-old prostitute named Florence Polillo, who lived a few blocks from where she had been found. Again homicide detectives Musil and May were among those assigned to the case. They heard that Polillo had been friendly with a lake sailor who sometimes functioned as her pimp, but he was never located. Polillo had allegedly been seen in a bar with a black man shortly before her death, but it was ascertained that she was already dead at the time the incident supposedly occurred. On February 7, when more pieces of the victim were found, it was determined that the various parts had been removed with clean strokes, not simply by hacking them off.

A detective sergeant told the press that the murder was not related to those of the two men found in Kingsbury Run. No doubt he was just attempting to calm the public. There was also a stronger reason for playing down the crime. The Republican National Convention was scheduled to open in Cleveland in June. An even larger event, the Great Lakes Exposition, would be held on the lakefront that summer to celebrate the hundredth anniversary of the city's founding. The GOP mayor was not anxious to be embarrassed in front of one thousand delegates from his own party. If it were reported that there was a madman running loose, attendance at the exposition might suffer. Visitors were supposed to leave their hearts in the city, not their heads.

Unfortunately, the man who was beginning to be called the Mad Butcher struck once just before the convention opened and a second time just before the exposition. Perhaps he wanted a share of the limelight.

On June 5, two boys, eleven and thirteen, taking a shortcut through Kingsbury Lane on their way to go fishing, noticed a bag. When one of the boys probed it with his fishing rod, a head fell out. Once again, police swarmed to Jackass Hill.

The bag with the head had actually been placed in front of the Nickel Plate Railroad police office. The rest of the corpse was found intact. The victim was a young man, well nourished, and his body had a number of tattoos indicating he was possibly a lake sailor. His identity would never be ascertained, but the coroner reported he had been decapitated while still alive. From then on, the cops had to quit pushing the line "nothing to worry about, folks," because it made them look ridiculous.

On July 22 another body was found just south of the city limits. This time it was the upper half of a torso with the head missing. After a search, the head was recovered but not the lower part of the body. There was blood on the scene, and the coroner declared that the killing had taken place on the site. The next day, firemen dragged the nearby sewers and turned up the victim's legs.

With six butchered murder victims found in just a year, the people of Cleveland were beginning to ask why the cops could not solve at least one of the cases. Ness had to respond to the public outcry and get involved in the work of Chief Matowicz and Insp. Charles Nevell, the commander of detectives who ran the investigation. One problem was that the police were aware Ness was there to nail a number of them, which did not encourage them to make their boss look good.

In October 1936 Ness presented the local prosecutor with an eighty-six-page report on corruption in the police department. Twenty officers were named, including a deputy inspector, two captains, two lieutenants, and three sergeants. For Ness it was only the beginning. In time, he would jail a number of cops and force scores of them to resign from the police department. In one instance, the wife of a captain convicted of corruption spit in Ness's face. While his actions won praise from civic reformers, Democratic politicians and a lot of ordinary citizens were not impressed by the fact that he was arresting cops for ten-dollar bribes they had taken from bootleggers five years earlier during Prohibition.

The 1936 county elections meant a changing of the guard in the coroner's office, with Samuel Gerber replacing Arthur Pearse. The tiny (five foot, three inch) Gerber was not only a doctor but also had studied widely in criminology and psychology and held a law degree. It was clear from the start that he wanted a major role in the Butcher investigation , and it was not long before he and Ness were clashing.

A coroner could choose how he wanted to run his office. Some stuck to determining the cause of death. Others ran virtually alternative detective bureaus, attempting to solve a homicide while making a number of public pronouncements about the investigation. In many places, like Chicago, the coroner was not even a medical doctor but rather a politician who hired medical experts as needed. In Cleveland the coroner was not the only elected official who poked his head into municipal police cases. Cuyahoga County sheriff Martin O' Donnell, a member of a faction of the Democratic Party led by the powerful congressman Martin Sweeney, also disliked Ness.

When the Cleveland police asked for help from the FBI, Hoover refused because he said there was no federal aspect to the case. Of course, Hoover had always been able to find a federal angle to matters he wanted to enter and to dodge cases he did not want to participate in by saying he did not have authority. Hoover knew that with Ness running the police, the FBI was likely to be upstaged.

Ness was now confronted with a coroner who considered himself a professional on crime and Ness an amateur, an FBI that gave him the cold shoulder, and many politicians out to do him in. Luckily for Ness, he formed a close alliance with another possible rival, the county prosecutor. While the coroner and sheriff could blow off as much steam as they wanted, they could not block an investigation. But without the prosecutor, the cops would have been severely handicapped.

Over the course of a year in which the Cleveland homicide detectives had to work on six Butcher victims—or more realistically seven, if the Lady of the Lake were counted—they began to tire out. Some detectives had started out optimistic about solving the case. However, they had followed promising leads and then hit a stone wall.

One lead the police followed was something the Cleveland cops called "nationality murders," a common phenomenon in midwestern industrial cities with large Slavic populations. These were patterns that came from Europe, particularly the Balkans, where different tribal groups supposedly engaged in distinct types of murders. For example, in the eastern portions of the old Austro-Hungarian Empire (home of both Dracula and Frankenstein), many men learned how to butcher animals. Thus a butcher-type killing might be carried out by persons of that background. Some nationalities valued skill with the blade, so possibly the killer was engaging in some kind of ritual.

After promising leads peter out, there are two strategies a police commander can take to revive his troops. The first is to essentially back off and wait until there is a break in the case. Possibly someone would see the Butcher depositing a body or had a strong suspicion of who he might be and would come forward. The second is to relieve the officers who have been working on the case and replace them with people who are fresh. This is one advantage large police departments have over small ones in complex investigations. When the initial investigating crew burns out in a small police department, there is nobody to replace them. In a big city, there is. The original homicide team was, to an extent, superseded by a new lead detective, Peter Merylo, who was a hard-charging, never-say-die cop. Physically, Merylo was a big man who, like all detectives of the time, wore a fedora in the winter and switched to a straw hat in the summer. His appearance immediately marked him as John Law. He was shrewd and imaginative and, with his partner, Martin Zalewski, had worked on the biggest cases. The two men liked to go right to the source of the problem. Many nights they would lie in the dark Kingsbury Run tunnels, ten to twelve feet apart, clutching their guns and watching one another. The idea was to see if they would be attacked. Other times they would pose as tramps, riding boxcars in and out of town or sitting around the fireside at hobo camps, listening to the gossip. Often they prowled through the dingy bars of the Roaring Third. Merylo was the kind of cop who, if he saw anyone suspicious, like some barfly bragging about his role in the case, he would pull him in for questioning, whereas other cops might have ignored him as a drunk shooting off his mouth. Like many detectives, Merylo and his partner adhered to the notion that criminals and oddballs were more likely to operate when there was a full moon. An FBI agent who reported that idea to J. Edgar Hoover would have been sent to view the moon from Anchorage, Alaska. However, there were indications of that correlation in many cities. Merylo studied medical textbooks, worked long hours, and made himself the master of the case. In later years, anyone writing about it would consult with him.

In October 1936 the Cleveland police got word from New Castle, Pennsylvania, that some thirteen headless bodies had been found there in the past ten years, one very recently. Sergeant Hogan of the Cleveland homicide squad and other officers went to New Castle, a town on the railroad across the state line from Youngstown, Ohio, about one hundred miles from Cleveland. The earlier bodies had been found in a swamp by the railroad yards, perhaps dumped there by gangsters. The most recent one had been lying on the floor of an old boxcar. The Cleveland police concluded that there was nothing definite to show that the New Castle murders were committed by the same person as the Cleveland murders. However, Detective Merylo tended to believe that there was a strong connection between the New Castle killings and the Cleveland Butcher.

In February 1937 there was a rerun of the Lady of the Lake murder. A headless female body floated up at Euclid Beach, where the 1934 victim had been found. Coroner Gerber said that she had been dead for just three or four days.

Next, a black woman's decapitated body was found underneath a local bridge. This time the coroner ruled she had been dead for about a year, which raised the question of where the body had been for that time.

Ness established a hotline at city hall to receive tips. While this is a device often used in big cases, given the publicity the crimes had received, the tip line was not likely to produce more than a lot of false information. Many people had developed their own theories of the case, and they were anxious to share them with the authorities. It also provided an opportunity to get back at someone the caller did not like by setting the cops on them. Detectives spent a lot of time running down false leads.

Like some detectives, Ness began to believe that the Butcher was not a low-class denizen of skid row but an upscale person who was familiar with the area, perhaps someone who had declined in status and now hung around the Third Precinct. The same kind of theories had been advanced in the time of Jack the Ripper. So Ness began to look at different social levels other than the ones inhabited by the bums and characters in the Roaring Third. Another possibility was that the Butcher was a railroad crewman or a ship's officer who made occasional visits to Cleveland but did not reside there, which would explain why there were long gaps between the commission of some of the murders. At the time, a locomotive engineer held the most princely of blue-collar jobs, and the captain of a lake steamer ranked as a gentleman. Some argued that the Butcher was a doctor, but the medical techniques he displayed were not up to that level. Instead, he might have worked at a hospital or have been an army medic.

Merylo, on the other hand, still felt the solution would be found in the dark tunnels or boxcars, where they would eventually run across the killer. Ness and Merylo would come up with diametrically opposed theories of the case. Had Ness been a police chief, he would have been in a stronger position to ride herd over Merylo, but he was in the ambiguous post of a director of public safety who was attempting to throw cops in jail.

Ness ordered detectives to look for a man of intelligence and standing. He calculated that the killer probably had a hideout somewhere near the scene of the murders and that a thorough search would turn it up. So he instituted the raiding methods he had used in Chicago, and officers were assigned to make a house-to-house canvas of the ten square miles where most of the murders had occurred. He especially alerted them to be on the lookout for the possibility that the suspect had his own crime lab where he performed dissections. To deal with constitutional limitations, Ness assigned fire inspectors to work with the task force because they possessed the legal authority to search for fire hazards without the necessity of securing a warrant. Nothing was found.

As good as Ness was with public relations, he did not know how to establish rapport with his officers. He failed to understand that men in any occupation had to be led, not driven. During his time, he provided one shining example of leading his cops. The county prosecutor, who was Ness's ally, undertook to raid a mob-controlled gambling casino outside the city limits of Cleveland. When he and his small force of investigators were refused entry and threatened with being shot if they tried to break in, the prosecutor called the sheriff for assistance. When the sheriff refused, the prosecutor called Eliot Ness, who technically had no jurisdiction. Although advised by the mayor to be careful about going outside the city, Ness decided to ride to the rescue. Shifts were changing in Cleveland police headquarters, so Ness went there, addressed fifty officers going off duty, and asked for volunteers to come with him to the aid of the prosecutor. One thing cops can be persuaded to do is to assist other cops in distress. So the officers volunteered and, toting machine guns, they went along with Ness to the casino. When the force from Cleveland arrived, the casino owners capitulated.

In April 1938 a leg was pulled out of the Cuyahoga River in the Kingsbury Run area. Then another leg was found in the river. Police searched the bridge and found a burlap sack containing a headless torso cut in half. The victim was a female who the coroner reported had been dead for about three to five days. In August a man and woman were found dead and decapitated near a lakeshore dump. One victim's head was found but not the other victim's. These would be the last official Butcher victims.

In 1939 Sheriff O'Donnell, assisted by a private investigator, arrested a fifty-two-year-old man named Frank Dolezal as a suspect in the murder of Florence Polillo. Later Dolezal was found to have been badly beaten while in police custody, and he eventually committed suicide in the county jail.

A suspect whom Ness favored was Francis E. Sweeney, a bona fide doctor who had done a number of amputations in the field during

World War I. However, Sweeney was not powerfully built and therefore not capable of carrying bodies long distances or overcoming physical resistance from healthy males. He was personally interviewed by Ness and given a polygraph test by the well-known expert Leonard Keeler of Chicago. Keeler believed that Sweeney was the murderer. There were a number of political complications, such as the fact that the doctor was the first cousin of Congressman Sweeney, who hated Ness. Congressman Sweeney was also related by marriage to Sheriff O'Donnell. Francis Sweeney eventually committed himself to an institution.

With the investigation at an impasse, Ness began to feel the pressures of his job. He divorced his first wife, remarried, and spent a lot of time socializing with the Cleveland elite. At Christmas 1941, while coming back from a party, he was involved in an accident with another vehicle. Ness stopped briefly to inquire if the other people were all right and then left the scene. Since his license plate said "ENI," it was not hard for cops to trace the car. By that time a new mayor, Democrat Frank Lausche, had taken office. Such was the respect that many people had for Ness that Lausche decided not to remove him. Eventually Ness went off to a wartime job, closing down houses of ill fame around military posts.

After the war, Ness went into business with the former dean of Harvard Law School, James Landis. For a time Ness was doing very well financially, but eventually the business collapsed. In 1947 he returned to Cleveland, ran for mayor, and was badly defeated. He did not have the knack of connecting with the ordinary voter. After that, Ness's career drifted downward. By the 1950s he was living in a small town in Pennsylvania with very little money. In New York he met a writer who was fascinated by Ness's career in Chicago and asked to write a book about him. Ness, whose health was failing, died in 1957 at the age of fifty-four, shortly before the book, *The Untouchables*, came out. Had he lived, he would have been both rich and famous. Given a normal lifespan, he would have been a much-sought-after figure during the 1960s and 1970s crime wave that plagued America. In the end, he has become a household name largely for what he did not do in Chicago.

Despite discontinuing police investigations in Cleveland, railroad police, professional as always, would routinely question hobos they picked up about the Butcher murders, even as late as the 1950s. Nothing turned up.

When the case is discussed, one of the reasons offered for the failure of police to solve it is that serial killings were so rare, or at least unrecognized as such, that cops just did not know how to handle them. Those that involved interstate killers were beyond the capacity of a single police department, and not until the FBI became involved in the phenomenon in the 1970s did serial killings become a major focus of detective work.

Detective Merylo always believed that the Butcher never stopped. He pointed to a number of cases where murdered individuals were decapitated, as in Butcher cases. In later years, Merylo would count two hundred murders in the Ohio–Pennsylvania area between 1920 and 1950 as Butcher cases.

Dr. Sam

Coroner Gerber continued to be regularly reelected to his office. In 1954 he had an opportunity to play chief of detectives. In July of that year, Marilyn Sheppard, who lived with her husband, Dr. Sam Sheppard, in Bay Village, Ohio, a Cleveland suburb, was bludgeoned to death in her bed. Dr. Sheppard, then thirty-one, was an osteopath who practiced at a family clinic along with his father and two brothers. He told police he was sleeping soundly downstairs when he heard his wife cry out. When he ran upstairs, he was knocked unconscious. When he awoke, he chased an intruder out of the house and down to the beach, where they tussled and Sheppard was knocked unconscious again. He lay with half his body in the lake.

It was one of those cases where several different departments were involved in the investigation. The small suburban Bay Shore police force had jurisdiction, but they called in Cleveland Police Department homicide detectives for assistance. Others who had authority to investigate the case were the county sheriff, county prosecutor, and county coroner. Based on their initial investigation and interrogation of Sheppard, the Cleveland homicide detectives recommended to the Bay Shore police that Dr. Sam, as he became known, should be arrested and charged with the murder. However, the mayor of Bay Shore was a close friend of Sheppard's.

The key figure in the case was Gerber, who since the 1930s Butcher investigation had developed a national reputation as a homicide expert and had built up his office into a large, modern agency. On any homicide case, he was always front and center with the media. Although he was a graduate of a third-rate medical school that had been out of business over twenty years, Gerber became a leader of the profession. At that time, MDs did not accept osteopaths as doctors and tried to put restrictions on their practice. In Cleveland, Gerber was hostile to osteopaths and also suspected that the Sheppards performed not only legal abortions but also illegal ones.

At one point in the case, the Cleveland commander of detectives was so upset with the way the matter was being handled that he withdrew his officers from the investigation. Finally it was agreed that Cleveland would have formal jurisdiction in the case and that the town of Bay Shore would pay the Cleveland police $5,000 for their services.

The local press played an important role in the investigation. Indeed, in the opinion of many, it played the next major role to Gerber. The *Cleveland Press* ran a front-page editorial headlined "Do It Now Dr. Gerber," which demanded a public inquest. The next day Gerber announced that he would hold the inquest. The newspaper ran another editorial, "Why Isn't Sam Sheppard Put in Jail?," which was alternatively titled "Quit Stalling and Bring Him In." That night Sheppard was arrested. At the time, the media reported stories about Shepherd's mistress. At the trial Gerber provided the state with a key element for the prosecution. No murder weapon had been found, but he testified that a blood imprint left on the pillow beneath the victim was made by a "two-blade surgical instrument with teeth at the end of each blade," such as a scalpel. Though never found, it pointed toward Dr. Sheppard as the killer. Sheppard was convicted at trial and given a life sentence in the Ohio State Penitentiary. Of all the participants in the case, Gerber received the most credit for his role, and he basked in it. However, the case was not entirely finished, and eight years later it would be reopened, much to Gerber's distress.

In 1961 Sheppard obtained a new lawyer, the then-unknown F. Lee Bailey. Bailey petitioned for a writ of habeas corpus, which the federal district court granted in July. Then the circuit court reversed the district judge's ruling, but the U.S. Supreme Court, by a vote of eight to one, struck down the murder conviction. In 1966 Sheppard was retried and acquitted.

Sheppard died in 1970 at the age of forty-six. However, many Clevelanders still believed that he was guilty of the murder. When his son, Samuel Reese Sheppard, attempted to sue the state of Ohio for wrongful imprisonment, an eight-person civil jury deliberated just three hours before returning a unanimous verdict that Samuel R. Sheppard failed to prove that his father was wrongfully imprisoned. Some jurors even stated that the verdict represented their belief that Sam Sheppard had murdered his wife.

Texarkana, Texas: The "Lone Wolf" Stalks the Midnight Phantom

Eight years after the last acknowledged Butcher murder, a similar case emerged in a much smaller and different type of community: Texarkana, Texas. The town straddles the border of northeast Texas and adjoining Arkansas. In 1946 Texarkana was not a city of one million, full of immigrants, like Cleveland but a regional center in the South. It was the kind of town where people said "good morning" and "howdy" and knew their neighbors' names and often a good bit of their business.

On paper, the case should have been solved. In a city of one million, an individual could go completely unnoticed. In a small community, it is reasonable to believe that some people must have at least suspected a particular person was carrying out serial killings.

In this case, the principal police department involved was a world-famous force: the Texas Rangers. This time the top cop was not a college boy who had become a revenue agent but a legendary figure who symbolized his agency and his state, Capt. Manuel "Lone Wolf" Gonzaullas. A larger-than-life individual, he claimed to have been born in Cadiz, Spain, where his naturalized American parents were visiting at the time of his birth. In 1911, when revolution broke out in Mexico, Gonzaullas, though only twenty, served as a major in that country's army. In 1915 he was appointed a U.S. Treasury agent, and in 1920 he joined the Rangers. In fact, he had been born in Texas and the yarn about his birth was meant to identify him as Spanish rather than Mexican.

Most people are roughly familiar with the history of the Rangers, at least from watching movies. Up until the 1930s, it was a loosely organized force and politics played a big role. In 1933, when Miriam "Ma" Ferguson was governor, filling in for her husband, "Pa," who ran Texas politics for a generation, she fired all the rangers, including men like Capt. Frank Hamer.

Hamer is generally regarded as the greatest ranger ever to serve in the legendary force. Born in the hill country of Texas in 1884, he joined the Rangers in 1906. During his career he was supposed to have been involved in fifty-two gunfights and killed twenty-three men. In acting as an agent of the Texas Department of Corrections, he tracked Bonnie and Clyde to Louisiana, where he and his team killed them.

In 1935 the state legislature created the modern Texas Department of Public Safety, consisting of the Highway Patrol, the Rangers, and the Bureau of Intelligence. The Rangers could be seen as the detective bureau of Texas, but its approximately hundred members were scattered throughout a huge area and there was still heavy emphasis on hunting dangerous criminals rather than solving mysteries.

Gonzaullas was appointed superintendent of the Bureau of Intelligence at its creation, which he made into one of the best crime-detection forces in America. In 1940 he returned to the Rangers as captain, commanding Company B, thus becoming the first American of Mexican descent to achieve that rank. Gonzaullas preferred to work alone, and the name Lone Wolf caught on with the public. With his Hollywood good looks, athletic build, and immaculate turnout, wearing a white ten-gallon hat and a spotless khaki ripcord suit, women swooned over him. Police knew him as fearless. Once, when he heard of a robbery being planned at a hotel, Gonzaullas went there alone and sat down with his two ivory-handled revolvers. When the robbers came in and announced a stickup, he killed both of them.

Gonzaullas was not the only ranger who worked alone. Once, one of them was sent to police a riot. When he got off the train, locals asked, "Where are the rest of your men?" To which the ranger replied, "There is only one riot." "One riot, one Ranger" became a catchphrase with the public.

As a matter of course, rangers carried two huge revolvers on their hips and were expected to use them if necessary. A ranger might have been one man, but he had a dozen bullets that he could fire quickly, and the state of Texas could always be relied upon to back him. If he were killed, his fellow rangers would track down the murderer and pump him full of lead.

When the serial killer struck in Texarkana, the local police were stymied, so Texas sent Lone Wolf to the rescue. The case had begun just before midnight on Friday night, February 22, 1946, when Jimmy Hollis, twenty-five, and his girlfriend, Mary Jeanne Larey, nineteen, were attacked on a secluded road known as a lovers' lane. The couple had arrived at the scene about 11:45, and ten minutes later, a man walked up to Hollis's side door and put a flashlight in his face, blinding him. The man produced a pistol and told him, "I don't want to kill you fella, so do what I tell you," and ordered the two to get out of the car. He told Hollis to take off his trousers. After he did so, he was struck in the head with a heavy, blunt object.

The assailant then demanded money from Larey, and when he learned that she did not have any, he knocked her down. She suspected he used an iron pipe. She started to run away, but he caught up with her. After sustaining a beating, she ran to a nearby house and woke up the owners, who called Bowie County sheriff Bill Presley. He arrived on the scene with three other officers, including his friend Jack Runnels, who was chief of police in the town of Texas City. The two victims disagreed on whether the attacker was black. For some reason police investigating the case did not believe the victims' story. Some insisted Larey knew who the attacker was. It was common in those days for a boyfriend who couldn't find his girlfriend at home to go down to the local lovers' lane and catch her with somebody else. Such altercations were a feature of small-town life. In any event, the police announced that the case was an isolated incident and further attacks were not expected.

On a Saturday night, March 24, Richard Griffin, twenty-nine, and his girlfriend, Polly Ann Moore, seventeen, were found dead in Griffin's car, parked in another lovers' lane. Passing motorists saw the bodies in the car and notified the police. Both victims had been shot once in the back of the head, and they were fully clothed. Moore's purse was beside her. According to an Arkansas state trooper who worked on the investigation, Moore had been killed on a blanket in front of the vehicle before being placed back inside. Sheriff Presley took charge of the investigation along with his friend Jack Runnels. One problem in the case was that there were too many cooks involved—there were city police, the Texas Rangers, and the county sheriff's department, plus the Arkansas authorities.

On another Saturday night, April 13, Betty Jo Booker, fifteen, finished playing her saxophone at a VFW club at about 1:30 a.m. She was scheduled be picked up by an old friend, Paul Martin, age sixteen, who had returned to town after moving away for a couple of years. At around 6:30 a.m. on Sunday, Martin was discovered lying on a road by a motorist. He had been shot four times. Booker was not found for several hours and then almost two miles away from Martin's body. She was fully clothed and had been shot twice. Sheriff Presley and Chief Runnels were the first officers on the scene of the murders.

On a Friday night, May 3, Virgil and Katie Starks, thirty-seven and thirty-six, respectively, were attacked at their farm. Mrs. Starks heard what she thought were shots fired and went to tell her husband to turn down the radio. A few seconds later, two shots were fired into the back of Mr. Starks's head. While using the wall-crank phone to notify the police, Katie Starks was shot twice in the face from the window, but she survived.

The police were becoming frustrated and quarrelsome over the case. One night Arkansas state trooper Max Tackett led a group of his men to the Starks' home, which had been closed off since the shootings. He announced that the probable killer might be hiding in the house and called upon him to surrender. After a while, a sheepish Lone Wolf Gonzaullas and a female reporter for a national magazine walked out of the building. As the case dragged on, on there were the usual tensions between the various investigators.

State Trooper Tackett arrested a man named Youell Swinney, whose wife, Peggy, claimed that he was the man locals were calling the Phantom Killer and recited in great detail an account of how he had killed Betty Jo Booker and Paul Martin. A wife could not be made to testify against her husband, and she was also considered unreliable. Instead, Youell was sent to prison as a habitual offender for stealing cars. Eventually, it was found that his fingerprints did not match any of the latent prints at the Booker-Martin crime scenes. Mrs. Swinney repudiated her accusation, and some law enforcement officers were convinced that her husband was not the Phantom. Other suspects were canvassed, but without results.

Eventually, Gonzaullas and the Texas Rangers quietly pulled out of the investigation. Many people misunderstood his mission. When a famous lawman is inserted into a case, it's not that his superiors expect that he personally will solve the crime. Rather, he was there to impress the media and other parties, such as elected officials. He also provided a cover for superiors because they could say, "We sent in the best man we have with a proven record of success, and even he could not crack the case."

A puzzling aspect of the investigation is that in such a small community no one ever came forward with any real, hard information that would lead to the killer. The fact that all the attacks occurred on weekend nights suggested that he might not have been a local resident but an individual from another town some distance away who was free on weekends to roam to Texarkana. Books have been written about the crime and several movies have been produced, but no definitive answer has emerged. Perhaps the killer moved on to a distant part of the country where he continued his activities. Yet no such linkage was made by the law enforcement agencies at that time.

A few years after the Texarkana case, Gonzaullas retired and moved to Hollywood, where he became a technical consultant for radio, TV, and movies. He was connected to the long-running 1950s radio show *Tales of the Texas Rangers*. While Eliot Ness could handle corruption and Lone Wolf could shoot down gunmen, like other American cops of their time, they were unable to apprehend serial killers.

7

The Inspectors Bureau in

the City by the Bay

San Francisco was the most colorful city in America. Its early settlers had come across the plains or oceans to the peninsula on the west coast of the mighty republic, and they always had the feeling that they were survivors of some great adventure. For San Franciscans who were alive at the time of the 1906 earthquake, it remained the most vivid memory of their lives. The city came back strongly after the earthquake because its citizens loved it. Instead of leaving, they stuck around through the dark postquake days. Other Americans loved San Francisco too and ranked it as their favorite city to visit. San Francisco—never "Frisco"—flourished through a combination of the allure of sophisticated Nob Hill, with its old families and tycoons, the shipping industry, and wide-open sin that attracted hordes of visitors. By the same token, the San Francisco police force was held together by its inspectors bureau.

In 1915 San Francisco hosted the Panama-Pacific International Exposition, a world's fair to celebrate the opening of the Panama Canal and San Francisco's recovery from the effects of the 1906 earthquake (though the city did not really recover until the 1920s). More police were needed to handle the expected throng that would attend. One of those hired the previous year was twenty-six-year-old Charlie Dullea, a San Francisco native who had six years of service in the U.S. Marine Corps, where he had spent most of his time on pacification missions in Central America.

Dullea was a natural for the police force. Like so many cops, he was born in the tough South of the Slot district, where the iron streetcar tracks on Market Street divided the city in half where the trolley cars were switched around. At six foot, one inch, 205 pounds, he looked like a marine on a recruiting poster and was made the captain's "dog robber" (a term so archaic that no GI today would understand it). The "dog robber" was the orderly who carried out various assignments for the company commander.

Dullea's hometown, where he would serve for the remainder of his days, had evolved out of the turbulent gold rush era of the '49ers, when vigilantes enforced the law. When it became a great seaport, linking America and Asia, the Chinese who came to the Bay Area were occasionally lynched. In the world-famous sin district, known as the Barbary Coast, sailors were regularly "shanghaied" (rendered unconscious and sent on a long trip to China). At the time of the earthquake, Frederick Funston, the army general commanding the local military base known as the Presidio, declared martial law, sent troops to maintain order, and shoot looters.

One of private detective William Burns's major cases occurred in San Francisco when he sent the mayor to jail for graft in the first decade of the twentieth century. During the investigation, bands of armed men raced through the streets beating or kidnapping their opponents. In one instance, a reform prosecutor was shot down in a courtroom. In 1908 the chief of police was being piloted across the bay in a launch when he allegedly fell overboard and drowned. The pilot went insane.

It was the only city in America where northern Italians, like Angelo Rossi, mayor from 1931 to 1943, were the dominant faction among their countrymen. The most prominent Italian in the city was A. P. Giannini, who founded the giant Bank of America. Since the Mafia was composed of southerners, it did not gain a real foothold in San Francisco, and when it tried, the police ran them out of town.

A question that always perplexed San Francisco's leading citizens was how to maintain what a prominent lawyer described as "the city's many-splendored nightlife" (including over three hundred bordellos) without corrupting the police force. It was a problem that could never be solved. In interwar San Francisco the role of liaison between local criminal groups and the police was performed by the McDonough brothers, Pete and Tom, a police sergeant's sons who were bail bondsmen and saloon keepers.

The police force that Dullea joined was organized in the same way as many big-city forces of the time. At the top was a board of three civilian commissioners drawn from men of standing. Under the board was the appointed police chief. Among his subordinates, the one with the most prestige was the captain of the inspectors bureau, the local name for detectives. The bureau maintained the usual special squads that most cities had, such as homicide and robbery, and its inspectors played the same role as the Chicago detective bureau, a citywide force controlled from headquarters. However, in Chicago, it was always clear that city hall was boss. In San Francisco, cops had more independent power. In addition, the police were united by an ethnic factor. Eighty percent of them were Irish, half of them born on the "auld sod." Cops were a proud outfit, and every year they paraded through the streets of the city to the cheers of onlookers. Given the composition of the force, it was almost a second St. Patrick's Day.

In 1916 the United States was in the midst of a presidential election, Charles Evans Hughes versus Woodrow Wilson. World War I raged in Europe, and the country was divided on whether to go to war on behalf of the Allies. Those who favored intervention began holding preparedness parades to alert people about the danger of the Germans. One was scheduled for San Francisco on Saturday, July 22. It was a bad time for such an event to be held. There had been a huge transit strike with bloody conflict between labor and management. Within an eight-month period, two policeman were shot dead by anarchists. The state militia was already on the Mexican border fighting Pancho Villa. Because the sponsor of the parade was the Chamber of Commerce, organized labor refused to participate.

At 1:30 p.m. on the twenty-second, Capt. Duncan Matheson, commanding officer of the traffic bureau, blew his whistle to start the parade down Market Street. Matheson was a Nova Scotia–born Scotsman noted for his stern morality and competence. He had joined the force in 1900 as part of the first civil service class. At that time, veteran officers complained that "book cops" would never be able to handle beats like the Barbary Coast. Years later, Matheson would boast that no member of his class had ever been charged with cowardice. At 2:06 p.m., as a contingent of war veterans passed Steuart Street, a bomb exploded on the sidewalk, killing outright or fatally injuring ten persons and wounding forty. Matheson realized that he had to do something to prevent panic, so he ordered the parade to continue and the vets, many dripping blood, drew themselves to attention and marched onward. Observers agreed that the captain's action prevented worse casualties.

In 1916 San Francisco did not have a detective force comparable in size or experience to those of much larger cities like New York and Chicago. On July 22, for example, one San Francisco detective, Lt. Steve Bunner, decided to wash down the bombing scene with fire hoses, thus removing a considerable portion of the physical evidence. In a hurried conference between Mayor Jim Rolph and police chief David White, Captain Matheson was put in charge of a squad to investigate the attack. Private detectives working for Pacific Gas and Electric (PG&E), the local utility company, focused on Tom Mooney and Warren Billings, radicals who had been involved in previous labor violence. Chief White himself, who had never been a cop, was a former executive of PG&E. Through the work of Matheson's detectives and the private eyes, a case was brought against Mooney and Billings for the bombing. At a trial, the men were convicted, and Mooney was sentenced to death (later commuted to life). Immediately, leftist groups took up the cry that the two men had been framed. However, no credible evidence has ever come forth to exonerate them. The slogan "Free Tom Mooney" echoed throughout radical circles for the next twenty years. When he was released in 1939, he was seen as such an unpleasant person that the left wing dropped him, and today he is almost totally forgotten.

World War I brought one great change in San Francisco. It caused the military to shut down the Barbary Coast, and the district never truly regained its old position. The downtown Tenderloin District became the city's leading vice and nightlife area. In 1917 the U.S. government, as a wartime measure, closed down all the great sin districts, such as Chicago's Levee and New Orleans's Storyville. In Philadelphia, when the mayor refused to cooperate, the U.S. Marines were sent in to do the job. After the war was over, the old-fashioned vice areas never regained prominence. The new vice district in Chicago became the Near North Side, three miles away from the Levee.

For his work on the bombing investigation, Matheson was made captain of inspectors. In 1920 there was an opening for chief of police, and he was offered the job on condition that he say that Mooney and Billings had been framed. Matheson refused. For the next decade he continued to command the bureau, during which time he was again passed over for chief of police because of the Mooney case. Finally, in 1929 after a scandal in the city treasurer's office, the mayor appointed him to fill the office, and he was periodically reelected until his death in 1942.

During his time as head of the bureau, Matheson trained a whole generation of future San Francisco detective inspectors, including Charles Dullea, who himself became the captain of the bureau and then chief of police. (Inspector was a title, not a rank like it was New York. Inspectors were usually civil service patrolmen and sergeants who received higher pay than their substantive ranks. A job in the bureau was generally considered the most desirable post in the police department.) Thanks to Matheson's efforts, the San Francisco inspectors bureau was rated on par with New York's or Chicago's. The captains in the city's fourteen districts also maintained local detectives, known as "special officers," and the collectors among them were called "bucket men." The district specials got no extra pay, but some of them made significant money on the side.

At first Dullea performed patrol as a motorcycle cop in the sprawling Richmond District of the northwest part of the city. His mentor was one of the old wise heads of the police force, Sgt. Oliver Hassing, better known as the Dutchman. Then Dullea became a charter member of the special shotgun squad that handled barricaded criminals and similar situations. Finally, he became an inspector, and in 1923 he was made a lieutenant. By the mid-1920s, he was the rising star of the San Francisco Police Department (SFPD).

As a homicide lieutenant he had many grisly cases to investigate. On February 24, 1926, Dullea and his partner, Insp. Francis Latulipe, the department's forensic specialist, were sent to a boardinghouse on a report of a dead body there. A man who had gone to visit his aunt, the landlady, had found her naked and dead in a third-floor bathroom. So gruesome was the scene that Dullea's hair stood on end. It turned out that the killer was a Canadian drifter named Earle Nelson who committed murders on both sides of the border and as far east as New York State. Eventually, he was captured in Canada and executed.

San Francisco's police force demonstrated its competence in its handling of a 1930s murder that shook the city. On April 29th the city experienced a total eclipse of the sun and the temperature fell twenty degrees in a short period of time. In a town that had been nearly destroyed by a natural phenomenon twenty-four years earlier (in the same month), many people wondered if they were about to repeat the earthquake experience or something similar. Yet life went on. At around 10:00 a.m., a cab driver picked up two employees of the Bank of America, one of whom was carrying a leather grip with $4,000 in it. The driver was directed to take them to a stevedoring company near Pier 26 on the Embarcadero, the twelve-mile stretch of waterfront where ships were loaded and unloaded. The money was to be dropped off to meet a payroll. As one of the bank employees slipped out of the cab, a short man came up to the driver and whispered to him, "This is a holdup." Just then, a thirty-two-year veteran of the force, Ofc. John Malcolm, came on the scene. The robber walked up to him and fired two shots into his heart. Malcolm uttered his wife's name and fell dead. The shooter and his accomplice fled in a blue Dodge. The press labeled the killer the Whispering Gunman.

Many veteran San Francisco cops knew Officer Malcolm and were shaken by the brutal murder. He had spent a number of years patrolling a tough beat on the Barbary Coast and was near retirement age. Captain Dullea took charge, and the entire police department was turned out and given orders to shoot to kill. Today an order like that might be challenged by civil libertarians, but it was standard in those times. A number of police "bathtubs" (motorcycles with sidecars) were mobilized and sent out to secure various spots in the city. Since San Francisco is surrounded by water on three sides, it wasn't hard to blanket an area with cops. By 4:00 p.m., a patrol car had located the blue Dodge about half a mile from Pier 26. Inspector Latulipe found prints in the vehicle and managed to link them to men previously arrested in Seattle and Tacoma. Finding the prints offered a shortcut in the process of capturing the killers; without the prints the inspectors bureau would have put enough pressure on every petty criminal and dive owner in town to make them talk. The fact that the men had fled the jurisdiction would not help them either. Any police force in America would work diligently to catch a cop killer.

Back in San Francisco a number of Embarcadero workers came forward to describe the robbers. Whatever hostility existed between management and labor on the San Francisco docks did not extend to street cops and dockworkers. Police were generally popular with the public. When the man identified as having done the shooting, Peter Farrington Jr., was arrested in Tacoma, a longshoreman captain named Claussen went up there and identified him as the gunman. Claussen angrily yelled, "That's the bastard, the son of a bitch." Farrington was returned to San Francisco, where he was hanged in San Quentin prison. The second man, George Berta, was killed in a gun battle with Seattle police.

In the Bay Area, crime and politics were often closely linked. In the 1930s Frank Egan was the city's public defender, an elected position that he had held since 1918. He was so important that he planned to run for mayor. Egan practiced law privately on the side and was known to have many older ladies as clients. Interestingly, he was able to persuade some of them to turn over their money and property to him. After one of Egan's clients, Jessie Hughes, was run over by a hit-and-run driver, Egan called Dullea to express his concern for her. The detective captain assigned homicide inspector Allan McGinn, a veteran of two hundred murder cases, to investigate Egan. The public defender was a well-connected man, and his influence reached into the office of William Quinn, the chief of police. Quinn was another South of the Slot man who, until his promotion to chief in 1930, had been an administrative sergeant in the previous chief's office. Quinn was much more familiar with the city's political landscape, including the McDonough brothers, than he was with robbers or murderers. He called Dullea in, made a speech about how Egan had been both a fireman and a policeman and was a thoroughly respectable citizen of San Francisco, and he warned Dullea to go easy on him. Suddenly Egan went missing. During his absence, he called Dullea and told him two men were holding him prisoner. Finally, he turned up and was arrested for the murder of Jessie Hughes. However, he managed to escape from jail and remain at large. Word began to spread that Egan knew so much about municipal corruption he could not be sent to prison. Nevertheless, he was recaptured, convicted of Hughes's murder, and jailed. The case shed some light on how the city was run.

While the killer of a landlady, a cop, or a law client got the headlines, robbery and burglary were the bread and butter of the inspectors bureau. Some robbers never carried a gun and confined themselves to strong-arm methods. Many burglars were smash-and-grab artists who broke store windows and ran off with the merchandise. These cases were usually handled by district special officers. The inspectors bureau concentrated on stickup men and burglars who broke into commercial establishments and wealthy residences.

Dullea made Insp. Richard Tatham head of the robbery squad that investigated the biggest heists. One group that was hard to nail was called the White Mask Gang by the cops; it was led by a character known as the Phantom. San Francisco detectives had a lot of informal rules, and one of them was that safecrackers known to use explosives were not allowed to come into the city. Today this order might be challenged, but back then California law enforcement was led by Earl Warren, the district attorney of Alameda County, across San Francisco Bay. He set the tone for vigorous police action. Once he ordered his investigators to seize gambling ships that operated outside the three-mile territorial limit, theoretically making them exempt from American law. When Warren's men went ahead and forcibly boarded the ships, his actions were characterized by a judge as "piracy." Even if the court ruled that an arrest and seizure was unlawful, it did not prevent the defendants from being tried and sent to prison because California did not follow the federal exclusionary rule. Warren served as an advisor to all police fraternal groups. His power was immense and grew to even greater heights when he was elected attorney general and then governor.

Warren held conservative views until he ascended to the U.S. Supreme Court in 1953. Then, knowing that he lacked the intellectual firepower to be chief justice and expecting a barrage of criticism from liberal lawyers and Ivy League professors, he switched his views 180 degrees. Eventually, he became the darling of civil rights advocates and the police came to despise him. Many of his old friends put up billboards urging that he be impeached. It was Warren, while running for governor, who was the force behind the 1942 roundup and removal of Japanese citizens from the West Coast. Surprisingly, the leading opponent of that move was FBI director J. Edgar Hoover, who staked his reputation on the notion that the Japanese on the coast were loyal citizens. Warren prevailed, and the history books have completely ignored his and Hoover's roles because it is not politically correct to criticize Warren or praise Hoover.

For a long time the White Masks pulled robberies and blew safes in San Francisco, and they were not averse to injuring people when they did so. Then they suddenly disappeared. The fact that they did gave some detectives a clue to their identity.

Among the minor local problems that bedeviled the police was the fact that San Francisco was an exceptionally rainy city. When cops would receive a call of a robbery in progress in a business district, upon arriving on the scene, they would find everybody running down the street to get out of the rain. However, one or more of those running might have a firearm on him that he had used in the robbery. That presented a problem. If an officer held a gun on a suspicious-looking character and found out that he was a respectable citizen, there could be trouble.

If he didn't put a gun on him, the officer might be shot. In those days the cops chose safety over a possible complaint.

Certain districts of the city required special handling. At the end of World War I, Chinatown was still a dangerous place. So-called tongs (Chinese associations) engaged in warfare that sometimes would end up with bodies in the street. It was also an area where gambling went on twenty-four hours a day, and police found it hard to make arrests because, when they entered a premises, an alarm would sound and the gambling would stop. The Chinese were noted for never cooperating with investigators, so if a policeman were accused of taking money from the Chinatown gamblers, the same rule would apply. They would not squeal to the district attorney or some other investigating body, even if they were sent to jail for refusing to do so.

Every American city where there was a Chinatown had a similar story. It goes like this. A young, Irish American girl was hired as a cashier in a Chinese restaurant because she was familiar with American currency. One night a local Caucasian tough walked in and stuck the place up. She happened to know who he was and her father was a detective, so she told him, and he arrested the man. To her surprise, the Chinese would not cooperate in prosecuting him. So the young girl quit her job and, a few nights later, came in and stuck the place up herself. A highly unlikely story but indicative of the basic situation.

In the 1920s police chief Dan O'Brien appointed a boyhood friend, Insp. Jack Manion, to take charge of Chinatown. Manion was known as an especially tough cop who had already proved himself by suppressing the mafiosos in the Italian North Beach section. Dan McKlem (later captain of inspectors) joined the force in 1925 and was assigned to the Chinatown squad. As he recollected years later, "Your effectiveness in the district depended on your contacts with the Chinese. They had to take a liking to you or they wouldn't give you the time of day. And even then there were some things they just would not tell you." McKlem recalled how Manion was able to end the tong wars by breaking the codes of secrecy and bringing the leaders of the groups together for a meeting that eventually resulted in a peace treaty enforced by the police. Yet to remain a prime tourist attraction, Chinatown had to still stress mystery and danger. Sometimes supposed tong hatchet men would chase "victims" down the street just to thrill the visitors. Manion worked for ten years in Chinatown, and when it was time for him to be transferred, the Chinese community demanded that he remain. So the department allowed him to remain in charge of the Chinatown squad until his retirement in 1946.

At the beginning of the 1930s, as the Great Depression hit, many San Francisco workers lost their jobs or had their paychecks cut. The International Longshoremen's Association, headed by Harry Bridges, put pressure on the employers for wage increases. Bridges, an Australian, was widely considered to be a Communist, though he would never answer that charge when questioned under oath. Since he wasn't even a citizen, shippers repeatedly demanded that he be deported.

In 1934 a virtual war broke out between police and striking longshoremen on the San Francisco docks. At first the strikers were able to close down the port. Mayor Rossi then ordered Chief Quinn to put the entire force, if necessary, on the Embarcadero and open it up again. The police action prompted Bridges to close down every port on the West Coast. In Washington Atty. Gen. Homer Cummings (the true founder of the modern FBI, not J. Edgar Hoover) urged President Roosevelt to call out the U.S. Army and suppress what he saw as a Communist revolution, but FDR did not listen to him.

Initially, nearly one thousand police officers (out of a total force of a little over thirteen hundred) were gathered to maintain order on the docks. The inspectors bureau, because of its prestige, was given a leading role in the affair. On July 3 seven hundred police in gas masks pushed boxcars in position to seal off the south side of the Embarcadero. Suddenly, the pickets began throwing rocks at inspectors, who returned the compliment by firing tear gas.

Bridges then called a citywide strike for July 5. That day the trouble began when strikers at the corner of Mission and Front Streets became violent and refused the orders of mounted police units to disperse. No one is certain who fired the first shot, but gun battles erupted in which two strikers were killed and many more were injured. The department canceled all leaves and called in auxiliary police with no experience, and the state government dispatched the National Guard to protect the railroads, which was the only way there was of getting food into the city.

McKlem, who was then an inspector, was stationed alongside one of the auxiliaries one night when the National Guard began shooting; the auxiliary policeman started yelling and crying, disgusting McKlem. McKlem remembered how bad conditions were: "The unions held everything up for two months. They stopped street cars and buses and we had to commandeer automobiles so we had cars enough for the police force. You'd tour around where the trouble was supposed to be and just hoped for the best."

July 5 became known as Bloody Thursday. After one hundred thousand union workers paraded through the streets, heading for the International Longshoremen's Association headquarters on Steuart Street, the police launched an all-out offensive. National guardsmen barricaded the streets with machine guns mounted on trucks, and the San Francisco police drove the strikers off. When strikers blockaded railroad tracks, SFPD captain Tom Hoertkorn ordered his men to fire shotguns into the mob. The police had won.

A shutdown of the West Coast would have delivered an economic blow to the country that the New Deal would not have been able to sustain. Roosevelt would have had to use the army. However, the president's critics had been calling for "a man on horseback" to put down the waves of disorder in the country. If he had sent the army to the West Coast, his chief of staff would have taken personal charge, as he had done in 1932 when troops were called out to suppress the Washington DC Bonus March. The chief of staff's name was Gen. Douglas MacArthur, and as President Hoover had found out, and President Truman would later learn, MacArthur was a loose cannon. The New Deal leadership did not want him leading troops on horseback, because many Americans might decide that the dashing and theatrical MacArthur should be the president.

Shortly after the strike ended, the White Mask gang began to operate again. This confirmed some detectives' suspicion that the gang included police officers, who had been busy doing seven-day, twelve-hour shifts along the waterfront. On Armistice Day 1934 the White Masks met their Waterloo. A woman heard an explosion at the Majestic Bottling plant. She called the police, reported that she had seen lights moving in the closed building just before the explosion, and said if the police hurried they could probably catch the burglars. Despite the police ban on carrying explosives, the White Masks had blown a safe. Seven cops from the Western Addition police station raced to the scene and surrounded the building. Ofc. John "Andy" Johnson captured two men coming down a ladder and turned them over to his colleagues. While still searching, he saw another man in a long black coat. When challenged he said, "Don't take me in. For the love of God, please let me go. You know me, Johnson, I'm an officer with the police. You know what this means to me. For God sakes, stand aside!" Suddenly, a fourth man went by and Johnson began chasing him. The man in the black coat then fled but was halted at the rear gate by another police officer. So he flashed his star, keeping his thumb over the number. Eventually, the prisoners were transported to the district station and charged with the burglary. The man in the long black coat turned out to be the Phantom, and he asked to see Captain Dullea. When Dullea met with him, he was stunned. It was his old mentor, Sgt. Oliver Hassing. Despite Hassing's pleas, Dullea ordered the processing of the prisoner to continue, and the sergeant received a fifteen-year prison sentence.

Finally, the police received payback for the Embarcadero affair. San Francisco was such a gaudy, wide-open town, anyone over twelve knew that some cops, usually district special duty men, were getting paid off. Before the Embarcadero riots, most San Franciscans didn't mind. Police were generally popular, and citizens had no objection to officers supplementing their income a bit. In those days a patrolman received only $175 a month, and for that he might have to stop a bullet.

The Depression changed some people's views. Many San Franciscans were unemployed or were making only seventy-five dollars a month, and they would have been happy with the salary a cop received. The real change came, though, after police shot and killed ordinary workers in the Embarcadero riots. San Francisco, unlike Los Angeles, had always been a workingman's town, and labor was part of the governing coalition of the city. Turning the police loose on them had been a big mistake.

One day in 1937 the collector of internal revenue for the San Francisco area made a speech in which he mentioned that his office was suing to get a police officer to pay income tax on the $100,000 that he possessed (the equivalent of over $1 million today). Obviously, the money had to have come from something beyond his salary. In the meantime, a grand jury convened by DA Matt Brady began investigating police corruption. A group of San Franciscans also hired Edward Atherton, a former FBI agent who worked as a private detective, to investigate the police. Between the grand jury and Atherton, San Franciscans were learning that police officers did not do too badly financially. The typical captain had between $40,000 and $70,000 in his bank account, a sum that today would be fifteen times greater. A prime target of the investigation was Captain Hoertkorn, the dashing cavalier who, during the strike, had ordered his men to fire their shotguns. The star of the inquiry was Patrolman James F. Madden, a cop since 1908. When he was called to testify, he brought a few dozen bank books with him. When the deposits in the bank books were totaled, they amounted to $834,000 (which would be more than $10 million today). Hoertkorn and some other captains were prosecuted and sent to jail. As a result of the furor, Chief Quinn was eventually forced to resign and Dullea was appointed in his place.

The appointment of Dullea as chief in 1940 promised better times for the San Francisco police. Most of his term, though, was consumed by the problems of World War II. San Francisco was loaded with servicemen, and nightlife boomed. As in the previous war, the U.S. government cracked down on places that were known to be responsible for high rates of venereal disease among their servicemen customers.

In August 1945 San Francisco, like all American cities, celebrated V-J Day. The first night was relatively orderly. On the second night, many of the celebrants were drunk, and they suddenly began smashing windows and overturning cars in the downtown area. The rioters were mostly young servicemen who were undergoing military training at the many bases in the area. They represented the boy next door who was fighting for "mom's apple pie and the girl next door." As one group was driven off, more would take their place. Finally, the violence overrode all bounds of decency. The rioters began attacking respectable young women who had been celebrating, tearing their clothes off and raping them. At the time women in San Francisco were regarded as the best dressed in the country. A respectable woman always wore a hat and white gloves when she went downtown. Reports of such women being raped on the street came as a great shock to the community.

The rioting was stopped only after two thousand military police and navy shore patrolmen were rushed into the city. Though there were numerous investigations of the matter, it was soon dropped. For years, there appeared to be an unspoken taboo about mentioning it. Eleven people were supposedly killed in the disorders, but other than one municipal worker who was identified, there seemed to be no details about the victims. In later years, if the facts had been known, it might have caused young people to ask their fathers or grandfathers, "You were in San Francisco on V-J Day; what did you do then?"

The riot was a huge black eye for Chief Dullea, who at the time was serving as president of the International Association of Police. Next to Commissioner Valentine in New York, Dullea was probably the best-known police chief in America, and it was an embarrassment when his colleagues asked questions like, "Charlie, what happened? We didn't have any trouble in our city."

Postwar San Francisco

After Dullea's retirement in 1947, the police department went on much as it had. The detective star of the postwar era was Francis J. "Frank" Ahern. Appointed to the force in 1930 at the age of thirty, he never held a civil service rank above patrolman. But from his inspector's post he played a large role in the department. At various times he commanded the narcotics squad and the homicide squad. Ahern was known as an absolutely straight cop. In 1945 he was assigned to clean up the abortion business in San Francisco. Abortion was always a mysterious subject among police officers. It was a lucrative criminal enterprise in most American cities, but it received little attention from law enforcement or the media. There was always a danger at abortion parlors that irate members of the patient's family, or her boyfriend or others, might suddenly erupt in violence. So abortionists were known to retain off-duty cops as guards. Occasionally there was a shoot-out in an abortion parlor, which would be reported as a robbery attempt. In my own city of Chicago, if abortion cases came to the attention of the regular police, they were quickly taken over by the state's attorney's office and disappeared from sight.

In San Francisco, Ahern's investigation led to the arrest of the three top abortionists in the city. In at least one case, $280,000 cash was put down in front of him to just walk away, but he refused and made the arrests.

Another San Francisco police star was Tom Cahill. Born in Chicago in 1910, he soon went back to the old country with his Irish American family and did not return to America until 1929, when he came back on his own. All his life he would retain an Irish brogue. In July 1942, at the age of thirty-two, he became a San Francisco policeman and soon made a reputation for himself on various assignments. When Ahern finished the abortion investigation he went to Chief Dullea and asked for Cahill (whom he knew only by reputation) to be assigned as his partner. Dullea agreed, but Ahern's request infuriated the captain of inspectors, Barney McDonald, who said, "Ahern, you've gone over my head, now you're stuck with Cahill as a partner forever." In fact, the two worked together for ten years and were involved in a number of important cases. Unlike many police officers, they were highly regarded by the FBI and were considered by some lawmen as the most knowledgeable cops in the country on organized crime. Because of this, they were detailed as investigators for the Kefauver Committee (the U.S. Senate Special Committee to Investigate Crime in Interstate Commerce, 1950–51, Sen. Estes Kefauver of Tennessee, chairman).

In January 1954 a kidnapping brought more publicity than any other crime in San Francisco between World War II and the 1960s. The Moskovitz family was one of the city's most prominent. The father, Maurice, was the founder of Rochester Big & Tall clothiers and owned other businesses. On Saturday, January 19, his son Lennie, age thirty-six, was working in the family real estate offices. When he failed to meet a client he was supposed to show a house to, the family became alarmed. Lennie was known for his promptness. Shortly before the meeting, two men had kidnapped Lennie, taken him to a house in the Ingleside district, and forced him to write a ransom note to his family. The note said he was being held prisoner by "some men and they want $500,000. Give it to them right away or you won't see me again." His father had already reported him missing to the police, and they were just about to send out a report on the teletype. Then, at 5:10 p.m., the ransom note arrived by special delivery, so the police teletype report was canceled and Frank Ahern and his homicide squad took charge of the investigation.

Meanwhile, news organizations were receiving reports that something big was going on in law enforcement. Such was the power of the police inspectors at that time that they were able to persuade every single media outlet not to mention the story for fear that the kidnappers might kill Lennie and flee the jurisdiction. In few other American cities would the police have been able to impose a total news embargo, but in San Francisco the inspectors bureau still ruled.

Cops fanned out across San Francisco. A special command post was set up to direct the operation. Every telephone operator in town was given the numbers of the Moskovitzes' residences so that they could immediately notify the police if a call went to one of them.

While negotiating with the kidnappers, the senior Moskovitz managed to get the ransom down to $300,000, but that increased the captors' ferocity, and they threatened to castrate Lennie if the money was not forthcoming. Finally, a call was intercepted by the police and traced to a phone booth. Insp. Al Nelder of homicide was the closest to the scene, and when he arrived he noticed someone in the booth. He immediately ordered him out at gunpoint, got on the phone, and determined that

that the caller had been talking to a Moskovitz number. The top brass in the command post ordered Nelder to bring his prisoner to them; he declined, however, because he felt that whoever was holding Moskovitz would probably kill him and disappear. So Nelder questioned the man he had apprehended, Joseph Lear, and persuaded him to tell him where Moskovitz was being held. How Nelder did this is not clear, but it is well known that a cocked, .38-caliber revolver held to a man's head can be very persuasive. Nelder, Ahearn, and the other homicide detectives then went to the apartment in the Ingleside district, where they rescued Moskovitz and arrested Harold Jackson. Both kidnappers were former private detectives in San Francisco. They were sentenced to life and would die in San Quentin prison.

Nelder might have run into some difficulty for the decision he made to go directly to the flat where Moskovitz was held, but it did not work out that way. Within a couple years, Frank Ahern was named chief of police. After his untimely death in 1958, he was succeeded by Tom Cahill. When Cahill stepped down in 1970, the post was given to Nelder.

In May 1960 students from the University of California at Berkeley and the University of San Francisco rioted when the House Committee on Un-American Activities held a hearing in city hall. The event made national headlines, and TV news showed cops dragging protesters down the marble steps of city hall. From then on, San Francisco was frequently the scene of protests. Watching the affair from the street, I had no idea I was witnessing the start of the 1960s era of protest.

In the 1970s some San Francisco cops were assassinated by radicals. In one instance, a bomb went off outside a church where an officer's funeral was being held. As the mayor and city supervisors (councilmen) grew increasingly radical, San Francisco became a mecca for vagrants and disorderly individuals from all over the country. In 1978 Mayor George Moscone and Supervisor Harvey Milk were murdered by ex-cop Dan White, who had just resigned from the Board of Supervisors. White's defense was that he had been temporarily unnerved mentally after eating too many Twinkies. When the news came out, Milk's gay supporters rioted, and eventually a deputy chief ordered all police to leave the Castro District and yield the streets to the rioters. Even the deputy chief would later write that his order demoralized the force, but he could see nothing else to do.

In 1975 Charles Gain, former chief of police of Oakland, was named to head the San Francisco police, whose cops had always regarded Oakland and its police department as, at best, second rate. Thus his appointment was a heavy blow to the morale of the San Francisco department. Gain preferred not to wear a police uniform but instead wore a business suit. He removed the seven-pointed star on the doors of police squad cars, replacing it with the tag *police services*, and allegedly took the American flag out of the chief's office so as "not to intimidate people." He was criticized for having his photo taken with Jim Jones of the People's Temple, who later committed mass suicide with nine hundred followers in the jungles of Guyana. Gain was widely assailed for the Castro District riots, which eventually became known as the White Nights. He was replaced as chief in 1980.

After San Francisco changed into the leftist capital of America and the streets filled with disorderly vagrants, the police department's glory days were over and the inspectors bureau, though important, no longer dominated the city. Among other things, inspectors failed to solve the Zodiac murders of the late 1960s and early 1970s, one of which occurred in the city.

The city of San Francisco that emerged out of the 1906 earthquake and the political upheaval that followed existed until the 1970s. Since then, the old San Francisco has lived only in the hearts of those who loved it. Once it was referred to as the Paris of America or the nation's favorite city. Although much smaller, its police department ranked in importance with those of Chicago and New York. Its famous inspectors bureau was the equal of the detective bureaus in those top two American cities. This is not the place to deal with the current changes in San Francisco but only to recall that its great police force was once a leader in American detective work.

FIG. 1. Allan Pinkerton, founder of America's most important detective agency. Under the name of Maj. E. J. Allen, Pinkerton served as head of the Union army's Secret Service during the early days of the Civil War. Though America's greatest detective, he constantly overestimated the size of Confederate forces. Pinkerton is seen here (*left*) standing alongside a prewar client, Abraham Lincoln, in 1862. Courtesy of Library of Congress, LC-B8171-7929.

FIG. 2. Detectives escort a Mafia killer, 1903. At left is Det. Lt. Joe Petrosino, head of the Italian Squad, and on the right are Insps. Arthur Carey and Jim McCafferty, the founders of the NYPD homicide squad. They are seen escorting mafioso Tomasso Petto, accused of the murder of an informant. Although Petto beat the case, he was eventually murdered in Pennsylvania. In 1909 Petrosino was sent on a mission to investigate the Mafia in Sicily, where he was assassinated in Palermo. Courtesy of Library of Congress, LC-USZ62-137644.

FIG. 3. NYPD commissioner Arthur Woods, 1914. A graduate of Harvard, instructor of English at Groton, and reporter for the *New York Sun* who married into the family of J. P. Morgan, Woods served as head of the NYPD detective bureau between 1907 and 1909. During that time, he studied European detective systems and introduced new investigative methods into the NYPD. From 1914 through 1917, as police commissioner, he was an outstanding administrator. Courtesy of Library of Congress, LC-DIG-ggbain-25793.

FIG. 4. San Francisco police interrogate Tom Mooney for the Preparedness Day bombing, 1916. Capt. Duncan Matheson (standing behind Mooney, who is seated in the center) was put in charge of a squad to investigate the bombing of the parade. Mooney was convicted and sentenced to death (later commuted to life in prison). The slogan "Free Tom Mooney" echoed throughout radical circles for the next twenty years. "Police grilling Mooney," photograph from the Thomas J. Mooney papers [graphic], BANC PIC 1945.003—PIC, box 2. Courtesy of Bancroft Library, University of California, Berkeley.

FIG. 5. William Flynn, director of the (federal) Bureau of Investigation, 1919. Before serving as the director of the Bureau of Investigation, Flynn had served as chief of the U.S. Secret Service and deputy commissioner in charge of NYPD detectives. At the time he was generally regarded as America's leading detective. Courtesy of Library of Congress, LC-DIG-hec-03690.

FIG. 6. Left: William Burns (*right*) talks to a reporter on the day of the Wall Street bombing, 1920. Burns, who had been hailed as "the American Sherlock Holmes" by Sir Arthur Conan Doyle, had fallen into disfavor in the years before the beginning of World War I. The bombing provided him with an opportunity to get back into the forefront of American detective work, and he quickly offered a reward for information and sought to take over the handling of the case. Courtesy of Library of Congress, LC-USZ62-137982.

FIG. 7. Above: Scene on Wall Street after the 1920 bombing that killed thirty-eight people. Seventeen hundred police responded to the incident, including detectives from the NYPD, the (federal) Bureau of Investigation, the U.S. Secret Service, and military intelligence. For a long time the case remained unsolved, but scholars today agree that the bomber was part of a gang of Boston anarchists that included Nicola Sacco and Bartolomeo Vanzetti. Courtesy of Library of Congress, LC-USZ62-67516.

Ranger Manuel T. Gonzaullas
Texas Rangers
On the Mexican Border near El Paso, Texas. in 1920

FIG. 8. Texas ranger Capt. Manuel "Lone Wolf" Gonzaullas early in his career, 1920. Gonzaullas was probably the best-known Texas ranger of his time and the first Hispanic to become a captain of the Rangers. He was a crack shot, with several notches on his gun. In 1946 he was sent, alone, to hunt for a serial killer in Texarkana, Texas. Even with a highly regarded professional lawman like Gonzaullas in charge, police could not solve the crimes. Courtesy of Texas Ranger Hall of Fame and Museum, Waco TX.

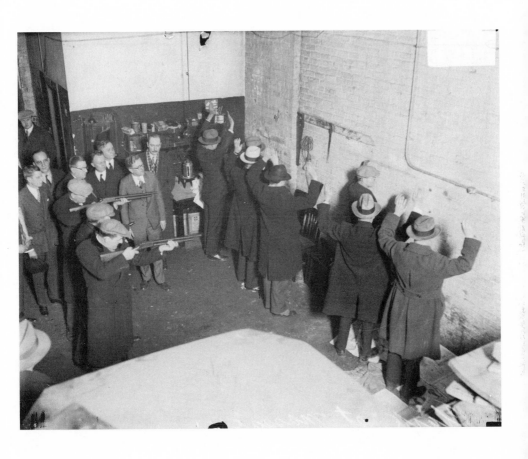

FIG. 9. Detectives reenact the 1929 St. Valentine's Day Massacre for the Cook County coroner. Chicago detectives demonstrate the machine gunning of seven rival gangsters by Al Capone's gunmen. Although no charges were brought against the killers, there was general agreement that they included a group of Capone's men and a member of the St. Louis Egan Rats. DN-0087705, *Chicago Daily News* negatives collection, Chicago History Museum.

FIG. 10. Capt. William "Red" Hynes (*left*), head of the Red Squad, and Chief James E. Davis, two of the top figures in the LAPD in 1934. Hynes was the leading security cop in the United States. He rode roughshod over civil rights, but nothing could be done to curtail him because he had the support of the Los Angeles business community. In 1938 he was demoted to patrolman and sent out to walk a beat. *Los Angeles Daily News* negatives (Collection 1387, [uclamass_1379_08788-00]), UCLA Library Special Collections, Charles E. Young Research Library, UCLA.

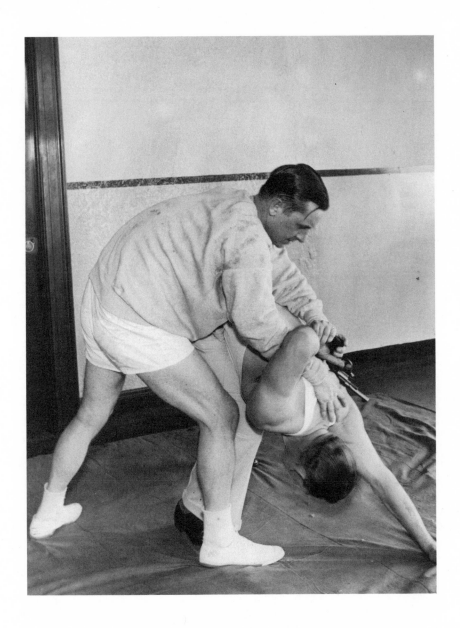

FIG. II. Eliot Ness demonstrates a disarming tactic, 1936. Though Ness was only a federal revenue agent and not a professional policeman, he received a great deal of publicity, mostly for what he did not do in Chicago, and is less well-known for what he really accomplished in cleaning up the Cleveland Police Department. Here Ness is seen practicing judo. Courtesy of Cleveland Public Library/Photograph Collection.

FIG. 12. The Cleveland coroner leads the search for a victim of the Mad Butcher serial killer, 1938. *Left to right*: Insp. Charles Nevell, chief of the city's detective bureau, Sgt. James Hogan, head of the homicide squad, and Coroner Samuel Gerber. Despite the efforts of the Cleveland Police Department, headed at the time by Eliot Ness, over a dozen Butcher killings between 1934 and 1938 remained unsolved. Courtesy of Cleveland Press Collection, Michael Schwartz Library, Cleveland State University. www.ClevelandMemory.org.

FIG. 13. An FBI agent on a stakeout in a kidnapping case, 1939. The photo exemplifies the image that FBI director Hoover projected for his agents: men who had a good appearance, were intelligent and resourceful, and used the latest investigative methods. So successful was the FBI in catching kidnappers that instances of that crime dropped considerably. By the end of the 1930s, the FBI was regarded as America's premier law enforcement agency. Courtesy of Federal Bureau of Investigation.

FIG. 14. San Francisco police chief Charles Dullea, 1940. In the 1920s Dullea commanded the SFPD homicide squad. From the time he took over the inspectors (detective) bureau in 1930 until he retired as chief of police in 1947, he was the leading figure in the San Francisco Police Department. Dullea earned a national reputation as an outstanding police officer and was president of the International Association of Chiefs of Police. Courtesy of San Francisco History Center, San Francisco Public Library.

FIG. 15. Los Angeles detectives examine the body of the Black Dahlia, 1947. Dets. Harry Hansen and Finis Brown (*middle, kneeling*) of the homicide squad peer at the badly mutilated body of a woman who would become known as the Black Dahlia. The case was hampered by rivalries within the police department and powerful influences that were sometimes brought to bear on the investigation. The case gripped the city of Los Angeles, and the failure to solve it reflected badly on the police department. To this date, there is no agreement on who the murderer was. Photo by R. L. Oliver. Copyright © 1996 *Los Angeles Times*. Reprinted with permission.

FIG. 16. Boston detectives interview Brink's and ADT employees at the scene of a $2.5 million robbery in 1950. The Boston police and the FBI—working together, but not in harmony—took six years to solve the case. Only when one of the suspects decided to break with his accomplices did they have sufficient evidence to make an arrest. Courtesy of *Boston Herald* and Boston Public Library.

FIG. 17. Boston detectives examine evidence in the Brink's robbery, 1950. Lt. Frank Wilson (*left*) and Det. John E. Gibbons examine one of the bags that the robbers used to carry the money away from Brink's. Wilson, a native Bostonian from an old and distinguished African American family, was very popular with his colleagues and noted for his skill and courtesy. Shortly after the close of the case and upon becoming deputy superintendent of police in charge of detectives, Wilson died of heart failure, presumably brought on by overwork on the Brink's case. Courtesy of *Boston Herald* and Boston Public Library.

FIG. 18. A San Francisco police detective arrests kidnappers in 1954. Insp. Al Nelder (*right*), later chief of police, with two kidnappers who had seized the son of a prominent businessman and threatened to murder him if they were not paid a ransom. The San Francisco police managed to keep his kidnapping completely secret so as to protect the victim's life. Finally, Nelder captured one of the men in a phone booth as he was making a call to the house of the victim. Courtesy of CriticalPast.

WILLIAM FRANCIS SUTTON,

FIG. 19. Willie Sutton, America's premier holdup man, 1950s. While he probably never said he robbed banks because "that's where the money is," Sutton became a legend for pulling off large robberies without injuring anybody. Sutton planned his jobs carefully and handpicked the few assistants that he used. He was the most successful robber in the United States from the 1930s to the 1950s. The hunt for Willie Sutton became a local sport in the New York area, and even when he was captured, no prison could hold him. Courtesy of Federal Bureau of Investigation.

FIG. 20. The most famous perp walk in American history, 1963. Presidential assassin Lee Harvey Oswald being taken from Dallas City Hall to the county jail. Ahead of him is Dallas detective captain Will Fritz (*far left, white hat, glasses*). An instant later, Oswald was shot and fatally wounded by Jack Ruby (*right*). The case brought much discredit to the Dallas Police Department and American detectives in general. Courtesy of Bettmann/Getty Images.

8

The Rubel Robbery, the
Disappearance of Judge Crater,
and the Elusive Willie Sutton

The Rubel Robbery

When Fiorello La Guardia was elected mayor of New York City in 1933, he was the first reform candidate to win the post in twenty years. La Guardia's chief rival for the nomination of the Fusion Party (a coalition of Republicans, Democrats, and independents) had been John F. O'Ryan, a lawyer and World War I general. So when La Guardia took office in January 1934, he named O'Ryan police commissioner, de facto the second most important post in city government. The two were not birds of a feather and disagreed strongly on police policies. When unions began staging sit-down strikes in Manhattan office buildings, O'Ryan wanted to disperse them with nightsticks. La Guardia, a former labor lawyer, did not favor that approach.

On the afternoon of August 21, 1934, when the two men met at city hall to discuss the situation, they were interrupted when word was flashed to them that an armored car had been held up in Brooklyn and the bandits had escaped with $427,500 in cash (about $7 million in today's dollars). It would turn out to be the largest cash robbery in American history up to that time. La Guardia, visibly upset, told the commissioner, "Break this case, John," to which O'Ryan replied, "I will put every man in the force on it." O'Ryan's statement was ridiculous; he was hardly going to take every cop off his beat and assign him to the holdup. Within a month, O'Ryan was out, replaced by Chief Insp. Lewis J. Valentine, a thirty-one-year veteran and a tough, demanding executive. He would remain police commissioner for the next eleven years.

At 12:45 p.m. on the day of the holdup, when the armored car approached the Rubel Ice plant on Nineteenth Street in the Bath Beach section of Brooklyn, guards William Lilienthal and John Wilson and driver Joe Allen scanned the streets for anything suspicious. As was standard procedure, Lilienthal opened the front door across from the driver and stepped down. Wilson started to follow Lilienthal, but as he did so a robber shoved a machine gun through the door and held Wilson and Allen at bay. Meanwhile, other robbers had pointed guns at Lilienthal and told him to keep walking into the Rubel office.

As the guards were neutralized, a second group of robbers pulled up in two cars, a Nash and a Lincoln, and began loading the money into sacks in the vehicles. Stunned onlookers watched them without moving. As the robbers departed, one of them started to enter the rear seat of the Nash, but it lurched, and he dropped his machine gun on the pavement. While the car roared away, the guard Lilienthal retrieved the machine gun, jumped into the slow-moving armored car, and with Allen driving, began chasing the getaway vehicles. Once they even got close enough for Lilienthal to fire a few bursts at the Nash.

At police headquarters the field general for the cops, Chief of Dets. John J. Sullivan, began issuing orders. With over eighteen thousand officers, the NYPD's resources dwarfed those of any other city in the United States. Sullivan ordered two hundred detectives into Brooklyn and assigned 75 of the city's 425 radio patrol cars to the manhunt. Within thirteen minutes, the NYPD had all the bridges and tunnels leading out of the borough covered by police squads with three-man crews, each including a sharpshooter. Within the area of the robbery, radio cars were stopping any vehicle with more than two men and searching them. The department's air force (two planes) took off to join the hunt.

Chief Sullivan's move was appropriate. If the gang could not get out of Brooklyn through the bridges and tunnels to the west and south, they would have to go north into Queens or east into the Nassau County section of Long Island. Riding around these semisuburban areas, they might stand out. In any event, the longer the gang had to keep driving, the more likely they were to be spotted by a police car. If they were local Brooklynites and went to ground not far from the scene of the robbery, this would also help the police, because they could begin rousting the local gangs, like Vannie Higgins's outfit or the curiously named Blah Blahs.

When police turned out in force to run down criminals, it was like a chase in a Western movie. In 1931 three holdup men ambushed the manager of a Bronx fur plant as he was taking a $4,600 payroll to his office. When a police officer guarding the manager reached for a gun, one of the robbers shot the cop in the heart. They then fled the scene, pursued by a motorcycle policeman, whom they shot and killed. An off-duty fireman grabbed the officer's gun and began firing until he was wounded. The gunmen sped from the Bronx toward Manhattan, shooting at everybody in their path. A couple and their four-year-old daughter in a passing car were wounded by gunfire, the child mortally. A detective and a patrolman joined the chase in a commandeered taxi and blazed away from the running boards. After crossing a bridge into Manhattan, the getaway car hit a truck and finally came to a stop. An army of pursuing police poured one hundred shots into the vehicle, hitting each of the three bandits at least a dozen times.

The Rubel robbers had some tricks of their own up their sleeves. Their field general, John Manning, was an unusual character to be involved in such a crime. He was a twenty-seven-year-old immigrant from Ireland who, despite his thin build, was nicknamed Fats, and the thick glasses that he wore made him look like a milquetoast. Unlike the typical New York City hoodlum, Manning did not hang out in the nightspots with a blonde on each arm. His goal was to buy a farm and raise chickens and pigs. Others in the gang were known criminals, but Manning had never been arrested. After Prohibition ended, his lost his job in the bootlegging business and became a slugger for waterfront gamblers and loan sharks. There he became friends with a more typical gangster,

Bernard McMahon, forty-one years old, who had a number of arrests, mostly for hijacking. McMahon, known variously as Bennie the Bum or Big Man Murray, and Manning were supposedly the original planners of the robbery.

A few months earlier they had been scouting the bathhouses on the Brooklyn waterfront to find some places to rob where there were no armed guards. One day they noticed an armored car delivering bags of money to a local bank. As bag after bag was carried in, the two robbers decided to hold up a bank. However, they were not experienced at that sort of thing, so they brought in Archie Stewart, a veteran stickup man who had done time in Sing Sing. Stewart was tough, and the others listened to him. He insisted that his friend Stewart Wallace, age fifty-one, known as One-Arm, be given a role in the robbery. Although Wallace actually had two arms, he was missing a hand, and it was not clear what good he would be in the robbery. If a witness noticed the missing hand, the cops would surely pick up Wallace for questioning. But Stewart insisted, and that was that. Next, Wallace suggested that two Albany men named John Oley and Percy "Angel Face" Geary be included. The two had been part of the Manney Strewl gang, which had kidnapped John O'Connell, nephew of Dan O'Connell, the powerful political boss of Albany, New York, the state capital. Oley also managed to get his brother Francis in on the upcoming caper. Because it was a crew put together only for a specific job, rather than an established gang with a leader, Oley had his way.

There was no hotter crime in 1934 than kidnapping, thanks to the ongoing search for the kidnapper of Charles Lindbergh's infant son and the O'Connell affair. No sensible robbery crew ever would have taken up with men whom the FBI was turning the East Coast upside down to find. An eighth man, named Joseph Kress, a getaway car driver who knew Brooklyn's twisting streets, was brought in to steal automobiles and drive one of them on the job.

The obscure Fats Manning was made field general not due to any special skills he possessed but because he had nerves of steel. It was Angel Face Geary, though, who began to play mastermind. Most of his ideas were not very sensible, but he did have one very good one. He knew that the police would try to seal off Brooklyn, so he suggested that they escape from the crime scene via a speedboat. For this purpose, the gang brought in two boat owners from the West Side of Manhattan. Thus a group of ten men who had never worked together before and would never work together again, some of them hotter than a two-dollar pistol on the Fourth of July, set out with a plan developed by a committee to tackle an armored car. The Rubel robbers made the Newton boys look like geniuses by comparison. Men like Willie Sutton, the reigning stickup man of the time, could only shake their heads in wonderment at what the heist world was coming to.

Following the robbery, the crew drove to the nearby waterfront and placed their sacks of loot aboard the two waiting vessels, which headed for an area adjacent to Queens. After a time, police received reports from waterfront boat owners that suspicious men had been seen transferring packages. Sullivan realized that the robbers had won the first round by avoiding the police blockade. Now the NYPD planes began swooping down on vessels traversing the harbor. But by this time it was already too late. So the police switched from a manhunt to a major criminal investigation.

Capt. John Ryan (later chief of detectives himself), who headed the detectives in south Brooklyn, sent his men out to canvas the area, and they quickly reported back that no local gang had been involved.

If the gangsters had won the first round, they lost the second. They decided to throw their weapons overboard in case there was a police reception committee waiting for them. McMahon was trying to loosen a shotgun that had gotten tangled with one of the money bags, when it discharged and blew off most of his leg. By the time they arrived in Queens, McMahon was unconscious. After unloading the money, Stewart and some of the others put him in the boat and took him back across the harbor to the West Side of Manhattan. En route, Stewart had the boat pull ashore and he walked six blocks to buy a bottle of whiskey to give to McMahon.

Upon arrival in Manhattan, Stewart and his wounded charge went to a combination gangster hideout and house of prostitution run by a hard-faced woman named Madeline Tully. Cops came around regularly to search her place, and she was anything but compliant; they had long marked her down as someone they would like to see in prison. At Tully's place, a mob-connected doctor amputated McMahon's leg. It was too late, and he died. So his friends had to dispose of the corpse. This necessitated cutting off both of his legs in order for the body to be put in a suitcase. Finally, the parts were packed and the case was dropped off on West Seventy-Fourth Street near the mansion of a New York millionaire. When a servant found the suitcase with blood leaking from it, the police were summoned. One of the detectives quickly identified McMahon.

The Irish appearance of some of the men and their MO screamed to detectives Hell's Kitchen" the neighborhood on the West Side of Manhattan that had produced heist men since before the Civil War. Most detectives were willing to make book that the crime would be cleared and the whole crew would wind up behind bars (or in the morgue) within a week.

In the ensuing investigation, Det. Frankie Phillips located a man named Tommy Quinn, who lived on West Forty-Fifth Street and owned some boats with a partner, John Hughes. They claimed they had rented their boats out.

Less than two weeks after the holdup, detectives had learned the names of virtually everyone involved. Usually the cops zeroed in on the weakest link in a gang and put pressure on him to confess, which would lead to the rest of the outfit being arrested and charged. However, because many of the gang were already on the run and those who were around were known as "standup" guys, the police had no success with this tactic.

Detectives showed some of the suspects to the guards, but they were unable to make an identification. It was claimed that the robbers had worn three days' growth of beard, although the fact that they had poked machine guns in the guards' faces might have had a lot more to do with influencing the witnesses to be silent. The guards' names were in the paper, and it would not have been hard for anyone to find them and kill them.

In the meantime, Brooklyn detectives led by John "Ha Ha" Murray of the Seventy-Fifth Precinct squad had been focusing on Joe Kress, whom they believed had played a part in the robbery. Kress had recently beaten a hijacking rap, but he was picked up to stand trial for assault with intent to kill one James "Ding Dong" Bell. With detectives like Ha Ha, gangs like Blah Blah, and victims like Ding Dong, Brooklyn was indeed a colorful place to work. The detectives showed Kress to the armored car guards, who, once again, were unable to make an identification. The failure of the guards to identify any of the robbers might have suggested that the crime was not a holdup but a give up. However, it was never alleged that the guards were in any way connected with the heist men.

After Archie Stewart held up a bank in New Jersey and was picked up in Manhattan by Phillips, the detective accused him of being involved in the Rubel robbery, but Stewart denied it. Stewart was released on $25,000 bail for the New Jersey job. However, while he was awaiting extradition to the Garden State, he and his gang held up a bank in upstate New York and got away with $15,000. They were chased by New York State troopers, who managed to shoot one of the robbers in the head. The police conducted a manhunt in the area, and when spotted, the fugitives decided to fight it out. Stewart was shot in the leg and another of the gang committed suicide. A fourth, "One Arm" Wallace, surrendered.

After a while, the Rubel investigation slowed down and almost came to a standstill. That in itself was strange. The largest cash robbery in American history and the largest force of detectives in the United States to investigate it, and nothing was happening. One possibility was that the cops and G-men were dangling a light sentence for the robbery in return for information on the O'Connell kidnapping. In the midst of the investigation of the Rubel robbery, the O'Connell case broke wide open.

In those days, *True Detective* magazine was a very helpful adjunct to police investigations. It published pictures of men wanted for serious crimes, and by 1936 two hundred people had been recognized by readers and apprehended. It was in fact the *America's Most Wanted* of its day. When I was a detective, I frequently read magazines like *True Detective*, and it was amazing the amount of useful information that could be obtained from them. A reader of the magazine in Denver, Colorado, saw a picture of Francis Oley, recognized him as the man who lived next door, and called the FBI. Agents searched Oley's car and found material indicating he had bought it in New York. When they checked with the salesman, he identified a man who had been with Oley as his brother John. Francis hanged himself, and John and Angel Face Geary were also caught and received seventy-seven-year sentences in Alcatraz.

In 1936 Fats Manning was shot to death in East Harlem. It is not clear why an Irishman was wandering around a Mafia stronghold far from Hell's Kitchen. It was rumored that he had been killed to keep him from talking. After four years, and despite repeated announcements by the police that a solution to the case was near, none of the gang had been charged in the Rubel heist.

The bulk of the NYPD continued to be split among Manhattan and Brooklyn, with the power and talent of the detective bureau in the former. The strongest unit in the department was the major case squad, commanded by Insp. John Lyons of the Manhattan central office. Lyons's right-hand man was Capt. Dick Oliver, who had been heavily involved in investigating both the Lindbergh and O'Connell kidnappings. However in the Rubel case the NYPD did not always field its first team.

The major case unit included detectives like Johnny Cordes and Johnny Broderick. The two men were as well known in New York City as the mayor. Broderick was famous for his rough treatment of gangsters. One of his tricks was to walk down Broadway with a newspaper rolled around a lead pipe in his hand. When he would see a known gangster he would give him what appeared to be a friendly tap with the paper, but actually he was hitting him over the head with the pipe. Broderick demanded all hoodlums tip their hats to him. Those who hesitated ended upside down in the nearest garbage can.

Among the two veterans' younger associates was Frankie Phillips, who, although he only was thirty, had already made first-grade detective and was on his way to becoming as much a legend as his mentor Cordes, although personally Phillips was less colorful. The secret to Cordes's success was that he probably had more informers than any detective on the force.

Possibly the major case detectives relegated the Rubel robbery to "a Brooklyn case" and would not work on it. Because the crime had occurred in Brooklyn, whatever the cops did, the criminals would have to be tried in Brooklyn. One problem with that was that the law enforcement machinery in Brooklyn was crooked. In 1938 the governor removed DA William Geoghan from office of a complaint by the New York Citizens Crime Commission. Geoghan's successor, Bill O'Dwyer (a future mayor of New York), failed to prosecute top mobsters in the Murder Inc. case. He then testified for detectives who had allowed a key witness to jump, or be pushed, out of a window on the sixth floor of a hotel where he was being guarded. Joe Adonis, né Doto, a top gangster (who had changed his name because he thought he was so handsome) was more powerful than the district attorney in Brooklyn. Equal to Adonis was Albert Anastasia, boss of the Brooklyn waterfront.

For a time Lt. "Big John" Osnato was put in charge of fifty detectives to work on the Rubel heist. During the Murder Inc. investigations, he distinguished himself by getting some of the people involved to talk. But Osnato's specialty was Italian gangs in Brooklyn, not Irish gangs in Manhattan.

Tom Dewey was a special prosecutor and later district attorney for Manhattan, where he earned a national reputation for his tough approach toward criminals. However, he had no jurisdiction in Brooklyn. Doubtless there were politicians and gangsters influential in the DA's office who would like a piece of $427,500. Thus the divide between Manhattan and Brooklyn likely hampered the police investigation.

In 1938 the police finally received a break in the Rubel case. Archie Stewart had a younger brother who had joined the NYPD. The rookie cop supposedly felt that his association with Archie would blight his career on the force, so he went to his brother in prison and demanded he come clean on what he knew about the Rubel robbery. Family loyalties ran high in those days, and Archie decided to talk. He named all the individuals who had been involved. But by that time Fats Manning was dead. Bernie McMahon had died from the gunshot wound. Frances Oley had hanged himself, and John Oley and Percy Geary were doing what amounted to life sentences in Alcatraz. Kress was serving sentences for his other crimes, and One Arm Wallace was also in prison. As a result of Stewart's testimony, police were able to arrest the boat owner Quinn, the doctor who amputated McMahon's leg, and the charming Madeleine Tully. The accessories received state prison sentences for their part in the Rubel case.

Despite Archie Stewart's cooperation, he continued to be held in custody for thirteen more years, although he was transferred from the state prison to various county jails to keep him safe from retaliation. Jail prisoners were either short-sentence petty criminals or serious ones awaiting trial, and because of the rapid turnover, inmates did not have the time to form highly organized gangs like those that existed in state prisons.

Today, with no one who worked on the Rubel case alive and the crime itself long forgotten, it is difficult to determine why it took so long to clear up. The notion that Archie Stewart talked because his brother wanted to persuade his police colleagues to like him is suspect. More than a few cops in the NYPD and other big city forces had close relatives in jail (in some cases, for killing a police officer), and their careers did not suffer.

The Disappearance of Judge Crater

In 1930 a prominent New York jurist disappeared from the face of the earth, and to this day the event remains a mystery. In April of that year Gov. Franklin Delano Roosevelt appointed Joseph Force Crater to the New York Supreme Court. Unlike most state supreme courts, New York's was not the highest judicial body in the state (that was the Court of Appeals in Albany). It was a trial court, but it was a great job for a Tammany stalwart. The judgeship paid $22,500 a year (the equivalent of $300,000 today) and carried with it a fourteen-year term.

At that time a former judge, Samuel Seabury, was conducting an investigation of New York City government and its judicial system. Seabury was a descendant of John Alden and Priscilla Mullins, who had come over on the *Mayflower*; another of his ancestors had been the first Episcopal bishop of New York. In 1916 Seabury himself had been an odds-on favorite to be elected governor of New York and was already eyeing the presidency. However, he was double-crossed by some of the party factions and lost the race. After that, Seabury no longer sought office, but he burned for revenge against those lesser beings who had failed to acknowledge his leadership. It was possible that if scandal engulfed Governor Roosevelt, Seabury might receive the 1932 Democratic nomination for president.

In July Judge Crater and his wife were vacationing in Maine when he suddenly decided to return to New York City. There he called one of his aides and asked him to meet him at his old law office to help transport various files to a new location. It was believed this was to keep them out of reach of Seabury, whose hot breath was beginning to blow on Crater.

When he practiced law in New York, Crater had been the recipient of many judicial appointments as a receiver. A receiver manages a failing property or company and is tasked with maximizing the value of the assets and then disposing of them. Before ascending to the bench, Crater had been made receiver of a twelve-story building in Manhattan known as the Libby. Within four months, Crater sold the Libby to the American Mortgage Loan Company for $75,000. Shortly afterward, the city approved a street-widening project in the area of the Libby and ended up paying American Mortgage Loan $2.85 million for it. Later a note to Crater's wife would be found among his papers. It advised her that he would soon be in line for a large payment over the Libby sale and that she should contact certain people about receiving it.

On the night of August 6, Crater purchased a ticket to a Broadway show. Before the performance, he joined a law colleague and the latter's girlfriend for dinner at a steakhouse in the theater district. The conversation became so engrossing that Crater missed the curtain, so he decided to catch a cab and head off into the night. It was the last time anybody was known to have seen him.

After Crater went missing, several members of U.S. senator Robert Wagner's law firm, where Crater had an office, visited his wife and expressed concern over the judge's disappearance. However, no official notifications were made to court officials or the police. Finally, when the court opened on August 25 and Crater was not there, his judicial superiors were notified. It was not until September 3 that the police were informed that the judge was missing. Detectives then began to search for him. Simultaneously the press learned about his disappearance and it became front-page material.

Various theories were advanced to explain Crater's disappearance. The most obvious was that he was trying to avoid having to answer questions from Judge Seabury. A second was that he had been murdered by gangsters who were former clients and were angry at him because they had been convicted. It would have been an amazing coincidence if these gangsters, provided they existed at all, had decided to strike just about that time. Most people believe that the story was a red herring.

Why did the police not proceed in an all-out fashion? The most obvious answer seems to be they did not want to embarrass their Tammany masters by solving the case. One interesting fact discovered in the investigation of Crater's papers was that, before his appointment to the supreme court, Crater had withdrawn $25,000 from a bank. Everyone in New York politics knew that the price of a judicial appointment was a year's salary, which in this case would have been $22,500. The money was probably delivered to Crater's Tammany district leader in Greenwich Village, but to receive the appointment from Governor Roosevelt, he also needed the approval of Senator Wagner. Governor Roosevelt was not so naïve as to expect that Crater would have been chosen by Tammany without paying the requisite fee. Politicians who were basically honest assumed such deals were a fixture of New York political life and there was nothing they could do about it, except keep their eyes closed.

In 1928 Tammany's control of the police department had been cemented when Mayor Jimmy Walker appointed Grover Whalen as police commissioner. Whalen was a lifelong party stalwart who had made his name as city greeter, arranging parades for the various celebrities who came to New York in the 1920s. He benefited from the fact that if he held the parade at noon, a ready-made audience of millions was on the streets heading for lunch. Later Whalen was made manager of John P. Wanamaker's department store at a salary of $100,000 a year. When he became police commissioner the store continued to pay his salary.

Whalen immediately set out to get rid of all the veteran police commanders. He dumped longtime chief of detectives John Coughlin and the head of the homicide squad, Insp. Arthur Carey, who had been solving murders since the days of Thomas Byrnes. The man who replaced Bill Leahy as chief inspector had been a traffic officer who worked with Whalen on the celebrity parades. So the police department in 1930 was a virtual Tammany fiefdom.

The real question in the Crater disappearance is not why did he leave, but why did he not come back after the heat had died down? Possibly Judge Crater found a pleasant place to relax, far from his wife, and had plenty of money to enjoy himself. However, money eventually runs out, and the individual has to ask those who supplied him in the first place to replenish the till. That could have raised questions about whether Crater would stay quiet. If there were intimations that he was beginning to crack and might make a full breast of things to Judge Seabury, he might have been murdered. However, in that circumstance, who had the power to order a hit? Surely Roosevelt and Wagner would not have been involved in that.

Some explanations for the disappearance appear to lack knowledge of how organized crime worked in those days. It has been suggested that Crater, who kept company with many chorus girls, had gone to a place like Stella Adler's well-known brothel in Midtown and died while overexerting himself. Adler then called her police friends to get rid of the body. Deaths in compromising situations occur more frequently than most people suppose and often involve individuals of considerable prestige. So the police had a procedure that was normally followed. They would take the man's dead body and move it to a dark street near a hospital. Then he would be found and the explanation would be that he was stricken while trying to reach the hospital. Even today, some New Yorkers are aware of such cases.

The Actor

Willie Sutton, known to his friends as Bill, was the perfect foil for the NYPD detective bureau. He was so well-known that anytime the cops were hunting him, it was news. When they caught him, they could hold a celebration like a Yankees World Series victory party. Of course, a judge then threw the book at him. But it didn't hurt Willie, because no prison could hold him.

Since Sutton never harmed anybody (in sixty robberies and burglaries no one was ever injured), hunting him was sort of like a sporting contest. Much of the time the one who chased Willie was his fellow Brooklynite Frankie Phillips, who rose from rookie detective to deputy chief.

Within the underworld, so respected was Willie by his peers, there were always plenty of people who wanted to work with him, but it was not easy to be chosen by the master. Sutton never had accomplices in the true sense; rather, they were best described as assistants, and he never took more than two of them on a job. He required that whomever he selected not be a drunk or a loudmouth. One of his nicknames was "the actor" because, in carrying out robberies, he frequently employed disguises, such as dressing up like a police officer. Willie also had rules about the targets he would pick. He never went for small scores but chose those that today would be in the million-dollar range.

In the 1920s he had managed to escape from Sing Sing prison, where he was doing time for robbery. In 1929 and 1930, while he was a wanted man, Sutton and his assistants perpetrated a string of jewelry jobs. One heist got considerable attention because they robbed a store on Broadway in midtown Manhattan and got away with $130,000 in gems. Unfortunately for the robbers, one of the accomplices' wives held a grudge against her husband and talked to the police. As a result, Willie and a partner were captured. To top it off, the judge gave Sutton a thirty-year sentence. In two years Willie escaped again. This time the cops set up a wiretap on the phone of an old buddy and picked up information that Sutton was in Philadelphia. Johnny Cordes and Frankie Phillips were among the detectives sent down there to grab him. While in the Quaker city, Sutton had hit a local bank for $60,000.

The top detective in Philadelphia, James "Shoey" Malone (later director of public safety for the city), paid the highest professional compliment to the New York team. No police department ever allowed outsiders to take the lead in their city, but because the New York cops were master detectives, the Philadelphia boys welcomed them. When Phillips and Captain Pat McVeigh broke into Willie's flat, he too was impressed, saying, "They sent the first team didn't they." Anything else would have been insulting to Willie.

Sutton was the type of criminal the public would root for, even though they wanted him captured. Such criminals were rare. None of the Rubel robbers would have ever fit that bill. Back at the turn of the century in Chicago, a slick character named Cooney the Fox pulled off a lot of hold-ups but slipped away each time just before the police could catch him. So he became a sort of local legend. A Washington DC burglar named Willy Pye, who was always ready to confess to every unsolved crime so that the cops could clear them off their books, became a popular local figure and police generally took it easy on him. Because, as was said, "Willy Pye was a regular guy, he took the rap for you and I."

Even today, with Sutton long gone, the public still regularly quotes his famous remark—when asked why he robbed banks, he replied, "That's where the money is." Of course it is doubtful that he ever really said it, but when the facts clash with the legend, print the legend.

One problem Sutton encountered was that he was an avid New York Giants baseball fan and there was nothing that he enjoyed more than going to the Polo Grounds. Once he learned that was Det. Frankie Phillips's favorite hangout, Willie had to forgo the pleasure of seeing his heroes play. It is interesting to speculate, if Phillips had spotted Willie and a chase developed, would the detective have shot him? The answer is probably yes. As Willie had his rules, so did detectives like Phillips, and they did not let a top criminal get away out of sentiment. But Phillips probably would have felt bad about having to do it.

Because of the heist Willie pulled in Philadelphia, he was sent to the Eastern State Penitentiary, but it did not hold him long. He studied the guards and learned that they were conscientious objectors who had chosen prison work as an alternative to military service. Thus they would never fire their weapons. So when Willie went over the wall, he just waved goodbye to the officers in the tower clutching their rifles.

Sutton was at large for a long time, but in 1952 a twenty-three-year-old clothing salesman named Arnold Schuster spotted a man he thought was Willie on a Brooklyn subway train and followed him. When the suspect went into a filling station to get a battery for his dead automobile, Schuster hailed a passing patrol car and told them about his suspicions. They went over and asked the man if he was, in fact, Willie Sutton. He replied, "No my name is Gordon." So the cops departed. In the precinct they told their story to a detective, who insisted on accompanying them back to the scene. Willie was still there, and when the detective questioned him he admitted his true identity.

The capture was a big news story, and when Brooklyn mob boss Albert Anastasia, who hated stool pigeons, saw it on television he ordered one of his goons to kill Schuster. Willie did not hold with murder and had no connection with Anastasia. Later, because of public sympathy, Sutton was released, after which he collaborated on a book and appeared at many law enforcement conferences. There he was treated like the legend he was. If all criminals had behaved like Willie Sutton, criminal investigation would have been a pleasant sport played between cops and crooks, with the public cheering both of them on. Nobody would ever get hurt except insurance companies, and they would simply raise their rates, which would constitute a form of admission to the public for the sport they were watching. Willie remains a popular figure long after Cordes and Phillips have been forgotten. It's always the way, the crook becomes the legend and the cops who ran him down are relegated to bit parts.

In 1956 Frank Phillips, the man who symbolized the old-time detectives, was slated to be made chief of detectives, but it did not happen. He was accused of visiting a gambling casino on Long Island. A by-the-book commissioner named Steve Kennedy was in charge of the force at the time, and he did not like high-profile detectives, whom he saw as prima donnas. Kennedy had started his own career as a police stenographer in La Guardia's city hall, where he was impressed by the educated and polished individuals he encountered. So he went to college and law school and substituted a Shakespearean voice for his Brooklyn accent. The cops hated him. Kennedy decided to make an example out of Phillips and compelled him to leave the force. Even though Johnny

Cordes came out of retirement to attempt to save Phillips, all their contacts with the press did them no good.

There was new thinking at police headquarters and in some press rooms about what constituted a good cop. From the 1950s on, many a police chief was far less interested in fighting crime then he was in appearing as an up-to-date police administrator. Such men essentially sought to please police reformers. At the same time, rules for criminals relaxed, and the ones for police were tightened. In New York City, a youth gang fight that resulted in murder was changed from a vicious crime into a Broadway musical and movie called *West Side Story*, where the street gangs were eulogized and the cops parodied. The day of the detective was ending.

9

The Kidnapping and Murder of

the Lindbergh Baby and the

Rise of Director Hoover

The Kidnapping of the Lindbergh Baby

Since the Hall-Mills case concluded in 1926, the New Jersey State Police had become leaders in law enforcement and were now ready for their supreme test. The commander of the force, Col. H. Norman Schwarzkopf, with his military bearing, was nationally known as the man who headed a spit-and-polish police force, much praised by police reformers. Instead of battling with the powers that be in his state, Schwarzkopf had cooperated with them to a degree. The basic arrangement was that his force would not interfere in urban problems and in return would be allowed to operate independently in the rural areas. He had even managed to team up with the big-city cops in Newark and Jersey City. Insp. Harry Walsh of Jersey City taught training courses for state police detectives and was always available to help the troopers. Walsh had been awarded the state police distinguished service medal for capturing the killer of a trooper. When needed, his detectives and a team from Newark would join with the troopers in working a case. Walsh was a special favorite of Mayor Hague of Jersey City, who had originally opposed the creation of the troopers, calling them "thugs" before the first one was ever hired. Since then, he had changed his mind.

On the wintry evening of Tuesday, March 1, 1932, the phone rang in the West Trenton headquarters of the force. The supervisor on duty at the time answered the phone in the prescribed manner: "New Jersey State Police, Lieutenant Dunn." When he hung up other troopers noticed he looked shocked and perplexed. When asked why, he replied, "Some guy said he was Colonel Lindbergh and his baby had been kidnapped. Now what am I supposed to do?" After verifying the call, Dunn dispatched state police units to the Lindbergh home in Hopewell. Trooper Joe Wolf was the first to arrive on the scene, followed by Dets. Lewis Bornmann and Nuncio De Gaetano. Later, Schwarzkopf himself and his second in command, Major Schoeffel, along with Lieutenant Keaten, head of the state police detectives, arrived accompanied by Cpl. Frank Kelly, a fingerprint technician. The local two-man Hopewell force was on the scene, but it was decided the troopers would take over and the locals were soon sent on their way. Unlike the Hall-Mills case, this time there would be no county detectives or small-town police to mess up the crime scene or go off in opposite directions. Schwarzkopf was going to be the boss cop and anyone who did not like it could call the governor, the attorney general, or Frank Hague. None of them wanted another Hall-Mills case, particularly on an international scale. In fact, Governor A. Harry Moore, a Hague man, ordered Schwarzkopf to take charge of the case.

Since his successful flight across the Atlantic in 1927, Charles Lindbergh had become a godlike figure to the American people. His stature contributed to the high level of publicity the case received. If it had not been for him, probably the crime would be no better remembered today than the O'Connell kidnapping in Albany or the series of snatches that were carried out in the Midwest by so-called public enemies.

Lindbergh had grown up in Minnesota, where his father was a populist congressman who lost his seat for opposing U.S. entry into World War I. Later, young Lindbergh would fly the mails and receive a reserve commission as a lieutenant in the U.S. Army Air Corps. He did not achieve a regular appointment because of the limited number of vacancies. His solo flight across the Atlantic to Paris had made him a national hero. President Coolidge sent a warship to bring him home to New York, where he arrived to tumultuous greetings. The Army Air Corps promoted him to colonel in the reserves and the media christened him "the Lone Eagle." The young pilot was a Hollywood version of a hero, a tall, handsome, seemingly modest mid-American. Lindbergh followed up with other aviation accomplishments and then married Anne Morrow, the daughter of Dwight Morrow, a principal partner in the J. P. Morgan investment firm and a leader of the Eastern bankers his father had inveighed against. At the time, Morrow was serving as U.S. senator from New Jersey. Though an aristocrat, Anne was a charming person, and she too became a pilot, accompanying her husband on a number of flying adventures.

Such a couple could not exist in contemporary America. The media that placed them on their pedestals would soon pull them down and there would be regular stories about them in the scandal sheets. In the late 1930s the American public would learn something about Lindbergh's extreme political views, including his great affection for Nazi Germany. After the war, it would be revealed that he had women friends in Europe and even illegitimate children. In 1932, however, he was the hero with shining wings who had married the Wall Street princess.

When the police questioned the family and staff, they told a straight-forward story. The house was not the only residence of Colonel and Mrs. Lindbergh, who often stayed at the fifty-room mansion of Anne's late father, Senator Morrow. This night, though, twenty-month-old Charles Junior had a cold and the family decided to remain at their new home, still under construction, in Hopewell. At 8:30 p.m. the baby's nurse, a Scottish girl named Betty Gow, waited until after young Charles had gone to sleep and then went downstairs to have a cup of coffee with the butler and cook, a husband-and-wife team. When Colonel Lindbergh arrived home, he and Anne sat in the living room. At nine o'clock he thought he heard a cracking noise outside. At ten o'clock Betty Gow went back to the nursery to take Charles to the bathroom and then tuck him in for the night. When she looked in his crib, he was not there. Thinking one of the Lindberghs had taken him, she ran downstairs to find the child. But Mrs. Lindbergh did not have him and suggested maybe the Colonel had taken the baby for a few minutes. When it was determined that the

Colonel did not have him either, Lindbergh took a Springfield rifle out of the closet and began searching the house. After a few minutes, he told his wife, "Anne, they have stolen our baby." He instructed the butler to call the Hopewell police while he made the call to Lieutenant Dunn.

Trooper Wolf was advised by the Hopewell police that they had located portions of a ladder near the house. In the nursery, Wolf turned his attention to an envelope that lay on the windowsill. He picked it up on the blade of a knife and placed it on the mantelpiece for safekeeping. Outside, Detective De Gaetano had come across a footprint near the house. Cursory examination showed that the shoe had apparently been covered with a heavy sock or similar material. Further search of the grounds turned up another section of a ladder. Detective Bornmann took all three sections into the house for closer examination, which showed that they were designed to fit together. Trooper Kelly dusted the nursery for fingerprints but found nothing. He then dusted the envelope, which provided only one smudge. With the permission of Lindbergh, the police opened the letter. Written in ink on a single sheet of notepaper, the misspelling of words and the scrawl of the author made it difficult to decipher.

> Dear Sir!
> Have 50.000 $ redy 25 000 in
> 20 $ bills 1.5000 $ in 10 $ bills and
> 10000 $ in 5 $ bills. After 2–4 days
> we will inform you were to deliver
> the Mony.
> We warn you for making
> Anyding public or for notify the Police
> the child is in gute care.
> Indication for all letters are
> Singnature

At the end of the note was a symbol of two interlocking circles in blue ink, each about the size of a quarter. Within the oval of the interlock was a solid ball of red ink, and the symbol was pierced by three holes spaced apart on the same line. The police decided to keep the signature secret.

With the baby apparently kidnapped for ransom, Colonel Lindbergh asked the troopers to back off and let him handle the case. However, a police alarm had already been sent out over the teletype in three states, and reporters had read it. The next day, the whole country learned that the national hero's baby had been kidnapped and demanded the cops break the case quickly.

The police investigation team included Inspector Walsh and his men from Jersey City, along with detectives from Newark and the troopers under Lieutenant Keaten, with state police captain Lamb in overall supervision. The strongman that every detective bureau needed to run interference was Schwarzkopf himself. Over two years of investigation, trial, and post-trial activity, the team held together.

Various theories of the case were open to choose from:

1. It was the work of a professional gang, possibly with inside help. Maids in rich households tipping off burglars was an old story in police work. Arguing against the professional gang was the size of the ransom eventually demanded, $70,000. By the time that was split up there would be very little money for the risks that the kidnappers were taking.

2. A nonprofessional had stolen the baby for ransom. This could have involved servants with outside help. Arguing for this notion was that servants were among the few people who knew the family was going to be at Hopewell that night, and $70,000 would look like a lot of money to low-paid employees.

3. The boy had been taken not for ransom but instead by a disturbed individual. The Sourland Mountain area around Hopewell was a mysterious place long known as a shelter for criminals and for strange happenings. Locals had warned Lindbergh when he moved into Hunterdon County that it was a forbidding area, but he wanted a remote home so as to discourage publicity.

Another mysterious place nearby was the New Jersey Pine Barrens, a wooded area inhabited by people descended from Hessian soldiers of the Revolutionary War and runaway slaves. Locals complained that "the Pineys" lived off the land without title, hunted without license, bought and sold wives, and were dangerous people. They cowed the neighborhood by occasional arson jobs on the barns of those who complained about them. The state police had found that the Pine Barrens and the Sourland Mountain area were the most difficult to police in New Jersey.

Initially the dominant figure in the case was Colonel Lindbergh himself. Given his high standing with the American public and the sympathy they felt for him, plus the fact that his wife's family was Wall Street royalty, no law enforcement officer would have dared defy him. Though an outstanding flier, his judgment was not always so good on other subjects, and he allowed a number of outsiders to play a role in the case. The first group was composed of racketeers and mobsters like Irving Bitz, Salvatore Spitale, and Mickey Rosner, who made contact with Lindbergh and persuaded him to allow them to engage in negotiations with the mob on his behalf. Lindbergh even announced publicly that they would be representing him in the case. Local bootleggers were particularly interested in getting the kidnapping solved because so many vehicles were being stopped on the highways that their beer trucks could not get through. Out in Chicago, Al Capone, who was about to head off to serve an eleven-year sentence for tax evasion, announced that if he were released he would "find that kid in no time." The Mafia, though, did not control all criminal gangs. John Dillinger and the various other midwestern outlaw groups operated on their own. If the kidnapper were a psychopath, Lucky Luciano, Al Capone, and the like would have no idea who he was.

Various prominent people tried to insert themselves into the investigation. An Episcopal bishop in Virginia reported that one of his parishioners, John Curtis, was already in touch with the kidnappers. Society millionaire Evelyn Walsh McLean recommended a former federal agent named Gaston Means, who had been sent to prison during the Harding Ohio Gang scandals. Special Assistant to the Secretary of Labor Murray Garson, later convicted as a Washington fixer, inserted himself into the case and, after turning the mansion upside down, declared that Lindbergh himself was the kidnapper.

The cases that came to city detectives routinely involved shootings and armed robberies, so they were used to dealing with hardened criminals. When the police questioned a Morrow family English maid, Violet Sharpe, they subjected her to a vigorous, third-degree-type interrogation. Allegedly, she became so shaken that she committed suicide. Later, it was revealed that she did not want to give information because she had been out with a man named Ernie, though she was engaged to someone else, on the night of the kidnapping. For a while, the cops believed that the man was a local ne'er-do-well whose first name was Ernie. Not until an ordinary citizen named Ernie Miller came in and volunteered that he had been out with Sharpe on the evening of the kidnapping was that notion discarded. Betty Gow, the nurse, had a boyfriend named Red Johnson, a crew member on the yacht of Thomas Lamont, Wall Street partner of Senator Morrow. Some people argued that the nickname Red came not from the color of his hair but from his leftist leanings and the whole thing was a Communist plot. That was eventually proven to be untrue as well.

For a time the case turned on Dr. John F. Condon, a retired educator who lived in the Bronx section of New York City. Dr. Condon was a publicity seeker, and he regularly provided his views to the local *Bronx Home News*, a paper far less read than the *New York Daily News* or other citywide journals. In the aftermath of the kidnapping, he wrote a letter to the paper stating that he stood willing to act as a conduit between Lindbergh and the kidnappers. Surprisingly, a reader of the *Home News* contacted Condon by mail, claiming he was the kidnapper and would be willing to use the doctor as an intermediary. Police were suspicious of the offer. However, when Condon mentioned that the letter from the kidnapper had some strange symbols at the bottom, the interest of the investigators rose. Eventually Condon, using the name Jafsie (a combination of his initials, JFC), met with a man who called himself John in a Bronx cemetery. Condon noticed that John had the same German accent that the writer of the letter had displayed, including the mispronunciation of some American words. John was scared off by noises that night, but the two men finally set up a meeting to hand over the money. Based on the advice of the IRS agents who had brought down Capone in Chicago, two ransom packages, containing $50,000 and $20,000 (the latter in fifty-dollar denominations) in gold certificates with serial numbers recorded were put together. In 1933 the U.S. government would recall gold certificates, so they became much more noticeable when passed.

On the night the money was to be turned over, Capt. Dick Oliver of the NYPD detective bureau, who maintained liaisons with outside police agencies, attempted to follow Condon and Colonel Lindbergh to the meeting place in order to sneak up on John and seize him. However, when Oliver weighed the awesome consequences if he failed, he backed off. Condon handed over the $50,000 package to John in a Bronx cemetery. The latter claimed he would not be able to turn the baby over for six or eight hours and gave Condon a location where the child would be. The kidnapper said he was on a "boad" called the *Nelly*. But no such vessel was found. When Condon returned from his mission, he boasted that he had saved Lindbergh $20,000 by not handing over the ransom package with the fifty-dollar bills. The Treasury agents were apoplectic. Fifty-dollar bills were easier to spot, and it would have been likely that the bigger ones would have been the first ones cashed by the kidnapper.

After the ransom was paid, a truck driver who stopped to relieve himself on a New Jersey highway not far from the Lindbergh home found the baby in a shallow grave. Searches by the state police had failed to turn it up. It was then realized that Gaston Means, the Virginia businessman Curtis, and all the others who inserted themselves into the case had been duped or were engaging in fraud. Detectives suspected that Condon himself was one of the gang.

The discovery of the dead body and the passing of the ransom bills opened the door for other law enforcement agencies to become involved. A man who burned to enter the case was (federal) Bureau of Investigation director J. Edgar Hoover. But the U.S. government had no jurisdiction in kidnappings until after the 1933 Lindbergh antikidnapping law was passed, and that could not be used retroactively. Nevertheless, Hoover pushed his way onto the fringes of the investigation, although the Jersey cops were tight-lipped with his agents. Even Frank Hague sought to be helpful. He assembled a meeting of the leaders of the various law enforcement agencies, including Hoover, who was not yet big enough to send a substitute in his place (as was his usual practice later). When the meeting adjourned, Hague invited all the participants to lunch, then sent the bill to the governor.

Facing the prospect of a new Democratic national administration in 1933, Hoover was worried about his job. Some of the leading Democrats had no love for him, dating back to when he had led the federal deportation drives known as the Red Scare and the 1923–24 Teapot Dome scandals, during which bureau agents tailed U.S. senators. Were Schwarzkopf to capture the kidnapper, he would become a national hero. This presented the possibility that he might be seen as Hoover's replacement, so that was an additional reason for the director to try to get a piece of the case. Among those who had reason to dislike Hoover was Thomas Walsh of Montana, one of the U.S. senators who had been followed by Justice Department detectives during Teapot Dome. In 1933 he was appointed attorney general. En route to his swearing in, he died of a heart attack in the railroad compartment that he shared with his new and vivacious young Cuban bride. If Walsh had taken over the Department of Justice it is almost certain that he would have fired Hoover.

The third component of the investigative group was a squad of New York City detectives commanded by Lt. James Finn, who had become acquainted with Lindbergh in 1927 when he headed the colonel's protective detail after the flight to Paris. The two men had hit it off, and when the kidnapping occurred, Lindbergh invited Finn to come out to the mansion and stay. But the New Jersey detectives froze him out.

Lieutenant Finn was a cop who thought beyond routine. He decided to consult a prominent New York psychiatrist, Dr. Dudley Schoenfeld, about clues to the kidnapper's identity. The psychiatrist posited that the motive for the crime was to demonstrate the kidnapper's superiority to an international hero like Lindbergh. The psychiatrist believed that the suspect subconsciously wanted to get caught; however, he would never talk if he were taken to a police station. So instead of being subjected to the usual grilling, he should be brought to a private setting, like a psychiatrist's office, and questioned in a soothing manner.

Finn was rowing against the tide even in New York. The public wanted the kidnapper caught and executed, not a rehash of the Loeb and Leopold case in Chicago. At that time the Chicago murder was less than ten years back, and it still left a bad taste in the mouths of law enforcement officers, who believed that once psychologists and social theorists like Clarence Darrow got into a case, they would find some excuse to save the defendant from the death penalty.

The investigative team largely allowed the New Jersey cops the primary role. The FBI agents under Tom Sisk looked for some chance to take over, and NYPD lieutenant Finn, who had tried to bring Dr. Schoenfeld into the case, was left with a squad of twenty-three officers tabulating ransom bills passed in New York City. By 1933 the gold certificates were clustering in the Bronx area where Condon lived. The Bronx was not a tiny place. It had a population of 1.5 million and occupied forty-one square miles, so the detectives' best hope was that someone could identify the bill passer.

In September 1934 an alert Bronx gas station attendant wrote down the license number of a car driven by a man who had passed him one of the gold certificates. The license was traced to Bruno Richard Hauptmann, an immigrant from Germany and resident of the Bronx whose home was in the middle of the area where the bills were accumulating. The police observed Hauptmann overnight. In the morning, when he came out of his house and got into his automobile, he was followed by three cars manned by nine detectives, three each from the New Jersey State Police, the NYPD, and the FBI. A block from his house he was pulled over, arrested, and taken to a deserted police station in lower Manhattan, where he was questioned by representatives of all three agencies. NYPD inspector John Lyons, commanding officer of the major case squad, took the lead in the interrogation, while others also pitched in until it became a babble of voices. The key FBI agent was Leon Turrou, an American who had been born in Russia. In World War I he had returned to Russia to serve with the czar's army. Afterward Hoover had made him an agent in the New York office, specializing in investigations of Communists. However, probing Reds was not politically correct after the early 1920s, and Turrou was used in a wide variety of cases. This gave the FBI an agent who was more sophisticated than most cops or troopers. But in 1934 the FBI was not so powerful that it could run the investigation. Later in the decade, when Turrou began getting publicity for catching Nazi spies, Hoover fired him. Only Hoover himself was authorized to get publicity.

The highlight of the grilling was when Dr. Condon was brought in to identify Hauptmann as the kidnapper. The wily doctor went down a lineup (composed of detectives) and then asked for time to talk to Hauptmann. He was granted it, and after a while, when asked to make an identification, Condon declined. Either he felt snubbed because he did not have a bigger role in the police investigation, or he simply wanted to continue his preeminent position. As Dr. Schoenfeld had predicted, Hauptmann did not confess. Nevertheless, the evidence against him was very strong. Approximately $14,000 from the ransom package was found in his house, and he was identified as having passed gold certificates. Wood similar to that in the ladder that the kidnapper used was also found in his house. Handwriting experts testified that it was Hauptmann's writing on the ransom notes.

The ever-helpful Clarence Darrow out in Chicago still enjoyed the limelight, and from a thousand miles away, he ventured an opinion that there was no evidence to support a murder conviction in the Hauptmann case. Possibly this was an attempt by Darrow to be retained by the defense so he could once more feel the spotlight shining on him while he delivered a sociological treatise that had nothing to do with law or the evidence. The defense was not willing to subsidize Darrow's last hurrah.

In January 1935 Hauptmann's trial opened in Flemington, New Jersey, seat of Hunterdon County. The lead prosecutor was David Wilentz, attorney general of New Jersey. Hauptmann's defense was led by a veteran criminal lawyer, Edward Reilly, known as the Bull of Brooklyn, whose fee was paid by Hearst's *Journal-American* in return for exclusive access to the defendant's camp.

The story was the biggest sensation of the time and, barring the Kennedy assassination, it probably remains the crime of the century. However, it was not a slam-dunk. No one had witnessed the kidnapping, and many people felt that Hauptmann was not alone in his actions. Reilly attempted the usual lawyer's tricks in the case. He intimated that it had been some kind of Red plot in revenge for the time when Dwight Morrow was ambassador to Mexico and helped to foil Communist influence there. Reilly, who was past his best, realized he held a losing hand. So he began playing every card in the deck. He called witnesses who had spent time in mental institutions. With a large law enforcement contingent at his disposal, Attorney General Wilentz had the resources to investigate every defense witness. So the bogus ones were quickly unmasked. Even Hauptmann asked Reilly, "Where are you getting these people?" In 1935 the jury found Hauptmann guilty of murder, and the judge sentenced him to death. Reilly told Hauptmann that there was no chance of avoiding the death penalty unless he confessed. A more prestigious Brooklyn lawyer named Sam Leibowitz was brought in and told Hauptmann the same thing. Eighty years later, people do not realize how strong the evidence against Hauptmann was.

It might have been expected that the successful resolution of the case would have brought accolades to the various authorities. However, many people were disappointed in the conviction. The governor of New Jersey, Harold Hoffman, a Republican who had been elected in 1934 despite a Democratic landslide nationally, was an ambitious man. Hoffman began to consult Ellis Parker Sr., chief of detectives in Burlington County, New Jersey, about the case. Parker had long held a grudge against the state police, and he was particularly angry because he had been barred from any role in the Lindbergh investigation. Governor Hoffman even made illegal secret visits to the state prison with the connivance of the warden, Mark Kimberling. Kimberling had been number two to Schwarzkopf at the state police, but with no sign of his boss leaving, he took the prison job. However, he still longed to replace Schwarzkopf.

As the execution drew near, a twenty-five-page signed confession was delivered to the eight members of the New Jersey Court of Errors and

Appeals, which was chaired by the governor. It was supposedly signed by Paul Wendel, a disbarred lawyer. The document did not contain any information about who might have prepared it, though a number of people, knowing of Wendel's friendship with Ellis Parker, had a suspicion of who it might be.

Wendel's confession, allegedly written at the dictation of Parker, was full of deliberate errors to show its lack of authenticity. When Wendel finally appeared, he reported that he had been kidnapped in New York City by Parker's agents, including Ellis Parker Jr., taken to Parker Sr., and forced to confess. As a result of Wendel's statements, the Brooklyn district attorney prepared indictments for the group of kidnappers he named, including Ellis Parker Sr., but Governor Hoffman would not allow the elder Parker to be extradited.

On April 3, 1936, Hauptmann was executed.

The case was not over for the senior Parker. He and his son were both indicted for violating the newly enacted federal Lindbergh law by kidnapping Wendel. The judge trying the case told Parker Sr., "I have the impression that your life as a law enforcement officer and your position in the community have given you the feeling that you are above the law, and that is the cause of your making a mockery of the processes of justice in New Jersey." Parker was found guilty and given six years in prison. He entered the federal penitentiary at Lewisburg, Pennsylvania, in June 1939 and died there in February 1940 of a brain tumor. For two generations, Parker had managed to con many journalists who should have known better and to promote the myth that he was an American Sherlock Holmes. In the end, he made the mistake of going up against the federal government.

The dénouement of the case came years later. Governor Hoffman was not considered for higher office by the Republican Party, but he did manage to fire Colonel Schwarzkopf and replace him with Warden Kimberling. In World War II, Schwarzkopf served as a general in command of the twenty-thousand-man Iranian gendarmerie and was decorated for his service. Later, he would be part of the CIA group that ousted anti-Western Iranian premier Mohammed Mossadgh. Schwarzkopf's son, H. Norman Jr., West Point '57, was commanding general of Allied forces in the Desert Storm Campaign. In 1954 Schwarzkopf Sr. was back in New Jersey serving as administrative assistant to the attorney general, overseeing the state police, motor vehicle department, and so on. It was an impressive title but limited in power. In his new job he was called on to investigate the state director of employment security for alleged irregularities in the running of his office, including telephone conversations with organized crime bosses. The director was former governor Harold Hoffman, who protested his innocence. In June he was found dead of a heart attack in a New York hotel room, and with him was a letter in which he admitted embezzling $300,000 over a period of years from a bank where he was an officer. All along Parker had been a phony and Hoffman a crook, yet important criminal justice matters in the Garden State were entrusted to Parker for years, and Hoffman was nearly able to sabotage the case in the crime of the century. An English observer once remarked about the American criminal justice system, "In a trial the criminal goes free and the jury is hung." In this instance the criminal did not go free, but the state police were hanged.

Many years after Hauptmann's execution the Lindbergh case still fascinates the public, and as with other such crimes, there is always a market for books that declare he was innocent. There were mistakes in the investigation that could have been avoided. For example, the troopers who responded to the call at the Lindbergh home did not conduct an adequate initial search of the house and grounds. The problem is that when officers arrive at a crime scene, they may not know if it might be a sensational case. So they usually operate in their normal manner, which is to get out of their cars and start looking around. In the 1980s a young man murdered a young girl in Central Park while engaging in "rough sex." The case became a front-page sensation. However, when the police initially responded to a call about a body in the park, some of the officers drove over the crime scene.

In the Lindbergh case, because there was a ransom note, police were quick to assume that a professional or semiprofessional gang had taken the baby, possibly with assistance from the servants. No one deduced from the ransom note that the person who had done the kidnapping might be psychotic and not an individual motivated by greed.

Because Lindbergh's requests could not be disputed, the police let him contact mob figures and allow Dr. Condon to assume a major role, all of which complicated the investigation. Police have learned that the victim should never be allowed to direct their work. Still, in 1932, who could have reined in the young god of the skies?

The fact that three law enforcement agencies were involved in the case meant that there would be rivalry, just as there is today. In the 1970s, when Frank Sinatra Jr. was kidnapped in the Los Angeles area, the FBI refused to turn over any information or work cooperatively with the LAPD. In 2002, when a so-called Beltway sniper began killing people in Virginia, Maryland, and the District of Columbia, the task of coordinating the investigation was left to a county police chief in Maryland, though his agency had no authority outside of his own state. Helpful "experts" on crime declared that "the shooter" was a lone white man, when in fact it was two black men.

Of course, innocent men have been charged with crimes. When an academic "expert" on policing was elected sheriff of Cook County, Illinois (greater Chicago), he charged a drifter with the murder of two young women. However, after the county prosecutor brought in forensic experts to review evidence, it became obvious that the accused, Benny Bedwell, was innocent. The state's attorney then dismissed the charges. The stubborn sheriff, Joseph D. Lohman, ambitious to be governor, would not accept the decision, and he continually told people that he had had the right man. Unfortunately, no one else agreed with him, and he did not become governor. Eventually he left Illinois to become dean of the School of Criminology at the University of California–Berkeley. He died in 1968 at the age of fifty-eight.

Director Hoover

In March 1932, when the Lindbergh baby was kidnapped, few Americans had heard of J. Edgar Hoover. His special agents did not even have police authority to make arrests, nor were they permitted to carry firearms. If an agent wished to arrest a criminal, he essentially had to call on the police to make the apprehension. This led to situations where cops stormed through the front door of a fugitive's house, guns in hand, while a bureau agent stood out back with a brick he had picked up in a vacant lot, ready to hit the offender over the head. Such was the majesty of the U.S. government that some of its agents had to fight like cavemen.

Hoover did not even look like a cop. William Burns and William Flynn, his predecessors as bureau director, were burly ex–Secret Service men who had personally made arrests at gunpoint and cracked big cases. Hoover looked like a clerk and dressed like a dandy. He never made an arrest before 1936, and then only after a U.S. senator criticized him for sending agents out to be killed and never taking any risk himself. After that, Hoover did make a few collars, but in all cases he was accompanied by a squad of agents who protected him. Hoover's skill was not as a law enforcement officer but as a public relations expert and master politician. Unlike local police, the average citizen never met a G-man, so they could easily be persuaded of the virtues of the agency by Hoover's propaganda. The agency's failures could be covered up, whereas ones by local police could not.

What many people never understood was that what Hoover wanted most was power. He never married but lived with his mother until her death. Many accusations have been made about his alleged sexual proclivities, but none have ever been proven, and there were plenty of people who would have liked to have gotten something on him. At one time, Hoover was trailed by the NYPD whenever he came to New York, but they found nothing. He did like to appear in celebrity places like the Stork Club, but marriage would have required that he have a more active social life than he had time for.

Hoover became FBI director in 1924, thanks to Larry Richey recommending him to Attorney General (and later chief justice of the United States) Harlan Fiske Stone. As director he began to have the power to put his ideas into effect. However, it was not the right time for him to step forward in American law enforcement. The national government of the 1920s was concerned with enforcing Prohibition, and Hoover wanted no part of that. Nor did he want to tangle with mobsters. After the St. Valentine's Day Massacre in 1929, when Hoover was offered the assignment to "get Al Capone," he dodged it because he knew that, given organized crime's political connections, there would be retaliation against the bureau. Instead the job was given to the U.S. Treasury's Special Intelligence Unit, which sent Capone to prison.

The New Jersey State Police and the NYPD really did not need any help in conducting the Lindbergh investigation. They were long-service professionals. In contrast, Hoover's agents back then were mostly young college men who had taken the job on a temporary basis during the Great Depression and would leave after two or three years. In the early thirties, an internal survey by the bureau revealed that only eleven agents were particularly qualified for work of a dangerous character.

At that time, wide areas of the Midwest and Southwest swarmed with former bootleggers and small-time criminals, who began holding up banks and kidnapping citizens. So Hoover recruited a number of tough lawmen from Texas and Oklahoma, still the American frontier, and sent them on missions against the gangsters. It was these so-called cowboys who shot men like John Dillinger.

Hoover won great acclaim for his successful war against "public enemies." He also became a favorite of President Franklin D. Roosevelt because the director was willing to carry out any mission the president wanted performed, regardless of the legality. As World War II approached, Roosevelt assigned Hoover to monitor the activities of isolationists and other antiwar groups, especially Charles Lindbergh at a time when the colonel was still a popular figure with many Americans. When the Second World War broke out, the FBI was in the forefront of rounding up possible spies and subversives in the United States. Hoover even lined up on the side of the angels by vigorously opposing the incarceration of Japanese Americans on the West Coast. During the World War II era, Hoover would try to sideline city police and simply use them as errand boys for his bureau. However, Mayor Fiorello La Guardia would not have it, and the New York Police Department formed large antisabotage and espionage squads. Throughout the conflict, Hoover engaged in a feud with the Office of Strategic Services (OSS), forerunner of the CIA. Even in wartime, his ego demanded that he always be in charge and not share with other agencies. Gen. George Marshall, chief of staff of the U.S. Army, commented that Hoover behaved "like a petulant child."

The only president with the prestige to have fired Hoover was Dwight Eisenhower, and he did not want to. Truman and JFK, professional politicians, would have loved to have been rid of Hoover, but they were afraid of the political costs of doing so. Throughout the 1950s, Hoover was continually able to highlight the "Red Menace" because the Communists in the Soviet Union did engage in widespread espionage and were very unpopular with the American public. In the 1960s, though, Hoover attempted to use Cold War methods against protesters from civil rights and antiwar groups, a policy that proved disastrous to his agency.

During the 1930s and the war years, Hoover did some outstanding things and laid the foundation for the creation of a great law enforcement agency. After the war, instead of leaving, he was like one of those people who stays too long at the dance and when the music changes does not know the new steps. In the end, it was his inability to move with the times that severely damaged his posthumous reputation.

10

Wall Street, a Day at the Fair,

and the Murder of Carlo Tresca

American police, unlike their European counterparts, were never skilled at security policing, a task quite different from regular criminal investigations. France, for example, because of its history of war and revolution, had always regarded state security as one of its major police responsibilities.

Regular police seek to identify criminals, put them in jail, and perhaps receive some mention in the newspapers before they move on to their next case. Security police are not so much interested in arrest as they are in keeping an eye on spies, subversives, or saboteurs. If the latter have to be arrested, security police officers are never identified publicly for their role in the case. In the years before World War I, the British Special Branch police uncovered a ring of German spies operating in Britain. Instead of hauling them in, they received warrants signed by the young home secretary, Winston Churchill, to keep these people under surveillance and intercept their mail. When Britain went to war with Germany in 1914, all twenty-one of the targets were hauled in.

In the early twentieth century, the NYPD's fight against subversive groups, anarchism, and so on, was led by Lt. Joe Petrosino's bomb squad until his death in 1909. Since most of the devices being exploded then were set or tossed by so-called Black Handers, it made some sense to give the bombing cases to the Italian squad. After the abolition of Petrosino's unit, Capt. Thomas Tunney's Special Service squad carried out the work of the bomb squad. When the war broke out in August 1914, Comm. Arthur Woods ordered the squad to be prepared to deal with German sabotage activities in the United States. To disguise its mission, Tunney's unit was renamed the Neutrality Squad. Dep. Comm. Guy Scull, a Harvard man, and his fellow Harvardian Dep. Comm. Nicholas Biddle, a member of the Philadelphia banking family and manager of New York's Astor properties (the city's largest real estate holdings), would supervise the neutrality squad in the same way Woods had run the detective bureau.

In 1914 the U.S. government also assigned the Secret Service, then headed by Chief William Flynn, and the Bureau of Investigation under A. Bruce Bielaski to prevent German espionage and sabotage. Bielaski, a lawyer and outstanding athlete, had originally been transferred from the Bureau of Engraving to the Justice Department to strengthen the latter's baseball team.

From 1914 on, ninety German vessels, caught unawares by the outbreak of war, were anchored in New York Harbor. Outside the three-mile limit, a squadron of British cruisers patrolled to intercept them. There were also several thousand German reservists in town who could not obtain the false papers that would allow them to sail home and join the army. This provided a strong force for German spymasters, like Capt. of Cavalry Franz von Papen, the military attaché (later chancellor of Germany), and Capt. Franz von Rintelen, a millionaire banker and naval reservist, who was sent to New York to direct sabotage operations. Career officers like von Papen and the naval attaché did not get along with the millionaire. One problem was that Rintelen had become a "von" after being adopted by an old lady. So in addition to not being a regular officer, he was not really an aristocrat. On the American side, the established U.S. Secret Service resented sharing duties with the Bureau of Investigation, whose agents did not even carry guns.

The German tactic was to manufacture bombs on the interned ships and then deliver them to English-hating Irish dockworkers, who would plant them on Allied ships. No American vessels were targeted for fear of bringing the United States into the war.

While Tunney and his men were crack detectives, they had little experience in dealing with foreign intelligence. So they secretly arranged to receive assistance from the British and French. Thirty-five Allied ships were sunk or damaged by the German bombs before a tip from French intelligence led Tunney's men to a German bomber in nearby New Jersey. With the assistance of the U.S. Secret Service, the bomber was arrested and eventually sent to Atlanta Penitentiary. The center of the bombing ring was in Hoboken, New Jersey, where the German shipping lines had their headquarters. So in the period before 1917, northern New Jersey swarmed with Secret Service operatives, Bureau of Investigation agents, and German-speaking New York detectives. When America entered the war, Hoboken became the principal point from which U.S. soldiers embarked for Europe. Because of the German influence and the antiwar attitude of the political boss of New Jersey, Mayor Frank Hague of Jersey City, President Wilson ordered the Secret Service and the army to take control of the city for the duration.

In 1915 Secret Service agents managed to steal the attaché case of a German diplomat who was the paymaster of the sabotage ring. While it contained insufficient evidence for prosecution, the contents were leaked to the newspapers and President Wilson was given an excuse to order most of the German spy and sabotage heads out of the country. This included the embarrassed paymaster, now known in the German community as the "minister without portfolio." Bielaski of the Bureau of Investigation had to learn of the Secret Service exploit by reading about it in the newspaper. The expelled von Rintelen, who did not have diplomatic immunity, was seized when his ship called at a British port and was held in custody until the United States entered the war. Then he was returned to American control and sent to the notorious Tombs jail in Manhattan.

Despite some successes, the security police failed to uncover a German safe house on West Fifteenth Street in Manhattan that was run by German opera singer Baroness Martha Held. Begun as a recreational establishment where German ships' officers could meet charming American ladies, during the war it became a center for spies and saboteurs. Von Papen was a frequent visitor and would often leave with a couple of beauties on his arm. Irish longshoreman who were carrying bombs in and out of the house had the toughest job. They had to sit listening to the baroness when she burst forth into Wagnerian opera, because nobody could leave before the fat lady sang.

Two years into the war, Allied agents had yet to beef up security at the largest ammunition dump in the United States, Black Tom Island, which was on a promontory off New Jersey, now known as Liberty State Park. (There are various explanations for the name. One is that from high in the air, it looked like a black tomcat. Another is that an early occupant of the island was African American.) On the night of July 30, a German sabotage team entered the island, which was protected by only a few private guards, and set off explosives, detonating the munitions. At 2:08 a.m., a huge explosion rocked the New York area. All over Manhattan and Brooklyn windows fell from buildings and people ran into the streets in panic. The Brooklyn Bridge swayed, terrifying motorists driving across it. The shock from the blast was felt as far south as Philadelphia. An even larger explosion followed half an hour later. Shells and shrapnel rained down on Ellis Island, and the immigrants there had to be evacuated to the mainland. When police arrived in lower Manhattan, burglar alarms were ringing in every block. Thousands of New Yorkers watched from their side of the Hudson as huge fires burned on the Jersey side. At least six people were killed, and a number of itinerants who slept near Black Tom simply disappeared. Had the Germans used stronger explosives, they might well have destroyed buildings in Hoboken, Jersey City, and Manhattan.

Bruce Bielaski of the Bureau of Investigation, always a day late and a dollar short, assured his Washington superiors that it had been an accident. British intelligence, with its much larger resources, determined that the saboteurs were Kurt Jahnke, a German intelligence officer who had been stationed in Mexico before the war, and Lothar Witzke, a German naval cadet who had been interned after his ship was scuttled off Chile. He escaped and made his way to the United States, where he placed himself at the service of the German sabotage ring. A third saboteur, Michael Kristoff, was an Austrian who worked at Black Tom.

Once the United States entered the war, members of the German spy and sabotage rings fled to Mexico. The security forces strengthened themselves by enlisting thousands of U.S. citizens as "Secret Service operatives" for Bielaski's Bureau of Investigation, many of them from a private group known as the American Protective League (APL), thus infuriating the official U.S. Secret Service. The NYPD formed a close association with the military intelligence division, and Nicholas Biddle was commissioned a colonel in charge of the New York office, while he continued to command a squad of NYPD detectives.

Under the espionage law passed in 1917 and a sedition law passed the following year, it became illegal to criticize virtually any aspect of the U.S. war effort. Thousands of volunteers from the APL surreptitiously entered offices of individuals suspected of opposition to the war. Anyone found guilty of such a thing was sent by administrative order to a detention facility at Fort Oglethorpe, Georgia. Finally, Bielaski instituted large-scale "slacker drives" in a number of American cities. These involved police, servicemen, federal agents, and citizen volunteers stopping individuals on the street and demanding to see their draft papers. Those who could not produce them were arrested. Many of those stopped had left their draft papers at home. Others were young boys, big for their age, or embarrassed off-duty cops who had left their badges at home. Older men whose vanity had caused them to dye their hair black now regretted their decision. All of these were held in crowded police lockups where they stood for hours waiting for someone to come and identify them. So many innocents were seized that a storm of criticism landed on Bielaski and he would soon pass from the scene.

After the armistice, the security forces faced a new challenge from American radicals who staged riots and set bombs in a number of American cities. In one instance a man carrying a bomb up the steps of the Washington home of U.S. attorney general A. Mitchell Palmer stumbled and blew himself up. If the blast had occurred a few minutes earlier, it would have injured or killed his neighbors Franklin and Eleanor

Roosevelt as they were walking home. It was generally believed that the bomber was an individual from an anarchist group in Boston led by Luigi Galleani, a lawyer and man of high culture who edited a small anarchist paper called *Cronaca sovversiva* (Subversive comment). Galleani was eventually deported from the United States, but his group, including Nicola Sacco and Bartolomeo Vanzetti, continued in operation.

The key government figure during the Red Scare was a night-school lawyer, J. Edgar Hoover, who had never served as a detective, military officer, or intelligence agent. Hoover found it difficult to win respect from more experienced people. Later on in his long career, he would always resent anyone who disagreed with him. In many ways he was a new kind of detective chief. He did not go out with his men or make arrests. Instead, he sat in his office, where he instituted a number of administrative procedures and showed a great ability to develop secret files. As a college student he had worked in the Library of Congress, where he learned how to categorize large amounts of material. He used this system to compile the names of sixty thousand suspects for his agency to keep an eye on. It was a huge amount of power for a young man from a modest Washington civil service family. It made Hoover equal to experienced detective chiefs like Flynn.

In general, U.S. security efforts in World War I were thought to be amateurish, and had it not been for the assistance of the more sophisticated British intelligence, there would have been even more failures in the Americans' work.

Wall Street, 1920

At noon on September 16, 1920, just as workers were heading for lunch, a bomb left in an old horse-drawn wagon outside the headquarters of J. P. Morgan at 23 Wall Street exploded, killing thirty-eight people and wounding scores more. NYPD police commissioner Richard Enright, following the traditional police practice of "throwing Blue at the problem," sent seventeen hundred cops into the narrow streets of lower Manhattan. If there had been a second bomb, as was common in other countries, it would have killed many of the responding officers. To add to the confusion, the management of the U.S. Assay Office, which handled $1 billion in gold every day, called for troops to be sent to the scene. So a regiment stationed on Governors Island boarded a vessel, landed in Manhattan, and double timed into Wall Street with bayonets fixed.

The porters at the assay office had just finished carrying gold into the building and had shut down for lunch. A police lieutenant suspected the explosion was a diversion to permit robbers to stage a holdup, so he commandeered every bluecoat in the vicinity and told them to form a line in front of the assay office and draw their guns.

Former police commissioner Arthur Woods had returned from the war a colonel, but his services were not required with any law enforcement agency. So he spent most of his time helping out at the firm of his in-laws, the Morgans. It had been assumed that in 1921 he would get a top job in law enforcement in Washington when Theodore Roosevelt, whom everybody expected to run for president in 1920, took office. However, Roosevelt had died in January 1919. Woods still hoped that his good record as commissioner and his connection with the House of Morgan would lead him back into some prominent post. Now he immediately went down to the Morgan building, where he found there had been considerable damage. A woman's head, with her hat still on it, was plastered to the wall outside the building. Inside, a Morgan administrator had been killed and other people injured.

Another man who heard the explosion was private detective chief William Burns. Once he been hailed as a genius and the American Sherlock Holmes. But during the pre-1917 period he had made the mistake of taking some business from the Germans and also had been found guilty of breaking into a law office and installing a Dictaphone. Burns hurried down from his office in the Woolworth Building to the site of the bombing and began talking to reporters. The shrewdest of all lawmen, he started planning how to use the explosion to step back into the limelight.

William Flynn and J. Edgar Hoover immediately boarded a train in Washington for New York. The presidential election was scheduled to take place in two months and everybody knew that it would result in a

Republican landslide. Thus the Wilson administration in Washington was tired and eager to leave. Atty. Gen. A. Mitchell Palmer, who had ordered the "Red raids" that led to the deportation of hundreds of radicals in anticipation that it would sweep him into the White House, now had little to say and gave direction of the bureau to Flynn.

America's top lawmen would vie for a major role in the Wall Street investigation. The first was New York police commissioner Richard Enright. As president of the Lieutenants Association, he had been outspoken in criticizing Comm. Arthur Woods and was passed over three times for captain before being sent to man a desk in a Flatbush precinct. The mayor's Tammany advisor, Grover Whalen, suggested Enright for police commissioner, and he was summoned to city hall. When told of his promotion above all the captains, inspectors, and deputy chiefs in the department, Enright was stunned. When the phone rang he immediately jumped to answer it, saying, "Lieutenant Enright speaking." Whalen assured him he was no longer a desk lieutenant.

The key figures in the NYPD investigation were Chief of Dets. Bill Leahy (soon to become chief inspector) and Det. Insp. John Coughlin (who would then be named chief of detectives.) The prewar NYPD security squad, which had gone into the army in 1917 and become the first U.S. Army counterintelligence unit, was back from the war with their commander, Insp. Thomas Tunney. However, Tunney and his squad had been favorites of the previous commissioner, Arthur Woods, and so they were not allowed to resume their work but were sent out chasing pickpockets. The bomb squad was now commanded by Sgt. James T. Gegan. One of his prominent squad members was the ubiquitous Det. Sgt. Irving O'Hara, the mayor's brother-in-law. Mayor Hylan, a puppet of publisher William Randolph Hearst, owed his job to his longtime opposition to the transit agency, which some years earlier had fired him as a motorman after he nearly ran over his boss.

William Burns announced that he had been retained by an unnamed client who offered a $50,000 reward for the capture of the bombers. To be eligible for the reward, an informant had to offer the information to the Burns agency exclusively. Some people believed the money was put up by the House of Morgan through Arthur Woods, while others thought that Burns himself was the client. If Woods did link Morgan with the Burns agency, it was a smart move. Burns was a Republican from Columbus, Ohio, and well-connected politically. In a few months, under the presidency of Warren Harding, the "Ohio gang" would take over the national government. Thus it was likely that Burns would have a lot to say about federal law enforcement. Woods himself was qualified to be director of the Bureau of Investigation, chief of the U.S. Secret Service, or commissioner of Customs, the latter two Treasury agencies that interacted with the House of Morgan. Without Teddy Roosevelt to sponsor him, the fact that Woods had served in Mayor Mitchel's liberal Democratic administration probably made him anathema to conservative Republicans. Still, one would think that the connection to the House of Morgan would trump everything else.

The various detectives never agreed on a theory of the case. Some thought the wagon had been transporting dynamite to a construction site and had accidentally exploded. Another group thought it was a cover for robbery.

Postal inspectors checked mailboxes in the area and found that sometime between the 11:15 and 11:30 a.m. pickups, five circulars had been deposited in a box that was a two-minute walk from the blast. Each contained a slightly different message, such as

REMEMBER
WE WILL NOT TOLERATE
ANY LONGER
FREE THE POLITICAL PRISONERS
OR IT WILL BE SURE DEATH FOR ALL OF YOU
AMERICAN ANARCHIST FIGHTERS

Several such circulars had been left at some other bombing scenes, including Attorney General Palmer's house. The discovery of the flyers made robbery or accident less likely explanations.

Burns believed the bombing was the work of Communists, who had recently seized power in Russia and were advocating a world revolution.

Flynn and Hoover had been investigating the Galleanists in Boston, and it was first thought that the bombing was revenge for the deportation of the group's leader. The circulars in the mail would also seem to point to the Galleanists, since they were anarchists who, by definition, were enemies of the Bolsheviks.

Edwin P. Fisher, a forty-two-year-old lawyer and former tennis champion who had once been a mental patient, had told friends weeks before the blast to stay away from Wall Street until after September 16 because sixty thousand pounds of explosives were going to blow up. He was taken into custody in Canada and brought back to New York. When he arrived at Grand Central Station he was wearing two complete business suits, one on top of the other, with a white tennis costume underneath. He told reporters he always wanted to be prepared for a game. As he was led through the station, he stopped to pick up three discarded cigars, declaring that although he didn't smoke he would keep them anyway. Detectives immediately pounced on them, expecting to find a message to Fisher from his confederates. Instead they turned out to be cheap cigars and nothing was found linking Fisher to the case.

In 1921, when the Harding administration took over the White House, Burns was named to replace Flynn as director of the Bureau of Investigation and J. Edgar Hoover was appointed assistant director. Burns announced that the man responsible for the bombing was a Polish anarchist named Wolf Lindenfeld, who, when arrested in Warsaw, confessed that he had carried out the act on the orders of the Communist International. He then repudiated his confession, and it was disclosed that he had previously been in the employ of the Burns agency. Russian Communists, who were new to the American scene, usually did not participate in bombings, preferring to concentrate on ferreting out U.S. industrial secrets and building disciplined cadres for the day they could seize power. At the time, the Soviet Union was trying to achieve diplomatic recognition from the United States, so it was highly unlikely Communist agents would have carried out the bombing. The failure to distinguish Communists from other radicals seemed to be a permanent weakness of the police right on through the 1960s and 1970s, when student protesters were mistaken for agents of Moscow or Havana.

Officially the Wall Street bombing case remains unsolved. Current researchers now concur that a Galleanist named Mike Boda or Buda probably set the bomb and then fled the country. Boda was a radical comrade of Sacco and Vanzetti, once such great heroes of the Left that a generation ago the governor of Massachusetts, Mike Dukakis, issued a proclamation exonerating them. Today they are not talked about very much.

Burns's acceptance of the Bureau of Investigation directorship led to a sad ending to his career. He was indicted for having his agents trail U.S. senators as a part of investigation of the Teapot Dome scandal. Hoover, who had been made assistant director of the bureau, managed to convince people he had no knowledge of such activity and, on the recommendation of Larry Richey to Atty. Gen. Harlan Fiske Stone, became director himself at the age of twenty-nine.

A Day at the Fair, 1940

The New York World's Fair of 1939 was meant to celebrate the 150th anniversary of the founding of the United States and to promote international peace and friendship. Unfortunately, it was held the year that World War II broke out. The fair, which was very popular, was a shot in the arm for the American people after ten years of depression. So it reopened in 1940 despite the fact that the United States was gearing up its national defense effort.

On Thursday, July 4, huge holiday crowds flocked to the site of the fair in Flushing Meadows, Queens. Two days earlier an anonymous phone call had been received at the British Pavilion warning that "the place is going to be blown up." Security was provided by private guards and an NYPD detail that operated out of a substation on the grounds. After the warning was received, the number of police officers assigned to keep an eye on the pavilion was increased and detectives were told to mingle with the crowds in the area.

At 3:30 p.m. on July 4 an electrician was working in a room on the second floor of the pavilion, where the air-conditioning controls were located, when he noticed a small (twelve-by eighteen-by-six-inch) canvas overnight bag sitting unattended. When he leaned down to examine it, he thought he heard ticking within. Even with a world war raging and spy plots making the news every day, the electrician concluded that it was probably just a radio that had been left behind; so he carried it down through a crowd of fifteen hundred people to the office of his supervisor. Then, in typical British fashion, everybody in the chain of command at the pavilion was notified and they gathered in a large room. The bag with the ticking clock was put in with them. Finally, someone thought to inform the NYPD. Two detectives who had been assigned outside were the first to respond. The fair security staff suggested the bag be doused with water, but Det. Fred Morlock explained that if it were an electric bomb the water might cause it to explode. In fact, two weeks earlier a device of that type had been left at a German commercial agency in downtown Manhattan. Morlock suggested that the bag be removed from the pavilion. So it was carried to an area fifty yards from the nearest building and placed alongside a cyclone fence that enclosed the grounds. At 4:45 p.m. bomb-squad detectives Joseph Lynch and Ferdinand Socha arrived on the scene.

The bomb squad had changed over the years since Petrosino had founded it in 1903. After World War I, it was incorporated into the NYPD Radical Bureau, and in 1935 it was combined with the forgery squad. Its detectives still lacked protective gear or special equipment, so they proceeded as best they could. They stood the bag on its end and cut a small hole in it, so they could look inside. When they peered in they saw sticks of dynamite. Detective Morlock walked over to a group of pavilion officials to notify them about the finding. Suddenly, there was an explosion. Detective Socha lost both feet and Detective Lynch was completely mangled. Both died from their wounds. Two other severely wounded detectives attempted to crawl away from the scene on their hands and knees. A patrolman and another detective were also injured, though less seriously. People at the fair heard the noise and thought it was just part of the Fourth of July fireworks, until police and fire units began pouring onto the grounds. Comm. Lewis Valentine and Mayor Fiorello

La Guardia both arrived. At headquarters, Chief Insp. Lou Costuma assembled a meeting of detectives and top brass. Costuma was noted as one of the toughest cops on the force. He had been chosen as chief inspector because American fascists had been beating up Jews around New York, and the cops did little about it. So La Guardia reasoned that bringing in a man of the Jewish faith like Costuma would reassure his coreligionists. Costuma knew that German Bundists and other pro-Nazi groups assembled nightly at open-air meetings in Columbus Circle, on the southwest corner of Central Park. So he assembled a squad of detectives to pick up every Nazi sympathizer there and bring them down to headquarters for a "third-degree" interrogation.

In the meantime, investigators concluded that if the bomb had gone off where it was originally placed, it would have destroyed the pavilion's roof supports, bringing the whole structure down. More than one thousand people would have been killed or severely injured.

There were a number of possibilities for the bombers. At the time, Germany was trying to keep the United States out of the war, and for its agents to kill one thousand Americans would not have been a very good idea. Nevertheless, a few detectives still argued for the Germans because some of their agents were loose cannons. Just before the bombing, one of them, Fritz Joubert Duquesne, had asked his superiors for permission to blow up President Roosevelt while he was attending church services in Hyde Park. It was also possible the bomb was in retaliation for the one set at the German commercial office in downtown Manhattan. At the time, the Germans worked closely with the Irish Republican Army (IRA), which was conducting a terror-bombing campaign in England in an attempt to force the British out of Northern Ireland. The chief of staff of the IRA, Sean Russell, was in New York when the bomb went off, receiving treatment for a serious illness. With the aid of the Nazis, he eventually reached Berlin but supposedly died on a German U-boat while being transported to Ireland. There were others who claimed he was murdered by either the Germans or the British Secret Service to silence him. Most of the IRA support came from the United States, and had it been revealed that IRA agents had set the bomb, support for their organization would have dried up and the U.S. government would have cracked down on the group's activities.

As might be expected, there were the usual rivalries and missed signals among the various investigative agencies. Commissioner Valentine announced that some bombs found in Philadelphia had been meant for the Republican National Convention, which was being held in that city. The Philadelphia Police Department denied the accuracy of the story. The Pennsylvania State Police would only confirm that there was a plot to assassinate their governor, and Hoover's FBI, which disliked the whole idea of the NYPD having a security investigative force, issued confusing statements.

Fritz Duquesne was the type to plant a bomb at the world's fair. He moved among a higher class of people than the usual Nazi agents. He took up with a non-German businesswoman who helped him in contacting U.S. corporations to obtain information on products of interest to the Third Reich. But at the time of the bombing he was under FBI surveillance. In June 1941 it was becoming clear that war was imminent. So the FBI rounded up twenty-nine Nazi spies in New York City, including Duquesne. Brought to trial in federal court, he was sentenced to eighteen years' imprisonment.

If the world's fair bomb had been set by German agents, files on it likely would have been found in Nazi archives after World War II. If the July 4 bombing was an IRA operation, they would have told the world about it by July 6. In both wars, German intelligence officers complained that the Irish were not sufficiently discreet. Frequently, they talked about confidential matters at the top of their lungs in Irish bars, where detectives were listening.

In 1916 the Black Tom bombers were known to British intelligence. In the 1920 Wall Street bombing, the Bureau of Investigation was on the right track in probing the Galleanists. If Burns had stayed out of the case, Flynn's men might have learned of Mike Boda and the Communists would not have been able to exploit Sacco and Vanzetti for their own causes. In 1940, there were no clearly identifiable suspects for the world's fair bombing.

The Murder of Carlo Tresca, 1943

The NYPD had one more unsolved puzzle in World War II. In 1942 Allied troops landed in North Africa, and it was likely that their next destination would be Mussolini's Italy. Before the outbreak of World War II, Mussolini had occupied a very different position in American life than the despised Adolf Hitler. Many Italian Americans admired him. In 1935, when Italy invaded Ethiopia, Mayor La Guardia, a strong antifascist, attended an Italian war relief rally at Madison Square Garden.

Now, in light of the coming occupation of Italy, the U.S. government was trying to pull all Italian factions together. One problem with this was that longtime antifascists would have had to work with men who, until very recently, had strongly supported Mussolini. One man who objected vigorously to this was Carlo Tresca, a veteran radical. Tresca had arrived in the United States in 1904. In Italy he had been a socialist, as was Benito Mussolini, although the two men detested each other. In the United States Tresca became an anarchist. Because he was tall, bearded, and unkempt, with a pronounced Italian accent, he fit the cartoon image of a bomb thrower. As far as is known, he never threw a real one in America, but he hurled plenty of verbal and literary explosives. He used his newspaper, *Il martello* (The hammer), to pound everyone. In addition to the usual denunciations of capitalism, he attacked corrupt labor leaders and their mob allies. His favorite enemy was Mussolini, who in 1931 put Tresca on the official fascist death list. Like anarchist leader Emma Goldman, who was deported in 1919, Tresca believed the Bolshevik government in Russia was a monstrous tyranny, thereby earning a place on the Communists' enemies list. Since World War I, he had been under attack constantly by factions of anarchists that labeled him a police spy. By 1943 Tresca's enemies were legion. Balancing the scale, he also had many friends among the non-Communist Left.

During wartime, New York City maintained a partial blackout. On Monday night, January 11, 1943, lower Fifth Avenue was practically deserted. At 9:30 Tresca and a companion emerged from an office building and crossed to the northwest corner of Fifteenth Street and Fifth Avenue, where they stood talking under a streetlamp. Suddenly, a figure appeared out of the darkness and fired three shots at Tresca, hitting him twice. The gunman then ran to a waiting dark sedan, which raced away. An ambulance removed Tresca to St. Vincent's Hospital, where he was pronounced dead. When cops asked the usual "who done it" questions of Tresca's companion, a man named Calabi, he told them that it was too dark and the attack too swift for him to have had a good look at the assailant. One of the officers found a .38 Police Special revolver behind a trash barrel. A few hours after midnight, a patrolling police squad found a Ford sedan sitting empty near Eighteenth Street and Seventh Avenue, half a mile from the Tresca murder scene. The doors of the vehicle were open, suggesting the occupants had made a quick exit. A state parole officer reported to the police that on the evening of the shooting, he had seen Carmine Galante hop into a vehicle that fit the description of the getaway car. Detectives were dispatched to bring in Galante, and that night they collared him as he left a gambling club on the Lower East Side. His alibi for the time of the murder was that he and a girlfriend, whose name he refused to reveal—"to protect her reputation"—had been in a Broadway movie theater watching *Casablanca*. When asked to describe the film's plot, Carmine could not recall anything about one of the most memorable movies ever made, though he claimed to have seen it twenty-four hours earlier.

Over the years, a consensus has developed that Galante killed Tresca, though there is no agreement as to why. One explanation relates to Italian politics: Tresca was murdered because he would not cooperate with a broad alliance of Italians who wanted to set policy in their native country after the Allies took over.

A second possibility was that he had offended the Mafia by criticizing its leaders and exposing some of its rackets. The individual boss most commonly mentioned in this respect was Frank Garafolo, a man who posed as a civic leader but was mixed up in strong-arm work and drug smuggling. At the time, Garafolo was Galante's capo, or crew chief, in the Bonanno crime family. Another hypothesis links Mafia involvement with Mussolini. In 1936 Vito Genovese, second in command to Lucky Luciano, had fled to Italy because prosecutor Tom Dewey was on the verge of indicting him for murder. Genovese's flight and Luciano's conviction by Dewey opened the way for Frank Costello to become the most important mob figure in New York. In Italy, Genovese maintained a lavish lifestyle but was totally dependent on the favor of Mussolini's government. In the 1920s the dictator had carried on a war against the Mafia, jailing hundreds of them, killing some, and pushing more into exile. At any time he might decide to throw Genovese into prison—or worse. According to some accounts, Genovese arranged to have Tresca murdered in order to curry favor with the dictator. As Luciano later told a biographer, "God dammit if Vito doesn't put out a contract from Italy on Tresca." However, various researchers tend to discredit Luciano's supposed allegation.

Another theory was that Soviet agents had Tresca killed because he continued to denounce them and posed an obstacle to their plans for gaining increased influence in Italy. A few years before his own death, Tresca had accused the Soviets of murdering a prominent New York Communist, socialite, and former Columbia professor named Juliet Stuart Poyntz. A founding member of the American Communist Party, she always adhered to Moscow's line. In 1934 she went to the Soviet Union, where, according to informed sources, she was trained for espionage duty by the GRU, the Soviet military intelligence agency. When she returned to New York, she began telling her friends that she could no longer support Stalin's regime because she was shocked by what she had seen at the Moscow treason trials of "old Bolshevik" leaders. In June 1937 Poyntz dropped out of sight. Not until six months later did her lawyer inform the police that she was missing from her apartment at the American Women's Association on West Fifty-Seventh Street. When an NYPD detective went there, he found her clothing hanging in the closet, her lingerie in the drawers, her passport in a desk drawer, and food left on the kitchen table.

In 1938 Tresca told the U.S. Attorney's office that he believed Poyntz had been "lured or kidnapped" to the Soviet Union. According to Tresca, a prominent Communist, formerly a resident of New York and subsequently connected with the secret police in Moscow, was sent specially to the United States for the purpose of delivering her to Moscow. The Poyntz disappearance was never solved. One theory is that she was murdered in New York City and buried behind the wall of a house in Greenwich Village. The police did not devote much time to trying to solve the Poyntz disappearance.

Galante was kept in custody for a year, during which time a police informer was placed in a cell with him. According to the informer, Galante admitted the murder. But because he had been used as a witness so many times by the district attorney, New York courts had ruled the informant's testimony could no longer be introduced in criminal proceedings. A committee of Tresca's friends was organized to press the authorities to solve the murder. It included such men as Norman Thomas, perennial socialist candidate for president of the United States, and Roger Baldwin, leader of the American Civil Liberties Union. On several occasions they inquired of the district attorney whether some aspect of politics, foreign or domestic, was preventing an arrest in the case.

In retrospect, the most likely explanation for Tresca's murder is that it was Mafia connected. Some prominent Italian Americans who before the war had praised Mussolini wanted to silence him. Although not regarded as gangsters, they had organized-crime connections that would have enabled them to put out a contract on someone. Galante was eventually released and rose to be the boss of the Bonanno crime family. In 1979 he was murdered during a power struggle within the New York mob world. If he ever revealed who was behind the hit on Tresca (and given his low rank at the time, he might not have known), the information has never been made public by law enforcement. Like the world's fair bombing, the Tresca murder gradually faded away. In both cases, a solution could have been embarrassing to many important people.

11

The Black Dahlia Murder
and Parker's Police

The LAPD's Greatest Mystery

On January 15, 1947, at 11:07 a.m., in response to a call from a woman pedestrian, the LAPD radio broadcast: "390 W 4015 in an empty lot one block east of Crenshaw between 39th and Coliseum Streets. Investigate code 2." Translated, the call meant a drunken woman (390 W) was indecently exposed (4015), and code 2 ordered the officers to respond quickly but without the use of the red light and siren. Supposedly, the call was originally broadcast as a man down, but it made no difference as long as the address was correct. The patrol car that caught the job was manned by Frank Perkins and William Fitzgerald of the University Division. Upon arrival, the first thing they observed was two men standing over what appeared to be a body. So both officers readied their revolvers. The men turned out to be a *Los Angeles Examiner* reporter and his photographer, who heard the call while driving in their radio-equipped car. Back then, the city had five newspapers and there was intense competition among them. Reporters in radio cars were one means of scooping the opposition.

"Hell, someone's cut this girl right in half!" Perkins exclaimed, and he told Officer Fitzgerald to put a radio call through to Lt. Paul Freestone, the watch commander on duty at University Station. In the meantime, the *Examiner* reporter, William Randolph Fowler (son of the famous writer Gene Fowler, who had named him for the owner of the newspaper where young Fowler now worked), went to the nearest pay phone and called city editor Jim Richardson. At first Richardson didn't believe it, but then he told Fowler to come into the office with photos and start preparing a front-page story.

Lieutenant Freestone dispatched Det. Lt. Jesse Haskins and Det. S. J. Lambert to the scene. Haskins noted the body was cold, white, and drained of blood. Since there was no blood on the grass, the murder had to have been committed elsewhere, and the corpse dumped there. Lieutenant Haskins, a division detective, received a call from Capt. Jack Donahoe, commanding officer of central homicide, who told him that the homicide response car was tied up and he was sending Sgt. Marty Wynn to the scene. When contact was made with the response car, manned by Sgts. Harry Hansen and Finis Brown, they were told to drop everything and proceed to Thirty-Ninth and Crenshaw and take over. Hansen had been running homicide investigations for a long time. Brown was also a veteran detective and the brother of "Thad" Brown, who was touted to be the next commander of detectives and possibly even chief of police.

When the homicide car arrived about noon, Sergeant Hansen did not like what he saw. Reporters had been allowed to trample all over the crime scene, and they had discarded cigarette butts and burned-out flashbulbs. The street had not been blocked off, and spectators were beginning to overflow onto the grass. Hansen ordered the University Division cops to clear the area and called Ray Pinker, the department's chemist and a crime scene expert. Along with Pinker came his boss, Lt. Lee Jones, commanding officer of the scientific investigation division.

Marty Wynn, a star detective, was close to Jack Webb, the actor, and was one of the first to suggest that Webb put together the real-life detective show that became *Dragnet*. Both Pinker and Jones, played by actors, were occasional characters in the series. It was a lucky break for Webb that he was sponsored by one of the dominant cliques of the department. Webb never became so successful, however, that he forgot his show rested on the favor of the LAPD.

Central homicide always took the big cases, no matter where they occurred. This meant that Captain Donahue was the most powerful figure in this case and Hansen and Brown were his boys. In policing it was important not only that the crime be solved but that it be solved by the right people. If someone outside the inner circle broke the case, it might lead to a shift in power within the organization.

Hansen declared that he had never seen a body so brutally mutilated as the one in the lot. The scene was so shocking that he had to stop a moment and compose himself. There were rope marks on the victim's neck, wrists, and ankles and severe bruises on the right side of her forehead, as though she had been repeatedly struck by a blunt instrument. Both cheeks had been slashed open from the corners of the mouth to the earlobes. Her breasts had been partially mutilated, and her arms were bruised, bent at right angles, and extended back above the shoulders. Her legs had been spread apart, and there were knife marks in the pubic area and on the upper legs. Perhaps most importantly, the body had been bisected at the waist in a neat and surgical manner, and some of the inner organs had been removed. The way the body had been placed indicated that it was posed and that the killer had left her just inside the lot so that she would be discovered by someone walking on the sidewalk. There was an empty cement sack near the body, and the detectives concluded that it had been used to transport the dead girl from a vehicle to the grass.

Police canvassing the vicinity of the crime found a newsboy who said he had seen an automobile at the murder site around four o'clock in the morning, when he was starting to make his rounds, but it drove off after a few minutes. Another witness believed it was about 6:30 a.m. when he saw an old, black Ford sedan. If the car had been near the scene twice, possibly it was to look for something that had been lost there the first time. Going over the ground, detectives found a man's wristwatch in the weeds near the body. It was not weathered and therefore did not appear to have been there long. Possibly, one of the persons who had dropped off the body had discovered his watch was missing and went back to the site to look for it.

At three o'clock in the afternoon, Fowler's paper, the *Los Angeles Examiner* (one of two papers in Los Angeles owned by Hearst), hit the streets with the story. It described the murderer as a "werewolf fiend."

LAPD detectives were able to take prints from the victim, but they could not forward them to the FBI in Washington because a storm there had knocked out the wires. The *Examiner* generously offered to allow the cops to use their new, special photo-transmission machine. Of course, that would give the paper the lead on the name of the victim. Not long after the FBI received the prints, they identified them as belonging to Elizabeth Short, twenty-two, originally from Massachusetts. She was five foot five, 120 pounds, blue eyes with dyed black hair. Short was not some downscale person, as with the typical victims of the Cleveland Butcher, but someone who could be turned by the press into an interesting figure. Of course, it would have been better if she had been a movie starlet, but she would do.

Examiner editor Richardson ordered a rewrite man to call Short's parents in Massachusetts, tell them she had won a beauty contest, and ask for details about her. The man assigned was almost ready to quit rather than carry out such a task, but he gave in and called. He spoke to Short's mother while Richardson listened and prompted him to ask various questions. Finally, Richardson allowed his man to tell the family the truth and say the *Examiner* would fly them out to Los Angeles to help in the investigation. Another lie, because Richardson just wanted to keep them away from other reporters.

While the story dominated the headlines for days, it was not an unusual event. Wartime America had seen thousands of young women go on the road. The experience provided a change from their routine lives, and with the Depression over, waitress and shop-girl jobs were easy to find. The men they met were not down-and-outers but the cream of young American manhood, men who had donned a military uniform. Los Angeles, a city filled with servicemen, had a pleasant climate and afforded access to Hollywood. Many young women believed the story that a girl having a soda at Schwab's drugstore in Hollywood might be tapped by a talent scout and offered a movie contract. At least they had heard that was how Lana Turner made it to stardom. In fact, as the daughter of a murdered gambler, she got there because of mob connections.

After ten days of Dahlia headlines, the media coverage dropped from earthshaking to only sensational. Then a package was mailed to the police; in it was the Dahlia's purse, Social Security card, and other items. The most interesting was Short's address book, with one hundred pages ripped out. Cops checked over the other pages, containing two hundred names, but they did not produce any leads. Did the hundred missing pages contain the murderer's name? Was this going to be a case like the London Ripper, where the killer supposedly sent mocking letters to the police?

Los Angeles city government had been cleaned up when reform mayor Fletcher Bowron was elected in 1938, but the police department was not. In 1947 it was being run by Chief C. B. Horrall, who appointed an assistant chief even though there was no such position authorized. Capt. Jack Donahue was commanding central homicide, but his scope of activity ranged widely and he often intervened when big-time gangsters were arrested. The vice squad was another unit with great power. There was also a gangster squad that reported directly to the police chief.

The leading mobster elements in Los Angeles were three in number. Jack Dragna was the local boss of the Mafia. The Mafia from New York and Chicago had been called in by Hollywood moguls in the early 1930s to break strikes. However, when the battle was won, the mob boys did not want to leave. Instead, they set their sights on gaining 50 percent control of Hollywood. In the late 1930s, Bugsy Siegel of New York represented the New York families, and Johnny Roselli was Chicago's man. There was also a non-mafia import from Cleveland named Mickey Cohen, a loudmouth lone wolf who embarrassed organized crime figures and outraged the police, although some of the latter were on his payroll. If the press could not find something colorful to write on any given day, Mickey was always there to fill the need.

The police continually warned against the threat from eastern gangsters, and they allowed their strong-arm squads considerable latitude in dealing with them. According to popular legend, they threw gangsters off a cliff overlooking Mulholland Drive, telling them to get out of town and never come back. While this might have happened on rare occasions, it seems unlikely. Such a fall would have caused serious injury, even death. Where were the hospital and coroner reports? Where were the roving press cars that might have responded to the scene and started asking questions?

During the war years, the U.S. government convicted the leadership of the Chicago mob for extorting money from the Hollywood studios and sent them and their man, Johnny Roselli, to prison. Bugsy Siegel was not involved but instead was active in taking over a large share of the racing wires. A few months after the Dahlia murder, Siegel himself was gunned down by Jack Dragna's boys at the request of Bugsy's eastern friends. Siegel had lost millions of dollars in the construction of the Flamingo Hotel and Casino in Las Vegas. What he didn't lose, his girlfriend, Virginia Hill, stole. After Siegel's untimely death she was "persuaded" to return the money to the New York mob.

The antigangster units were also active in the Dahlia case, and supposedly Finis Brown fed them information. Often the police spent more time spying on each other than they did looking for the killer.

During the investigation, journalists trampled evidence, withheld information, and roamed freely through the police department's offices, sitting at officer's desks and answering their phones. Many tips were not passed on to the police as the reporters who received them rushed out to get "scoops." Florabel Muir was still around and trying to solve the case apart from the police. It was the press that hung the Black Dahlia name on Elizabeth Short after a reporter supposedly learned that was what she was called in a bar where she drank. This discovery (or invention) gave the case a catchy name. It also linked the case to a film Paramount had released the year before, set in Los Angeles and entitled *The Blue Dahlia*, which was about a man who was suspected of killing his wife. With the popular team of Alan Ladd and Veronica Lake as the leads, it did well at the box office.

The first hot suspect the LAPD turned up was one of the many men the victim had known in Los Angeles. Robert "Red" Manley, though married, had been seeing a lot of Short just before her death. Supposedly a military pilot, he turned out to have been an army band musician who had been discharged as a Section 8 (psycho). Captain Donahue called him the best suspect yet. In many communities in those times, the fact that a man who was close to a woman who was murdered was himself officially certified as a psychopath might have led to him being "persuaded" to confess. In which case he would have been executed in the gas chamber or electric chair, on the scaffold, or by a firing squad, depending on what state he was in. The case would have then been marked closed. However, in the Dahlia murder, the Los Angeles press would have checked every facet of the suspect's background and relationships and blown up the police case.

A more sensational theory that many clung to was that the Dahlia was made pregnant by a powerful man and he had tried to force her into getting an abortion. When she resisted, he enlisted the support of the police, who in turn called in gangsters.

During the investigation, the police determined that one man who had known the Dahlia was movie actor Arthur Lake, star of the *Dagwood* series and a genuine Hollywood celebrity. Lake, in turn, was friends with Norman Chandler, publisher of the *Los Angeles Times*, the most important man in the city. According to the story, police contacts (Jack Donahue was always mentioned) obtained the services of Bugsy Siegel, and it was Bugsy and his men who had kidnapped and tortured the Dahlia, with Siegel being the eventual killer. To spice up the story, Lake was married to the "niece" of Marion Davies, William Randolph Hearst's mistress. In fact, everybody in the know believed Mrs. Lake was the illegitimate daughter of Davies and Hearst. It was a great yarn and as a movie would have been a box office sensation, like the 1974 film *Chinatown*.

Anyone experienced in detective work knows that prominent men sometimes get young girls pregnant. However, they usually did not have them killed, but instead bought them off. If the girl continued to bother the VIP, he might ask the police to persuade her to take the money and leave town. The cops would then point out to the girl the legal consequences of engaging in extortion and mention that the women's prison in the state was a really lousy place. Invariably that was enough to get rid of her.

The LAPD allowed a layman to enter their ranks and assume a role in the investigation. Dr. Paul De River, supposedly a top psychiatrist, offered his services to the department, and when a Miami bellboy wrote a letter to the police about the Dahlia case, De River encouraged him to come to LA and assist in the probe. After the young man arrived, he was held incommunicado for days and urged to confess that he was the killer. Finally, he was released and sued the police department. Later, it was disclosed that "Dr." De River was not a medical man and his claim to have attended top schools could not be verified.

Among the red herrings pushed by the police was speculation that the murderer was a lesbian. The department investigators did not actually believe this, but it kept reporters running around on wild-goose chases. As late as 1960, when I was briefed on the Dahlia murder, I was told that it was probably done by a woman. In recent times, LAPD detective Steve Hodel has named his father, a physician, as the killer. However, most people feel his claim does not check out. In another book, a woman claimed that her father was the killer. The famous LA detective John St. John, who worked on the case, declared, "It is amazing how many people offer up a relative as the killer."

While the Dahlia case dragged on with no solution, in 1949 the old police system broke apart. One night Det. Elmer Jackson of the powerful vice squad was sitting in a car on a lonely road with a lady friend when a man attempted to rob them. Jackson managed to draw a gun from his ankle holster and kill the would-be robber. Afterward it was revealed that the lady in the car was Brenda Allen, the city's top madam, boss of 114 prostitutes. Allegedly, she was paying $900 per girl to the police, and the man had not intended to rob the couple but was a hit man sent to kill Allen for not making payoffs to the right local people. After the Allen-Jackson case, the investigation of the Dahlia murder had to proceed along with the various police scandals, gangster wars, and journalistic capers.

The Brenda Allen scandal would spell the end of Chief Horrall. William Worton, a marine general, was made interim police chief.

Worton admitted he did not know whom to trust in the department, so policing continued to be dominated by the central homicide, vice, and antigangster units.

Much of the police efforts at the time were directed against Mickey Cohen. Many people wanted him dead. After he had been shot at a few times, reporters and detectives began trailing him around, waiting to witness his murder. On the night of July 27, 1949, Cohen decided to stop at Sherry's nightclub on the Sunset Strip. Though the strip was in the heart of Hollywood, the county had jurisdiction. Sheriff Eugene Biscailuz ordered his men to stop and search Cohen every time they saw him, which sometimes could be five times in a single night. Yet no deputies were around Sherry's that evening. The place was managed by Barney Ruditsky, who for twenty years had been a New York City gangster-squad detective with a career so fabulous that he became a major character in his hometown. Ruditsky had been at Johnny Broderick's side when, with guns blazing, they had foiled the escape of three convicts who had murdered the warden and a guard at the Tombs jail. After his 1941 retirement, he went to Los Angeles, where he was on friendly terms with gangsters but not the police department. Ruditsky was one of the people who joined Joe DiMaggio, Frank Sinatra, and some top private detectives in a raid to get the goods on DiMaggio's estranged wife, Marilyn Monroe. The private eyes got into the wrong apartment and ended up with a heavy lawsuit on their hands.

Cohen and his entourage arrived at Sherry's about 3:45 a.m. and were observed by reporters and detectives. Fred Howser, the attorney general of California, was in the process of becoming involved with gambling enforcement in Los Angeles by taking over some of the payoffs previously given to the cops. He assigned a bodyguard, a six-foot-six bruiser named Harry Cooper, to accompany Cohen everywhere he went. Also present were Florabel Muir and her husband, a publicity man.

Ruditsky was patrolling outside the place, as he claimed he did every night to protect his customers as they were leaving. But apparently he did not notice two men hiding across the street, both of them armed with shotguns. When Cohen got out of his car they fired seven blasts, striking him in the shoulder, killing his muscleman, Neddie Herbert, wounding one of Mickey's blonde girlfriends, and hitting Florabel Muir in the rear end. The attorney general's bodyguard, Cooper, was severely wounded. Muir later claimed the gunmen were LAPD detectives trying to eliminate Cohen because he knew too much.

Cohen survived, but the cops made life tough for him. Once when he caught a plane for Texas, they wired ahead, and as soon as he arrived, Capt. "Lone Wolf" Gonzaullas of the Texas Rangers put him under arrest. Cohen then got a message from the governor saying, "If you are thinking of coming to Texas, stay out. If you are in Texas, get out." Since everyone knew that notches were common on rangers' guns, Cohen decided to listen to the governor's advice.

Parker's Police

The Brenda Allen case and the various other problems in the postwar LAPD, not the least of which was the failure to solve the Dahlia murder, led to the creation of a new police department, one sometimes ranked as the best in the United States. Two major figures reflected the blend of elements in the new LAPD.

The best features of the old LAPD could be summed up in the career of Thaddeus "Thad" Brown, a Missouri miner who had worked for seventeen and a half cents an hour. With local prospects dismal, he moved from Joplin, Missouri, to Los Angeles. In January 1926 he joined the LAPD. Eventually he teamed up with a veteran detective from Oklahoma, W. A. "Pappy" Neely, who only had a sixth-grade education but was a shrewd investigator. For a dozen years before 1940, Brown worked in the detective bureau, where he handled a variety of cases, particularly homicides. His style was not that of a hard-charging Dirty Harry but of a folksy schmoozer who persuaded people that "fessing up" was the best thing to do. As a lieutenant at the start of World War II, Brown was the department's liaison with the armed forces. During the war, crime zoomed up in Los Angeles, and the total number of annual murders rose to seventy-eight (about the same number that would occur in some months later in the century). In 1943 Brown was promoted to captain

THE BLACK DAHLIA MURDER

and put in charge of homicide. Always popular with cops and crime reporters, he rose to be chief of detectives five years later. In 1950, when the city sought a new police chief to replace interim chief General Worton, Brown was the choice of three of the five police commissioners.

Brown's only real rival for the position of chief was William H. Parker, who had come to Los Angeles in the mid-1920s and had driven a cab while he attended law school at night. In 1927 he joined the LAPD. As Brown would later observe, "Parker never worked the detective bureau in all his years on the force. . . . As a matter of fact, outside of traffic work, he never did much police work at all." Most of his assignments were administrative. As a lieutenant, he ran Chief Davis's office during the Shaw administration, although none of the corruption of that time washed over onto him. Essentially Parker bided his time, waiting for the day when the Los Angeles power elite would realize that to be a world-class city would require a modern police department. After World War II service as a military police captain in Europe, Parker returned to the department and headed the internal affairs section under General Worton.

No one ever found Parker a warm colleague; rather, they described him as a harsh and extremely ambitious man. Though General Worton was desirous of being named the regular police chief, under a law devised by Parker in his capacity as a Police Protective Association lobbyist, the candidates were confined to ranking officers of the LAPD.

Parker finished first in the examination and Brown second. So the choice was clear: an honest, hard-working veteran detective versus an administrative type always scheming to gain personal advantage. Brown finally removed himself from the running, telling friends he would much rather have Parker standing in front of him than behind him, ready to put a knife in his back. The LAPD was headed for a new regime and a new era, but it would continue some of the methods of the old.

There was much to admire in Parker's policing system. His force of only forty-five hundred officers covered 455 square miles, the largest area of any metropolis in the United States. New York had five times as many officers. Part of the reason Parker could get by with so few cops was that the department was highly selective in the recruits that it accepted. Only one out of twenty-five applicants was appointed to the force, whereas in some cities, almost anyone who could pass the height exam and had a little political influence could make it. LA cops were strictly supervised and discipline was tight. An officer who gained a few pounds after being appointed was called on the carpet and ordered to get his weight back to what it had been or lose his job.

The chief's position was civil service, so Parker did not have to worry about being removed by the mayor unless he made a huge error. Because the department was so independent, he made it virtually a fourth branch of government. The city council and the mayor had little choice but to go along with the police. Only the courts issued independent decisions, which the chief routinely denounced.

Parker's great weakness was that he was a falling-down drunk. His bodyguard, Daryl Gates (later chief of police himself), had to carry his boss to bed every night. When word reached the conservative Republican who was mayor of the city, he called in Parker and threatened that if he did not stop drinking so heavily, he would report the fact to the city elite. This would have meant Parker's dismissal. So the chief cut down on his drinking, but it made him more difficult than ever to deal with.

From the days of Det. Lefty James around World War I, through "Roughhouse" Brown and his partner "Sweety" Sweetnam in the 1920s, to "Red" Hynes's outfit and Mayor Shaw's intelligence unit, the department always had a strong-arm squad to crack down on gangsters, radicals, and enemies of the regime. Its modern version, the gangster squad, was kept intact and utilized by Chief Parker. One new feature in the 1950s was an airport squad, which covered incoming planes bringing eastern gangsters to Los Angeles. The usual procedure was to grab them as they got off the plane, take them into the men's room, push their head under the faucet, and put them back on an outgoing plane. Parker created a powerful intelligence division and placed it under the command of his confidant Capt. Jim Hamilton. He also managed to have all the information in the intelligence files legally designated as the property of the chief, so that they could not be subpoenaed by any individual or agency.

When two out-of-town stickup men, Tony Trombino and Tony

Brancato, were murdered in LA, the media played it up big. It annoyed Parker that someone would dare to pull that kind of hit in his town. The reason for the killing was probably that the two Tonys had stuck up a gambling game in mob-controlled Las Vegas and were getting punished for it. It was not the custom in Vegas to shoot people there, because it would scare off tourists. So the mobsters usually waited until their target went somewhere else, which was often Los Angeles, and plugged him there. Parker and Hamilton took charge of the investigation and held the suspects for five days at a downtown hotel while they were questioned. It was generally believed that the shooter was Jimmy "the Weasel" Fratiano, a Los Angeles gunman out of Cleveland, available to do hits for out-of-town gangs. But he did not confess.

The intelligence squad also went after critics of the LAPD. The usual method was to uncover some of a man's lady friends or the fact that he had once belonged to a far-left organization. It was intelligence that gave Parker a means of control. In an age when information was increasingly necessary to hold power, the various LAPD units furnished plenty of it to the chief, which he used as he saw fit. While the detective bureau handled the routine criminal investigations, it was the intelligence and gangster squads that supplied the lifeblood of the Parker administration.

In 1961, when Sam Yorty, a leftist firebrand since the 1930s with a thick dossier in the chief's intelligence files, was elected mayor there was some worry that he would crack down on the police department. Instead, he shrewdly calculated that it was better to be pro-police than anti-police and became a strong supporter of Parker and the LAPD.

In the 1960s Parker assigned Det. John St. John to review the Dahlia case. St. John received the nickname Jigsaw John after putting together the pieces of a body that had been cut up. He was so highly regarded that the chief awarded him detective badge number one, and his assignment was meant to show that the department was working diligently on the Dahlia case. However, according to contemporaries, St. John largely spent his time talking to reporters.

In examining the Dahlia murder, the key question is not who killed her but why the police did not solve the case and why they continuously put out red herrings for public consumption. Most likely, it was necessary to protect some prominent person who was at least peripherally involved with the Dahlia.

Over the twentieth century, police agencies in Los Angeles, including the sheriff and the district attorney, were known to cover up cases for important people. In the 1920s, Edward Doheny was one of the richest men in America, estimated to have the equivalent of $5 billion in today's dollars. Doheny had been caught up in the Teapot Dome scandal when he allegedly bribed Secretary of the Interior Albert Fall. Doheny's son Ned and Ned's secretary, Hugh Plunkett, were also enmeshed in the case. In January 1929 young Doheny was found shot to death in his Beverly Hills mansion and near his body was Hugh Plunkett, also dead. Neither the Beverly Hills police nor the sheriff wished to handle the investigation, so the district attorney took over.

The generally accepted story is that young Doheny was trying to persuade Plunkett to commit himself to a mental institution so that he would not have to testify in the Teapot Dome trials. Plunkett refused and, according to the official account, he then killed Doheny and shot himself. The district attorney's forensic investigator concluded that it was probably the reverse that was true. Young Doheny had shot Plunkett to protect his father and then committed suicide. For a while the story dominated the front page. Then, suddenly, it disappeared completely, and the district attorney, who had promised to pursue the investigation vigorously and prosecute guilty parties whoever they were, accepted the explanation that it was Plunkett who had killed young Doheny. Not a word was then written about the case in the newspapers. It was a demonstration of how money and power could buy silence, even in murder cases, and no one in the law enforcement system or journalism would dare to object.

In 1931 a former "crusading" assistant district attorney, Dave Clark, shot and killed Charles Crawford and a journalist while talking with them in Crawford's office. At the time Clark was running for municipal court judge and appeared to have a bright future. Throughout the 1920s, Crawford was generally believed to be the fix man for gamblers, bootleggers, and vice operators. Clark claimed that Crawford, who was armed, tried to shoot him and he had fired in self-defense. The general consensus was that, just as the sheriff's office and the district attorney had covered up the Doheny shooting, the LAPD did the same for Clark's shooting of Crawford and the journalist, and he was acquitted.

Later in the twentieth century the LAPD would be confronted with a number of sensational killings that took years to solve. And as the investigations dragged on, other victims were murdered.

Over a four-month period in 1972 and 1973, ten young women were raped and murdered in the hills of northeastern Los Angeles County. The press named the murderer the Hillside Strangler. It turned out that there were actually two Hillside Stranglers operating independently. The case dragged on into the 1980s before arrests were made.

Beginning in 1972, the Trash Bag Murderer killed and mutilated twenty-eight people. Eventually, in 1977, a man named Patrick Kearney was convicted of the crimes. In 1974 a Skid Row Slasher began a series of throat cuttings of nine men, mostly derelicts. Finally, Vaughn Greenwood was convicted and sentenced to life imprisonment for the crimes. Starting in 1974, a so-called Sunset Slayer began killing victims he chose off the Sunset Strip. He particularly liked to shoot out the brains of prostitutes while he was having sex with them. In 1983 Douglas Clark was convicted of six of the murders and sentenced to death. In 1979 police apprehended three men on suspicion of killing at least twenty-two men and young boys. A fourth suspect committed suicide after his arrest. The men's MO was to pick up hitchhikers and hold them in the back of a van, where they were tortured for days. Because most of the victims were strangled and dumped near freeways, journalist began calling the murderer the Freeway Strangler.

At the same time, the LAPD and the county sheriff could never manage to control the Crips and the Bloods, two violent gangs. A young man growing up in the inner city had to choose which one he wanted to belong to. Since one gang wore red and the other blue, they could easily be distinguished. If a person in blue appeared in a red neighborhood, his or her life was likely to be forfeited.

In 1995 the LAPD was embarrassed when the O. J. Simpson case was lost. Essentially, the defense was allowed to hold a trial within a trial about whether LA detective Mark Fuhrman, and by implication the whole police department, was racist and had framed Simpson. The jury apparently bought the story.

Twice the city was consumed by a major riot: Watts in 1965 and the protests against the Rodney King verdict in 1991. In both cases police were slow to respond to the situation and, being unable to control it, had to call out strong military forces. In many instances, the esprit de corps of the police department and its high reputation actually worked against the department's willingness to change strategies and tactics.

Why were there so many problems in the LAPD? The department was not only outwardly impressive, but many of its commanders and other personnel were clearly well above average. It was always near the top of the list of best American police departments. One possible reason was that most police and many residents came to the city from elsewhere. Joseph Wambaugh, the great chronicler of the department, portrayed LA police in his first book as centurions: professional soldiers, like those of Rome, who policed an alien population and, in many cases, were aliens to the city themselves. He also illustrated how the department was dominated by a harsh bureaucracy that often drove, not led, its officers. Los Angeles cops never trusted anyone, except possibly another cop.

Following the Rodney King riots, under Chief Gates the city finally ended the old Parker system of policing. Afterward, police chiefs were confined to two consecutive five-year terms, and public officials had much more input into the department. Police chiefs in Los Angeles were also urged to switch their model from hard-nosed enforcement to community policing.

The same cry was heard in many cities, though there was no form of community policing that actually defined the model. What the future will bring is as uncertain in Los Angeles as in any other city, but the Parker system is, at least for the time being, dead. However, Hollywood and those who are attracted to its lifestyle are still around.

12

The Brink's Robbery

At 7:27 p.m. on January 17, 1950, the first alarm to come into Boston police headquarters was when a caller shouted into the phone, "This is Brink's. We are cleaned out. We are cleaned out." A dispatcher immediately broadcast a message to cars in the First Division: "Calling 1-A, a report of an armed robbery at Brink's 165 Prince Street. Calling 1-O, backup the 1-A car at Brink's." At 7:31 the first patrol car arrived on the scene. There they learned that seven men in masks had held up five Brink's guards, tied them up, and stolen at least $1 million. Soon police cars from every downtown division were on the scene, led by police commissioner Col. Tom Sullivan and department superintendent Edward Fallon. At the same time, reporters were being rousted out of their homes or from bars by city editors and told to go to Brink's.

In 1950 Boston was a quiet place for a city of nearly eight hundred thousand. The ruling elite of the state were still the fading Yankees descended from the Puritans and other early seventeenth-century settlers. The politically powerful group in Boston was the Irish who had come over from their famine-ridden land in the nineteenth century. The two groups did not mix well. To the Yankees, the Irish were a bunch of rowdy hoodlums. They did not take account of the fact that the Catholic Church in Boston was as puritanical as any Yankee congregation. To the Irish, the Yankee Brahmins, sitting atop Beacon Hill, were a bunch of bigoted snobs living off the money and accomplishments of their ancestors.

The police department was an interesting amalgam of the two groups. Traditionally, the civilian commissioner was appointed by a Yankee governor, not the mayor of Boston. The cops were mostly Irishmen, and the superintendent who ran the force was a career officer who was invariably Irish.

The leading Irish family in the city was the Kennedys. In 1914 Joe Kennedy, son of Patrick Kennedy, the political leader of East Boston, married Rose Fitzgerald, daughter of Mayor John "Honey Fitz" Fitzgerald. After World War I, when Joe became a multimillionaire, the family largely lived in places like New York and London and the sons went to Harvard. In 1946 Jack Kennedy was elected to the House of Representatives.

When detectives began questioning the Brink's employees who had been held up and examined the scene, they were amazed at how easily the heist had been pulled off. Around 7:00 p.m., the robbers had picked a few locks and gone up to the second-floor vault room, where they surprised the guards who were counting money. The robbers were wearing masks of cartoon characters like Captain Marvel, navy pea coats, and chauffeur's caps. Some of them tied up the guards while the others scooped up the money and departed. When one of the guards worked loose from his ropes, he managed to hit the ADT alarm and then phoned the police. Standard procedure called for the six bridges that connected downtown Boston to the mainland to be blocked. However, by the time the order was carried out, it was too late to accomplish anything except creating traffic jams.

In the world of law enforcement, the Boston Police Department was not noted for its efficiency or leadership. The only thing it could claim was that it had a higher ratio of police to population than most cities. A generation earlier, the department had been rated by many experts as the best in the country. The commissioner then, Stephen O'Meara, was a retired newspaper publisher who, despite being an Irish Catholic, stood in high favor with the Brahmin elite. In effect, they made him an honorary Yankee. Appointed to the post of commissioner by the governor in 1906, he had run a tight ship. Compared to most Americans cities, there was little corruption, and the police were rarely accused of using excessive force.

In 1918 O'Meara died in the worldwide flu epidemic and was replaced by a Yankee gentleman, Edwin Curtis. During the war, police salaries had been frozen while inflation raged, and after it ended the cops wanted a raise. When they didn't get it, they sought to form a union. The commissioner refused to allow them to have one. As a result, in September 1919 three-quarters of the 1,544 patrolmen on the force went out on strike. Local hoodlums immediately took advantage of the situation, looting stores and engaging in general disorder. The Yankee governor, Calvin Coolidge, ignored requests to settle the strike and instead called out the National Guard. All of the striking police officers were discharged and replaced by World War I veterans.

With the onset of Prohibition and the rise of organized crime, Boston police became just as corrupt as in any other place. In the 1930s William Whyte, in his famous sociological study of Boston youth entitled *Street Corner Society*, presented a chapter on the police. He found the same sort of arrangements as existed elsewhere between police and gamblers. He noted, though, that there was a core of honest officers, and whenever a problem developed, such as a gamblers' shooting war, these men were put in charge of the police department until the crisis passed. Afterward they went back to running the traffic division, teaching recruits, or handling various administrative tasks. Whyte, who knew little of policing, shrewdly calculated that without this core of "untouchable cops" any future scandal would require the complete overhaul of the department by outsiders, something no one wanted in such a traditional city.

In the 1930s Leonard Harrison, a Harvard expert on policing, found a certain smugness about the way the Boston department functioned and a resistance to change. The most powerful local politician in this era was James Michael Curley, who served several terms in Congress, four separate ones as mayor, one as governor, and two prison terms. In

1936 Governor Curley, who was despised by the Brahmins, appointed Irish American Joe Timilty as the civilian police commissioner. Serving under him as superintendent was Edward Fallon, who had joined the force right after the 1919 strike. Both men were in their late thirties when they took over the top jobs.

In 1942 a fire broke out at the popular Cocoanut Grove nightclub, killing nearly five hundred people. In the aftermath, charges were made that fire regulations had been violated by admitting too many occupants to the building and locking exit doors to prevent customers from slipping out without paying their checks. The investigation, led by the attorney general of Massachusetts, then turned into a probe of gambling, resulting in Commissioner Timilty, Superintendent Fallon, and a number of captains being indicted, though not convicted. In 1943, when Timilty's term ended, a popular Yankee governor, Leverett Saltonstall, appointed "Colonel" Tom Sullivan, an Irish Catholic civil engineer and militia colonel, as police commissioner.

This was the police force that was faced with the task of solving the largest cash robbery in American history. Eventually, it was determined that about $2.5 million in cash and negotiable securities had been taken. In many ways, the investigation resembled that of the Rubel heist in New York in 1934.

Boston detectives, like those in other cities, were expected to know the composition of the local underworld and who was likely to have been behind a particular big crime. In 1934 NYPD detectives figured out quickly that the armored car robbery in far-out Brooklyn had its roots in the notorious Hell's Kitchen district on the West Side of Manhattan. In the Brink's case, the grapevine began to hum with the names of local criminals who might have been involved. Detectives put together lists of heist men likely to have taken part in the crime. Among thirty names on the list, ten were the actual robbers. Still, just as it took four years to officially solve the Rubel case in New York, it took six to clear up the Brink's case in Boston. In both instances, many people questioned why it took so long.

In Washington, FBI director J. Edgar Hoover, now the top cop in America, was eager to take charge of the Brink's investigation. On the night of the holdup, two hours after the police arrived on the scene, some stern-looking men in gray suits entered the building. They were FBI agents who had learned of the crime via commercial radio broadcasts, not through notification by the police department. This was not surprising, since the two agencies did not get along. Only at the top, where Colonel Sullivan and FBI special agent in charge (SAC) Ed Souci were on friendly terms, was there any kind of cooperation. Beyond that, Boston cops and FBI men did not trust each other. To further complicate the matter, most of the Boston Police Department didn't like Colonel Sullivan.

Some of the G-men looking around noticed that the money had been wrapped in bands from the Federal Reserve Bank. They gathered those up as evidence of possible federal jurisdiction over the crime. Eventually, the U.S. attorney ruled that there was sufficient legal justification to open an investigation. The bureau created a file on the Brink's case labeled Robink 91-5535 (robbery Brink's, 91 for bank robbery, and 5535 for the number of investigations of this crime since the 1934 federal bank robbery law was enacted). Before the investigation was over, every FBI field office in the country would contribute to it.

Because Boston crooks were not considered big-timers, suspects in other cities were canvassed. Chicago had experienced several recent robberies of Brink's armored cars, and one of them had resulted in the murder of two guards. There, the gunmen had not even given the guards a chance but simply shot them down when they got out of the truck. The men eventually fingered for the Chicago job were no bigger crooks than their opposite numbers in Boston. New York had a lot of good heist men, and it was common for them to go into New England to pull a job. However, New York detectives in squads like safe and loft always had their ear to the ground, and there were no rumbles about local people being involved with the Brink's robbery. Canada had some high-powered robbery gangs, but their MO was not to take a long time planning a job; instead they would come in with guns blazing, pull off the score, and head back to Canada. The chances of southerners or westerners pulling a job in Boston were nil. Most good old boys had learned that what works in Texas brings disaster "up north."

Willie Sutton, who was J. Edgar Hoover's choice as the chief of the robbers, was on the loose, but his MO did not fit the Brink's job. He never would have gotten involved with a large group, and anyone who worked with Willie had to meet his exacting standards. Alternatively, Hoover thought it might be underground American Communists robbing banks to support their cause. That was how Joe Stalin made his name in prerevolutionary Russia. But Communists in the postwar era were not out pulling holdups. Their student imitators in the 1960s tried it and, because they were amateurs, it was usually their downfall. Probably the most famous robbery of that era was of the Brighton Bank in Boston. In 1970 some radical coeds from Brandeis and professional criminals stuck up the bank and killed a policeman. They were all caught and, aside from the one who blew himself up in prison, they were given stiff sentences.

At first, detectives favored some local jewel thieves as the robbers. Cops always overrated jewel robbers. (In one instance, when the chief of detectives of a major city retired, he organized a jewel robbery gang. After a few capers he was caught and sentenced to fifteen years, during which he could contemplate the un-wisdom of his choice.)

One of the men near the top of the list was Anthony Pino, forty-seven, a medium-height, overweight professional thief. Pino was the type who was always joking, even with cops. Born in Sicily and brought as a baby to Boston, it did not take long for him to become involved in crime. At fifteen, while escaping from a burglary, he was shot in the rear end by a Boston police officer. As an adult he was a robber and safecracker and would do any kind of criminal work as long as it would bring him money. But he was not a leader. While other criminals respected his ability to plan a job, he was not the kind of individual who secured instant obedience from other men. He also had a propensity to commit crimes when it wasn't necessary. If he went shopping for underwear, instead of purchasing it, he would steal it. Pino's brother-in-law, Vince Costa, age thirty-six, who was also on the list, would never have had the ability to carry out a crime like Brink's, and he relied on his in-law to keep him working. Both men, though Italian, were from the Irish stronghold of South Boston.

Another Southie man who turned out to be involved in the Brinks job was Thomas "Sandy" Richardson, forty-three, a longshoreman with a long criminal record and a reputation for violence. His pal James Faherty, forty-one, also of Southie, had once stuck up a railroad express truck with a machine gun. The third musketeer was Mike Geagan, forty-two years old, also from South Boston. All three were known as heavy drinkers who liked to spend a lot of time carousing, even though they worked at regular jobs on the docks. They had the toughness to be leaders but not the smarts.

One member of the group was a surprising addition. Adolph "Jazz" Maffie, thirty-nine, was basically a bookmaker with only a minor criminal record. His nickname came from the jazzy way he dressed. He had been a high school football star known for his ability to plunge through the opposing line. Maffie was a man of class and regarded Pino as a slob. If Jazz had been a regular professional criminal, he might have been the best one to lead the gang. But he was essentially a gambler who occasionally liked a thrill.

Then there was Joe McGinnis, forty-seven, a policeman's son from Providence, Rhode Island. McGinnis was tall, powerfully built, and didn't mind whacking people around. He was also clever about the underworld ways, but he was disliked, distrusted by many criminals, and suspected of being a police informant. Still, many later accounts would wrongly label him the leader.

Stanley "Gus" Gusciora, only thirty-one years old, was probably more of a criminal than most of them. He could not conceal his hatred for the police, and he was frequently reckless. Gusciora teamed up many times with Joseph "Specs" or "Speckie" O'Keefe, another denizen of South Boston. Specs, forty-two, was known as a tough holdup man, but some of his colleagues felt there was something wrong with him mentally. He drank heavily and could get very angry.

Two other men were brought on later in the planning stage. Joseph "Barney" Banfield was a getaway car driver, a heavy drinker, and a friend of McGinnis. Henry Baker, forty-four, the only Jewish member of the gang, was an accomplished safecracker and lock picker. Of the group, only O'Keefe, McGinnis, and Pino were capable of being leaders, but the first two scared some of their colleagues for various reasons, and so Pino was allowed to direct the job.

During the planning phase, it was understood that Pino would remain in the robbers' truck with Banfield, and his brother-in-law, Costa, would stay outside as a lookout. That meant they would not have to risk the chance of stopping a bullet inside Brink's and would have a better chance of getting away if an alarm sounded. Most underworld gangs did not have a chief who led from the rear.

Unlike the Rubel gang, who had never worked together, some of the men in the Brink's group teamed up frequently. In 1947 Pino, Geagan, and Richardson, along with two other men, had committed a stickup that netted $110,000, the largest in Boston history up to that date.

One unusual factor about the Brink's job was that the robbers pulled their holdup in the North End, the center of the local Mafia. In a lot of cities that would have upset the mob boys because it meant the FBI would be swarming through the area, bringing a lot of heat with them. In Chicago, there would have been a hefty "mob tax" collected on the proceeds. Although the angle was not explored in the investigation, Joe McGinnis had a relationship with Carlton O'Brien, the longtime leader of organized crime in Providence, Rhode Island. Was McGinnis, with the help of O'Brien, planning to take most of the money after the job went down? We will never know, because O'Brien was assassinated in Providence in 1952, and the leadership of local operations went to Raymond Patriarca, boss of the New England Mafia.

The actual robbery went off smoothly. The robbers found it easy to get into the building and surprise the guards at the vault. Once the doorbell rang, throwing everyone into a panic. But it turned out to be a maintenance man, and when he got tired of waiting for someone to open the door, he entered by another door and went to a remote section of the building to eat his lunch. Pino had been smart to send seven men into the building, because they had a great deal of money, the disguises, and other things to carry out. Even with so much to carry, they were gone for about fifteen minutes before the Brink's employee was able to hit the

ADT alarm and use the phone, bringing police, who broadcast alarms area wide. Most of the gang had made it to their homes or hangouts before the investigation really got underway.

Originally each member of the gang received an advance of $100,000 from the Brink's money. The other $1.5 million was hidden away. Allegedly, McGinnis, who took care of some of the money for the others, held out on them. Jazz Maffie, of all people, had to confess tearfully to Specs O'Keefe, who had given him his $100,000 to hold, that he had lost the money gambling. One plus for the gang was that Boston's run-of-the-mill street criminals, regardless of nationality, subscribed to the Irish hatred of informers. Since the Mafia had its own code of silence, the city was always a difficult place for detectives to work.

To add to the gang's problems, O'Keefe and Gusciora had stuck up the Statler Hotel the day before the Brink's robbery and taken $47,600. So the police were canvassing the city investigating that crime. When Pino heard about it, he was furious. But because he did not command sufficient respect, he could not discipline the two tough guys.

The Boston Police Department's top detective on robberies was Lt. James Crowley, who had been a cop since 1921. There was a Crowley in every big city, a police officer who took charge when a big score went down. They knew every crook and informer in town, though sometimes they knew them too well. After a major heist occurred, they began rattling the bars, that is, questioning their informers and possible suspects. In New York, Lt. Johnny Cordes was the best man on those types of cases. In Chicago, it was Lt. Frank Pape. In St. Louis, it was Lt. Lou Shoulders, who, like the others, was a freewheeling, do-as-he-pleased cop.

Crowley had an odd relationship with Pino. Back in 1936, New Hampshire wished to extradite the gangster for a robbery in their state, but Crowley testified that he had seen him in Boston at the time the crime occurred. Strangely, this situation was to develop again in the Brink's case. Crowley went to see Joe McGinnis on the night Brink's was held up to talk about the Statler Hotel robbery, and while he was there Pino came along. Crowley later testified that he had seen the two men at 7:10 p.m., which would have absolved both of any involvement in the holdup. The FBI flat out did not believe Crowley, and so from the beginning, relationships were poisoned between the Boston Police Department and the G-men.

Among the other members of the Boston Police Department who played a large role in the case was Det. Lt. Frank Wilson, an African American. He could easily pass for white, but as a member of a distinguished, old Boston family (his father was a prominent lawyer for many years), he chose to retain his ethic identification. Wilson was very popular with his colleagues and had been a member of the force for twenty-four years. Eventually he would rise to deputy superintendent in charge of the detective bureau.

To clear the air with the FBI, Commissioner Sullivan should have sent Lieutenant Crowley and his partner to an outlying division with orders not to go near headquarters and instructed the detective bureau that anyone who supplied them with information on the Brink's job would be fired. Instead there was a sort of compromise solution. Frank Wilson, who everybody knew was an absolutely straight cop, was promoted to the rank of captain, but he was too much of a gentleman to be able to control Crowley.

Given that the authorities knew who the leading suspects were, they should have carefully analyzed who might accept a large reward in return for talking. It was not a Mafia affair, so there would be no worldwide manhunt for the squealer. Once he got a thousand miles from Boston, he would be home free. However much the underworld hated informers, some people would talk under the right circumstances, such as an offer of $200,000 in cash (the equivalent of $2 million today) and safe passage out of Boston to some unknown place. On the surface, one of the most likely was Jazz Maffie, the gambler. He was happily married and might not have refused such a large sum of money. The same might be true of Henry Baker, who was not Irish and had a relatively stable background. McGinnis was a man who always looked to help himself rather than his comrades, but any reward he would accept would have to have been larger than $200,000. One problem was that the state and federal prosecutors would have had to agree to any deal, but the U.S. attorney could be ordered to accept one by the attorney general of the United States, and the governor of Massachusetts could have reassigned the case from the district attorney of Suffolk County to the attorney general of the state. However, there was reluctance among the prosecutors to cut a deal, even if it would convict ten robbers.

Within the police department, certain changes were also necessary. Colonel Sullivan himself should have been replaced. An official from the state police, a force that still had a military aura and spent part of their time living in barracks, might have been a good choice for his replacement. State police standards of integrity were higher than in the city force. Other men in New England had distinguished war records. One of the best possibilities would have been Maj. Gen. Ernie Harmon, the famous tank leader of World War II who commanded the U.S. constabulary in occupied Germany. At the time of the robbery, Harmon was serving as head of a military school in nearby Vermont. Harmon's stature as a war hero and his rank in the army would put him on par with a man like J. Edgar Hoover. But no internal changes at the top of the Boston Police Department were contemplated.

Six months after the Brink's heist, Specs O'Keefe and his sidekick Gusciora were arrested in Pennsylvania after Gusciora broke into a sporting goods store and stole five pistols and Specs burglarized a haberdashery, taking away luggage and new clothing. The FBI had alerted police departments outside of Boston that O'Keefe and Gusciora were on their way back from the west. Gusciora received five to twenty years for the gun thefts and Specs got three years for the burglary he committed. Gusciora's sentence was exceptionally long, and it was possible that the FBI discussed his case with the judge.

The FBI investigation faced a deadline. The federal statute of limitations on robbery ran only three years, so on January 17, 1953, the agency's official jurisdiction in the case would end. Hoping to break the impasse, the U.S. government impaneled a grand jury and summoned all the robbery suspects before it. O'Keefe was sent to jail for refusing to answer questions, but the grand jury was unable to determine that the other members of the gang were lying. Despite the tolling of the federal statute of limitations, the FBI remained on the case in a big way, but they were somewhat subordinate to state prosecutors, who operated under a six-year statute of limitations.

In 1954 O'Keefe was released from jail in Pennsylvania, but Gusciora was still held there. O'Keefe contacted Henry Baker and asked him for money. When Baker refused, the two men got into a gun battle, but both missed their target. O'Keefe was now seen as a menace to the gang, and Pino called for a professional New York hit man to deal with him. Elmer "Trigger" Burke was a decorated war hero who had been released from prison to join a special army commando-type unit. When he came back, he began killing people around his native Hell's Kitchen, including his best friend. Burke was on the Ten Most Wanted list, and the FBI was hunting him throughout the Northeast. By bringing in a psychopathic New York murderer, Pino was escalating the situation. One night in June, Burke ambushed O'Keefe with a machine gun but did not manage to kill him. Ten days later, the same thing happened. Based on information from New York, Boston detectives were able to capture Burke, and he was confined in the Charlestown jail while awaiting extradition. However, with the aid of some lock pickers who were also there, he managed to escape. He then fled to South Carolina, where he was apprehended by the FBI, returned to New York, and executed in the electric chair. If Pino had been a strong leader, he would not have called for outside help and certainly not from a walking bomb like Burke.

In January 1956 the state statute of limitations would run out. The robbers would then be free to spend the stolen money on television, if they so desired. The only hope was to break Specs O'Keefe, who was furious over losing his money and being shot at by Burke. Still he refused to talk to FBI agents. A new SAC, Edward J. Powers, son of a Chicago police sergeant, had taken over in Boston and realized that if the Brink's robbers got away with it, he would be one of Hoover's scapegoats. So agents concentrated on trying to turn O'Keefe. All efforts were unsuccessful. Finally Powers himself took a hand at it, and the two men hit it off very well. Based on O'Keefe's testimony, eight of the Brink's robbers were arrested (Banfield was dead and Gusciora was dying). The state jury in Boston began to consider the verdict at 10:00 p.m. on October 5, 1956. Three hours later, they returned with a finding of guilty against all of the defendants on all the charges. The men were given life sentences.

In 1969 and 1970 the remaining living robbers (McGinnis and Baker had died in prison) were released. Col. Tom Sullivan retired in 1957, and another civilian was appointed in his place. One of the saddest things was what happened to Frank Wilson. In September 1958 he was named deputy superintendent in charge of the detective bureau, but three months later he died of a heart attack. Friends and family believed it was from overwork on cases like Brink's.

In 1960 NBC-TV ran a program entitled "Biography of a Bookie Joint." Their camera was fixed on a key store in Boston that was supposedly a front for gambling. Men who looked like Boston police detectives were photographed going in and out of the place. Complaints to the department had no effect, so raids were finally made on the store by Massachusetts State Police and U.S. Treasury agents. The scandal led to the Boston Police Department being returned to the control of the city and the appointment as commissioner, in 1962, of Ed Namara, an FBI agent who had worked the Brink's case. He would serve as commissioner for ten years.

The Brink's case would be dramatized in various forms. A movie, *Six Bridges to Cross*, portrayed individuals who resembled Pino and Lieutenant Crowley. It was sympathetic to the two men and took the position that Crowley had not betrayed the force. A 1978 movie, *The Brink's Job*, was made as a comedy and meant to portray the holdup men as clowns. It starred name actors like Peter Falk as Pino, Peter Boyle as Joe McGinnis, Warren Oates as O'Keefe, and Paul Sorvino as Jazz Maffie. The film did not mention the FBI–Boston police rivalry.

Only $50,000 was recovered. The money that had originally been handed out to the robbers had largely been spent on drinking, gambling, or lawyers' fees. The FBI justified spending an estimated $29 million on the investigation on the grounds that it would be bad for public morale and for young men contemplating criminal careers to believe that individuals could get away with such a large heist.

Boston since Brink's

The FBI-police rivalry in Boston would continue. A generation later, some bureau agents would form an alliance with a predominantly Irish gang led by "Whitey" Bulger, a notorious criminal from South Boston, and use information from him to bring down the local branch of the Mafia. Agents covered up information about murders by Bulger and his cohorts and always kept him informed of what other law enforcement agencies were doing. Investigations by the Boston police and the Massachusetts State Police were allegedly sabotaged by the bureau. Out-of-town detectives investigating murders by Bulger and his associates that occurred in their jurisdictions would be stonewalled by the FBI. Later, when some agents were finally exposed for their dealings with Bulger, it seemed obvious that higher-ups had known about the cover-ups. While other agents were sent to prison or died of a heart attack while facing a murder trial, bureau supervisors and U.S. attorneys were not charged.

After Bulger was tipped off by FBI agents that he was about to be arrested, he fled the scene, and for fifteen years the FBI could not find him. Gov. William Weld was a former U.S. attorney and had been chief of the criminal division of the U.S. Department of Justice. Yet he was a close ally of Whitey's brother, Bill, who was leader of the Massachusetts Senate. Weld even appointed Bill Bulger, who had no credentials in education, to be the president of the University of Massachusetts. Despite being called in many investigations, Senate President Bulger claimed he had no knowledge of his brother's activities or whereabouts, yet he and his brother were known to have been very close. When Mitt Romney became governor, Bulger was fired as president of the university.

There were always rumors (some of them planted) that Whitey and his girlfriend were living abroad and would never be found. Finally, a woman in California recognized him as a wanted fugitive. To collect the $2 million reward placed on him, she contacted the authorities. The involvement of the bureau with Bulger's group and its role in frustrating other law enforcement agencies' investigations put the FBI into great disfavor in the Boston area.

Another case in which the bureau has been severely criticized began in the early morning hours of March 18, 1990 (in the aftermath of Boston's St. Patrick's Day celebrations). There were only two guards on duty at the Isabella Stewart Gardner Museum in Boston's Fenway area, despite the fact that it held hundreds of millions of dollars in valuable paintings. When two supposed Boston cops came to the security door, a guard broke the rules and let them in. The two men then persuaded him to call the other guard to the desk. There, both were taken prisoner. They were not discovered until the next morning, when another guard arrived to relieve them. In the meantime, the intruders had crudely cut many valuable paintings from their frames and had taken them from the museum. The total value of the stolen paintings was placed as high as $1 billion. The museum has offered a $5 million reward for information leading to their recovery.

The FBI took over the investigation and allegedly failed to cooperate with the Boston police. Despite periodic announcements by the Boston office of the bureau that the men who committed the robbery were known and the paintings would soon be recovered, there have been no arrests or recoveries in the twenty-seven years since the crime occurred.

At the time of the 2013 terrorist attack in Boston that killed four people, out-of-town reporters noted how extremely unpopular the FBI was in the area. Boston, more than most cities in the United States, is still haunted by the tribal rivalries of its past and the intense politics of its present. Both of these play a large role in law enforcement. The Brink's case, the murders committed by Whitey Bulger and his associates, and the Isabella Gardner Stewart Museum theft are not shining moments in the history of American law enforcement.

St. Louis Blues

In the early 1950s experts named Los Angeles, Cincinnati, St. Louis, and Milwaukee as the top police forces in the country. In St. Louis the department was run by a board of commissioners appointed by the governor, and the commissioners, in turn, chose a career officer as chief of police. The city itself was one of the top ten in America, with a thriving economy. Among the power blocs in St. Louis there were no deep divisions similar to the Irish-WASP feud in Boston.

In 1953 a stickup gang from Chicago, led by a nationally known bank robber, came into St. Louis and held up the Southwest Bank. When a teller hit the silent alarm, the police responded. One of the first two officers to arrive was wounded, but others immediately sealed off the area to prevent any possible escape. When the shotgun-toting gang leader, Fred Bowerman, attempted to seize a woman hostage, he was shot dead. Bowerman was a man nearing sixty who had been a highly rated bank robber for many years. But he was slowing down, and men who might have gone with him on the job a few years earlier declined. So he recruited his crew from a bunch of young Chicago hijackers. One of them, Frank Vito, when he realized he was trapped, committed suicide. Two others were captured. For a while, there was considerable attention paid to the death of Vito, and the public was supposed to feel sorry for him. What wasn't reported was that he and his mates in the hijacking gang had been killing each other for some time in an unsuccessful effort to locate an informer within the group. My personal opinion (without any evidence to back it up) is that the traitorous informers were wiretaps that the FBI had planted on the gang's phones. But the members never figured that out. As a police officer watching film of the bank robbery on TV, I cheered for the quick, tough, professional way the St. Louis Police Department foiled the crime, and I managed to withhold any tears for the fallen hijacker and the professional bank robber.

In 1953 there was another major crime in Missouri. A middle-aged woman came into an exclusive Catholic school in Kansas City and announced she was there to pick up her six-year-old nephew. The nun who spoke to her was not suspicious of her story as the woman explained that the boy's mother had suffered a heart attack that morning and she was going to take him home. The school allowed her to leave with Bobby Greenlease, the son of a multimillionaire owner of a chain of auto dealerships. Not until the afternoon, when the nun called the house and Mrs. Greenlease answered, did anyone suspect Bobby had been kidnapped.

The Kansas City police were notified, and they alerted the FBI. When a demand was made for a $600,000 ransom, both agencies urged Mr. Greenlease not to pay. However, he gathered the money, put it in a bag, and dropped it off at a specified location. It was the largest ransom paid in America up to that time. Sadly, Bobby was already dead, murdered by the kidnappers, Bonnie Brown Heady and Carl Austin Hall, and thrown in a lime pit. Heady was a plain, middle-aged woman while Hall was a handsome man from an upper-middle-class private-school background who had served as a wartime marine. After running through his small inheritance, he began sticking up cab drivers in Kansas City and was sent to the state penitentiary for fifteen months.

The kidnappers immediately headed for St. Louis. There, Hall left Heady with just $2,000 and moved to a motel, where he began paying taxi drivers to procure prostitutes for him. By then the kidnapping was front-page news, and one of the cab drivers notified his boss that there was a man spending a lot of money in a motel. The cab company owner called a St. Louis police lieutenant he knew, Louis Shoulders. Accompanied by Cpl. Elmer Dolan, a uniformed officer he had commandeered, the two went to the motel where Hall was staying, arrested him, confiscated the ransom, and later arrested Heady. It was another great triumph for the St. Louis police.

At the same time, FBI director J. Edgar Hoover was putting both feet into his mouth. He leapt in to announce that the case had been solved by his bureau and identified Heady as a notorious criminal. Actually, the FBI had no role in the capture of the kidnapper; Hoover had mixed Heady up with another woman with the same name. The FBI also bought Hall's story that the crime had been committed by one Thomas Martin, and they ordered a nationwide search for him. Eventually, it was determined that Hall's account was false. Hoover's efforts to claim unwarranted credit for breaking the case, his misidentification of Heady, and the wild-goose chase for Martin made the FBI look bad.

When FBI agents interrogated Hall, he claimed that when he was arrested he had most of the $600,000 ransom with him at the motel. However, Lieutenant Shoulders vouchered only half of that amount. The lieutenant was a Crowley-type officer in that he usually was assigned to the big cases and had a very good record of crime fighting. However, he more or less made his own hours and worked according to his own rules. The chief of police should have dealt with him long before. Now Shoulders and Dolan were charged with perjury in their testimony to the grand jury about the money and sentenced to three and two years' imprisonment, respectively. Dolan was eventually given a presidential pardon. Hall and Heady were executed in the Missouri gas chamber. The best law enforcement agency in America and the highly rated St. Louis Police Department had both stumbled badly in the case.

Shoulders was an old story. The cop who is too friendly with underworld figures is likely to get a lot of tips on crime, but his loyalty will be to his pigeons, not the police department. A detective commander never liked to have some star investigator of this type working for him. If the boss doesn't crack down, the rogue cop is liable to disgrace the unit. If he does discipline the detective with a friend in every newsroom in town, the cop will claim that the boss knows nothing of detective work and is punishing him for being successful. Every city had a Crowley or a Shoulders in its police department. The New York version was Lt. Johnny Broderick, who went along for years winning accolades, until he was finally caught in incriminating conversations with mob figures on a district attorney's wiretap. After which, despite having many powerful friends, he was forced to resign from the police department.

Running a detective squad, or an entire bureau, is a difficult task, which is why some lieutenants, captains, and above stick to patrol or some cushy administrative job. One unfortunate aspect of policing is that twenty years of good work can be wiped out in a single day by a wrong judgment in an investigation or a wrong tactical move in the field. The only way for a boss to avoid mistakes is to hide in his office and not become involved in any controversial matters. However, that will not gain him the respect of those working for him.

13

A Death in Dallas

At the end of World War II, many American businesses looked toward postwar expansion. This included an organization known as the Chicago syndicate, the local name for what many people called the Mafia (years later *syndicate* was dropped in favor of *the outfit*). At the time, the Chicago mob was reeling from its disastrous move into Hollywood, which resulted in a federal prosecution that brought down most of its top leadership and led to the suicide of longtime mob boss Frank Nitti. In a few years, the syndicate would enter Las Vegas in a big way. That too would ultimately prove to be a disaster that would fatally damage several big-city mobs.

The Chicago mob just could not pick winners beyond its boundaries, whereas Frank Costello in New York established a large gambling operation in Louisiana. Probably the situation was a reflection of the fact that New York was a cosmopolitan city with many talented entrepreneurs, while Chicago was, at heart, an industrial city where old-fashioned businesses, like meatpacking and railroads, flourished.

In 1947 a proposal was put before Chicago mobsters Jake Guzik, secretary of the treasury for the syndicate, and Murray Humphreys, its secretary of labor, to expand to Dallas. The individual advocating this was a drug dealer named Paul Jones. That in itself was surprising. Drug dealers were not popular with the Chicago bosses, and Jones himself was a nobody. The kingpins whom Jones approached were strictly local boys. Guzik had started in the family business, pimping; his brother Harry was such a big-time brothel keeper that his notoriety played a large role in the enactment of the Mann Act in 1910, which outlawed the transportation of females across state lines for immoral purposes. (Many people believed that it applied only to commercial sex, but in fact in the early days it was used to prosecute individuals such as the son of a high federal official who took his girlfriend from Sacramento, California, to Reno, Nevada, for a fun weekend. In the 1940s the U.S. Supreme Court would rule that its provisions applied only to commercial sex, not private dalliances.) Humphreys was an old-time labor racketeer who negotiated contracts with a gun in his hand.

The two men asked Jones how Dallas gamblers would take to a Chicago incursion in Texas, where even noncriminals packed guns and policemen and the Texas Rangers were judged by the number of notches on their revolvers. Jones blithely assured the two that there would be no opposition, particularly since he was representing the newly elected Dallas County sheriff, Steve Guthrie, who was anxious to make big money.

Jones's assessment of Dallas must have been made when he was high on one of his own products. As in many southern cities, local gamblers carried great weight in Dallas, particularly with the police department, and the good old boys played rough. In 1946 the city recorded eighty-two homicides, or about thirteen per one hundred thousand, many of them suspected to be related to problems in organized crime. Chicago, with six times the population, had a little more than two hundred homicides that year, or six per one hundred thousand.

The gangster in Dallas who drew the most attention at the time was Hollis Delois Green, known by everyone as "Lois." He controlled a mob of ex-convicts the newspapers called "the 40 Thieves," who specialized in safecracking, armed robbery, and prostitution.

Green was a sharp dresser who favored late-model automobiles and was on a first-name basis with many members of the police department. He maintained an exclusive home in ritzy Oak Cliff, surrounded by flood-lights. When he came home at night, he usually rode around the block several times before turning into his driveway. Then he would honk his horn and his wife would push a button from inside the house to open the garage doors. Green would then drive in, close the doors, turn off the floodlights, and, carrying a shotgun with him, run from the garage to the front door. Once inside, he would turn the floodlights on again.

Finally, on Christmas Eve 1949, while attending a party at the Sky-Vu Club, Green was shot down from ambush as he left the affair. Detectives found five shotgun wounds in his body. Green was only thirty-one years old at the time he expired.

The next Dallas resident to obtain notoriety, including nationally, was a local gambler named Herbert Noble. In 1946 he sustained his first wound from an assassination attempt. While driving to his ranch near Grapevine, he was shot at by men in a car that followed him. He man-aged to get to the hospital, where a .45 slug was removed from his back. Ten more such incidents would follow over the next few years. Noble's troubles caught the attention of national publications, and anyone who could read should have known what the situation was down Texas way.

Noble did not cooperate with police investigations, telling officials that he would take care of it himself. In May 1948 he was back in the hospital with his arm mangled by a shotgun blast. Eight months later a bomb was placed his car, but a friend saw someone putting it under the hood and alerted Noble. A few months later, he arrived at a hospital with a gunshot wound in his leg.

In November 1949, on a day that he had an appointment in Fort Worth, he told his wife, Mildred, that he would like to borrow her Cadillac because it handled better on the highway. She, in turn, could take his Mercury. A couple of hours later his wife left the house on a shopping trip. When she stepped on the starter, the car exploded. Noble buried her in a $15,000 casket, the most expensive one ever sold in Dallas. Noble himself was soon back in the hospital after a rifle bullet shattered a bone in his left arm and lodged in his hip. This was attempt number six. While he was still in the hospital, he was shot by an assassin, armed with a high-powered rifle, from a position across the street.

In six years Noble survived eleven attempts on his life and, since he knew it was only a matter of time until they got him, he had long since made his funeral arrangements. Not until August 1951, though, did he finally lose his war. Leaving his home, he stopped to check his mail and was killed instantly when a high explosive charge, set at the base of the mailbox, ripped him and his automobile to pieces. Investigators found wires leading to a clump of scrub oak, seventy-five yards away, where they were connected to an auto battery. That was the kind of local climate that Paul Jones was going to bring the mob into.

The Chicago bosses designated one of their gambling supervisors, Pat Manno, to accompany Jones to Dallas to start negotiations for the move-in. The arrangements for a meeting were made by Lt. George Butler of the Dallas Police Department. Butler was one of those police lieutenants who roamed widely through his department and carried far more weight than his rank would indicate. In this, he was the equivalent of Lieutenant Cordes in New York, Lieutenant Pape in Chicago, Lieutenant Crowley in Boston, and Lieutenant Shoulders in St. Louis. Later, he would found the Dallas police officers' equivalent of a union and maintain it through many confrontations with city hall and the police brass.

At the meeting with Sheriff Guthrie, Manno presented the Chicago deal. He explained, "Once you get organized you don't have to worry about money. Everything will roll in a nice quiet manner, in a business-like way." Manno said he did not believe in having a half a dozen joints scattered throughout the city. He wanted just one big place, hidden out in the county. In addition, he pledged mob support in hunting down any ordinary criminals who might commit robberies and burglaries. It would have been interesting to watch killers who had developed their skills in the beer wars of the Windy City battling real western bad men who had perfected their shooting while blazing away at the posse chasing them. For going along, Guthrie would receive $150,000 annually (a sum equivalent to well over $1 million in today's dollars).

Unbeknownst to Jones and Manno, the meeting was recorded by Texas Rangers and photos were snapped of them entering and leaving. Lieutenant Butler had set the whole thing up to trap the Chicago emissaries. Manno returned home, and attempts to extradite him to Texas failed. Jones was arrested, convicted, and given three years in jail for attempted bribery.

One Chicagoan who went down to Dallas at the time was one of Humphrey's minions, a small-time hoodlum named Jacob Rubenstein. It's not clear whether he was sent there to work on arrangements for the gambling casino or whether he went on his own because he had a relative there and wanted to make a new start. Instead of returning to Chicago, he remained and operated strip joints. He made many friends with the police and in 1963, by which time he was known as Jack Ruby, he was able to enter police headquarters and kill Lee Harvey Oswald.

The fact that Dallas was a town where gamblers played a big role in setting law enforcement policy made it no different from many cities in America, especially southern ones. Even in northern cities, the same situations existed. In New York a bunch of gamblers in Brooklyn were put into business by the top NYPD brass. When the situation exploded, the mayor had to flee to Mexico. In Chicago, "America's richest cop," Capt. Dan Gilbert, chief investigator for the state's attorney, spent part of his time running county law enforcement and the other part serving on the governing board of the syndicate. In 1950 he was defeated in a run for county sheriff, bringing down the entire Democratic ticket with him, including U.S. Senate majority leader Scott W. Lucas.

Despite the claims of reformers, a city where organized crime flourished did not necessarily have an incompetent police department. San Francisco was one of the most wide-open American cities but the police there were first rate. Cops in any city adhered to the local customs. Everybody knew the situation, and most people accepted it.

Some elements of the Dallas Police Department, especially the detective bureau, were as competent as a similar group in any American city. The star of the bureau was Capt. Will Fritz of homicide. John Will Fritz joined the Dallas Police Department in 1921, when he was twenty-six

years old, and quickly became a detective. In 1934, as a captain, he organized the department's homicide and robbery bureau. Fritz became
widely known among American homicide sleuths for his successes in
investigating murder cases. Most years he cleared about 98 percent of
all cases reported in his city, whereas some communities were lucky to
clear 50 or 60 percent.

Recording a crime as cleared is different than stating that it is solved.
Even though the police may know who the killer is, they cannot claim
statistical credit unless he is arrested and booked for it. However, if the
wanted man is dead or incarcerated in a jurisdiction that will not return
him for trial, then the authorities may claim an exceptional clearance
on the case.

Between 1940 and 1951, the Dallas homicide bureau recorded 713 murders and cleared 750. Only eleven murders remained unsolved in eleven
years. Fritz explained how the bureau could clear thirty-seven more
murders than were actually recorded. He took homicides from previous years, investigated and solved them, and then wrote up clearances,
which would count in the year in which they were received. All of these
maneuvers were totally legitimate under FBI Uniform Crime Reporting
rules. The gamblers' wars put a little dent in the homicide clearance
rate. For example, by 1955, five of fifty-nine murder cases reported went
uncleared, including the murder of Mrs. Herbert Noble.

Legal charges were a different story. It was common for locals who
were arrested and charged with murder to be released when the grand
jury declined an indictment, that is, returned a no bill. A "good old boy"
who shot someone in broad daylight might be declared innocent if he
could prove that the other fellow needed killing. In Chicago, the same
thing applied, but the defendant was often required to go through a
regular trial and be acquitted by a judge or jury.

Most of these procedures were just bookkeeping. In the end, the bad
guys were kept in line and the not-so-bad guys did not suffer too much
from the criminal justice system. Officers who did not care for this system of selective justice and catering to good (or bad) old boys usually
worked in police units that did not deal with gangsters. However, they

could comfort themselves with the fact that, in the end, the bad guys got their due (often from each other) and the cop was around to see the mighty fall. By the 1960s, Captain Fritz and the homicide bureau were able to handle the local "conventions" and still become a legend in American law enforcement.

On the fateful day of November 22, 1963, the police department was deployed to protect Pres. John F. Kennedy during his visit to the city. Prior to the visit, there had been some trouble in Dallas from right-wing elements. UN ambassador Adlai Stevenson had been bopped over the head by a sign-carrying demonstrator. A couple of years earlier, Sen. Lyndon Johnson and his wife, Lady Bird, were roughed up by a Dallas crowd while walking to lunch at a downtown hotel. Some of JFK's advisers urged him to skip Dallas on his western swing, but he declined. The police and city government were not controlled by right-wingers, and the local chief of the Secret Service, Forrest Sorrels, and Chief of Police Jesse Curry believed that they could handle any trouble. One hundred and sixty-eight police officers were assigned along the parade route. Two dozen police reservists would take care of midblock security. There would be three motorcycles riding in advance to alert the command center to the progress of the parade. Five more would precede the lead car, two would be placed on each side of the presidential limousine, and two more officers on motorcycles would bring up the rear of the motorcade. At the president's destination, the huge Trade Mart complex, there were fifty-six detectives, fifty patrolmen, and nine supervisory officers stationed.

The story of the events that occurred outside the Texas School Book Depository has been repeated so many times that every American knows it. When word was flashed that the president and Texas governor John Connolly had been shot, Captain Fritz, still going strong at sixty-eight, rushed quickly from the Trade Mart to the book depository. There, he and his men determined that shots had been fired from a sixth-floor window of the depository. Officers found a rifle hidden beneath a stack of books near the stairway at the northeast corner of the floor. A building official reported that only one employee who had checked in that morning was missing. His name was Lee Harvey Oswald.

While that investigation was going on, Ofc. J. D. Tippit, patrolling solo in the Oak Cliff section, had been assigned to an at-large status covering a nearby district that had been vacated by other squads during the course of the emergency. At about 12:45 p.m., Tippit came on the radio asking for additional information on the supposed shooter. He had spotted a man who looked like Oswald walking in the street, and he drove his vehicle to catch up with him. As he got out of the car, Oswald pulled a handgun and fired several shots, killing Tippit. Shortly afterward, a call came from a cashier at the nearby Texas Theater saying that she had observed suspicious actions by a man who had just entered. Ofc. Nick McDonald arrived just seconds ahead of other squad cars, coming from all directions with sirens blaring. As McDonald spotted the suspicious character in the sparse matinee crowd, Oswald rose and shouted, "This is it, it's all over now," and pulled a gun from beneath his shirt. McDonald lunged at Oswald, grabbing him around the waist, and they both fell in a row of seats, wrestling for the gun. Oswald pulled the trigger but the weapon misfired. Half a dozen officers arrived, jumped in, and overpowered the suspect. Oswald was immediately taken to police headquarters at city hall and transferred to the custody of Captain Fritz, who started his interrogation at once.

Fritz concentrated first on the killing of Officer Tippit. A district attorney's office official who had arrived felt there was enough evidence to charge Oswald with the death of Tippit. After further investigation, Fritz charged Oswald with killing the president. So far, other than the status of the first victim, the case was not different from most Dallas homicides where an individual killed a citizen or a policeman and was quickly apprehended.

Many Americans have seen the TV footage of the attempted transfer of Oswald from city hall to the county jail on Sunday morning. Captain Fritz was among the officers present when Jack Ruby entered and fired, killing Oswald. That did it for the reputation of the Dallas Police Department. In three days it had received two crushing blows: the president of the United States had been murdered in its city and the man alleged to have killed him had been shot dead in police headquarters by an individual who had close associations with some cops. So far the Dallas police, though, had done nothing illegal. That fell to the White House staff, who tried to take control of the investigation and were successful in removing the president's body to Washington, a violation of Texas law. Captain Fritz pointed out that the assassination was a state homicide and there was no federal jurisdiction. Some have speculated that the president's people did not want an autopsy performed by persons outside of the federal government because it would have revealed Kennedy's illnesses that had been concealed from the public.

If the president had used the bubble top on his limousine, the killing never would have occurred. Later, the Warren Commission, containing politicians friendly to Kennedy's successor, Lyndon Johnson, did a poor job of investigating the assassination, and its credibility was limited. CIA director Allen Dulles, who had much to conceal, was allowed to be a member of the commission, and J. Edgar Hoover was treated as some kind of nonpartisan outside expert, even though his agents were supposed to have been keeping an eye on Oswald.

If the case had gone forward as a Texas murder, the trial would likely have resulted in the conviction and execution of Oswald. That is what happened in 1901, when President McKinley was killed in Buffalo and the state of New York prosecuted and executed the assassin, Leon Czolgosz.

The transfer of Oswald to the county jail on Sunday was normal procedure because the security there was greater than at police headquarters in city hall. In an attempt to cooperate with the national media, the Dallas police had alerted the TV networks to the time that the transfer would occur and told them that they would be allowed to film it. Perp walks are common in American law enforcement and are done to please journalists. One unforeseen problem was that not only was Ruby very close to police officers, he also had a background in Chicago that could label him a mob associate, though not a made member. Yet such characters abound in American policing. Dive owners who have a habit of picking up tabs for cops are often treated as hail fellows by the men in blue.

The fact is that the assassination could have happened in any American city of the time. Prior to 1963, presidential security was poor in most places. In 1961, when I was assigned as part of the bodyguard detail for President Kennedy on a visit to Chicago, I was stunned at how slipshod his protection was. Teenagers galore made their way up the back stairways of his hotel to try to get near the president. Almost anyone with a rifle could have killed him because he went around the city so openly. In 1968 Robert Kennedy was assassinated in Los Angeles, which was considered to have the best police force in the country. Recently, a lone man entered the White House grounds, overpowered the single agent inside the front door, and ran down the hallway leading to the president's quarters.

The Disintegration of Detectives

One result of the Dallas fiasco was to help discredit American local detective bureaus. Fritz, who was an outstanding investigator and had a good team of detectives, was made to look like some bumbling movie sheriff. Already the disintegration of American detective bureaus had begun in, of all places, Chicago.

The hostility to detectives came not from criminals but police reformers. Police brass often became dissatisfied with the detectives because they would write in their activity reports that they spent X number of hours talking to an informant, when a superior suspected they were sitting in a bar talking to their friends. Of course, sitting in a bar talking to certain people was a very good way to gather information.

In Chicago in 1959, a group of young patrolmen in a North Side district organized a burglary ring utilizing the services of a professional burglar. When the burglar would break into a store, the officers in the ring would surround the area so that no other cruising police could interfere. If a call came over the air of a burglar alarm or a citizen hearing noises, members of the ring would respond to it. It seemed like a foolproof scheme except that the burglar began to worry that his police friends were going to kill him because he knew too much about their activities. It would be easy to shoot him down while he was committing a burglary in a store. Before the cops could act, the burglar went to the Cook County state's attorney and told all. Eight police officers were simultaneously arrested.

The repercussions of what was called the Summerdale (District) scandal shook the city. Initially no detectives were involved, just a bunch of loosely supervised patrol cops. The police commissioner himself was compelled to resign and O. W. Wilson, dean of the School of Criminology at the University of California, Berkeley, was brought in to run the department. His appointment was a shock. Most Chicagoans thought it was just a temporary arrangement designed to get the heat off and soon things would go back to the way they were. This was not how it worked out. Wilson had been named chairman of a committee to investigate the police department, thereby enabling him to sit in judgment on all the top officials. Then he was recommended for the top job in the police department by a group of reformers, whose headquarters was located at 1313 East Sixtieth Street, near the University of Chicago campus. In the 1950s some right-wing writers had attacked the 1313 reformers as a secret leftist group attempting to take over American government. In fact, they were just a bunch of public administration researchers who wanted to improve local government. Wilson was an occasional consultant to them on police matters. They were neither left nor right wing but good government advocates. After the 1954 death of Bruce Smith, the police reform leader, Wilson became the informal leader of the police administrative reformers. He was also strongly endorsed by the Chicago Crime Commission. (Full disclosure: later, as part of Harvard's Kennedy School of Government public administration crowd, I was well acquainted with Smith's New York Institute of Public Administration and various public administration people around the country. I would probably be considered an ally of the group that I have been describing.)

Mayor Daley wanted a white knight to head the police department in order to contain the damage from the Summerdale scandal. However, Wilson was not a good choice for the top job. Like his mentor, August Vollmer, who served as LA's police chief in 1924, he knew little of big-city police work. In Wilson's case, he had not been a cop for over twenty years, and then as the chief of police of the small city of Wichita, Kansas. Nor was he a real academic. He only held a bachelor's degree and, at the time, was in the process of being removed as dean of Berkeley's

School of Criminology because the university authorities felt it was not engaging in scholarly work. A better appointment as Chicago's police superintendent might have been Harold Sullivan, a career cop in the LAPD who had served as deputy chief, came close to becoming chief there, and was later commissioner of the California Highway Patrol. It was almost impossible for a man to come into Chicago and do a good job if he had not previously worked in big-city policing.

In an attempt to cut down on corruption, Wilson closed seventeen of thirty-eight police district stations and virtually eliminated the old-time detective bureau. Later, when community policing ideas were introduced, a number of stations had to be reopened. The evaluation of detectives was always a dilemma for efficiency experts. How many arrests and crime clearances per month was the correct figure for the average detective? How do you rank a murder arrest against one for petty larceny? Some murder arrests were "smoking gun" affairs where the killer waited on the scene and handed his weapon to the first officer to arrive. Some larcenies involved complex schemes that required extensive investigation. What weight should be given for talking to an informer? Often the problem was exacerbated by the fact that many top brass had never been detectives. If they had, they could have seen through the various claims of detective subordinates and arrived at a good estimate of who was working and who was not. Police brass often condemned all detectives for the incompetence of a few, and reining in their bureau ranked high on the reformers' hit list.

Instead of having a number of detective generalists working out of districts (precincts) as well as detective specialists from headquarters, Wilson combined the two groups and divided them into six geographic areas and five specialized squads: homicide, burglary, robbery, auto theft, and general assignment. No longer would detectives roam the streets, keeping an eye on criminals and picking up information. Their job became strictly casework. The district detectives who had been generalists were now converted to specialists, and nobody in the districts could take over their task of keeping track of criminals in an area of one hundred thousand people. The detective bureau, which had once been feared by hoodlums and respected by all, was gone. At first criminals did not believe it, and then they had a field day. There was no one to stop them. Detectives did not patrol, and patrolmen did not know much about dealing with professional criminals. District uniformed cops were trained not to look at the local crime picture in depth but to respond to 911 calls. Needless to say, crime rose.

In New York until the 1950s, the detective bureau was run by powerful leaders such as August Flath and Conrad Rothengast, who, after serving as chief of detectives, moved up to chief inspector (the NYPD's top career job). But after the Harry Gross scandal in 1950, when high-ranking officers were charged with being paid off on a regular basis by Brooklyn gamblers, a number of top brass were fired. The Gross case did not actually involve detectives but rather vice cops who were not members of the detective bureau. Nevertheless, the detectives lost prestige. A clear sign of the decline of the bureau came in 1956, when a bookish commissioner, Steve Kennedy, compelled Dep. Chief Frank Phillips, longtime stalwart of the bureau, nemesis of Willie Sutton, and a colorful cop with friends all over the city, to leave the department over a minor incident.

In the 1960s Howard Leary, a mediocre Philadelphia police commissioner, was appointed by Mayor John Lindsay to head the NYPD because he agreed to support the introduction of a civilian complaint review board (CCRB) like the one in Philadelphia. No one asked whether the Philadelphia CCRB worked or was just a political ploy. As it turned out, it was the latter, and soon the Philadelphia Police Department and eventually the entire city were taken over by an old-fashioned, tough cop named Frank Rizzo, who became police commissioner and then mayor. During Leary's time in New York, rivalries between the various units were fierce. For example, the detective bureau refused to furnish a copy of a report to the internal affairs bureau of the department. So a plan was arranged for the internal affairs chief to stage a midnight raid on the detective bureau office. The chief of detectives was tipped off, and during the raid, he and the internal affairs boss began swapping punches. The newspapers jumped on the story, and the department looked ridiculous.

In 1970, when Pat Murphy became commissioner, the detective bureau, which he had never favored, would be a prime target of change despite the fact that it had saved the city. No sooner was Murphy in office than uniformed officers, angry over a back pay dispute, refused to go on patrol. Murphy canceled days off and assigned the city's thirty-two hundred detectives to work twelve-hour shifts in radio cars. Thanks to them, the city remained quiet, and the patrol officers returned to their duties. When the strike was over, however, Murphy announced a number of plans to overhaul the detective bureau. For example, he would end the practice of promoting detectives to first or second grade and just leave third. That would cost a lot of veteran detectives the opportunity to make higher salaries.

In some ways Murphy was a great reform commissioner who ended "the pad" system, whereby vice cops handed over regular monthly payments to top police brass. In contrast, a detective's violations might involve getting free meals in a fancy restaurant or a break on the price of an expensive appliance. For some businessmen, this made sense because they had situations where they sometimes needed to call on detectives to help them out informally. When Johnny Broderick would hear that a local punk was trying to intimidate a storekeeper, or when a Broadway producer called him to say that some hoodlum was trying to force a chorus girl into becoming a prostitute, he would pay the creep a quick visit and leave him upside down in a garbage can. This usually solved the problem. To protect a decent young girl alone in the city, it was sometimes necessary to use methods not cited in the rule book.

Even past cases where detectives had been hailed began to be seen in a different light in the 1960s. In 1954 Dr. Sam Sheppard, a prominent physician, had been convicted and sentenced to life for killing his wife (see chapter 8). At the time Coroner Gerber and the homicide squad of the Cleveland detective bureau took most of the credit for the successful resolution of the case. In 1961 Sheppard was serving his life sentence when the courts struck down the murder conviction.

Washington DC police were notoriously inefficient. It was said to be the safest city in the United States—in which to commit a murder. In the years just before World War II, seven women were raped and murdered in the district and five more viciously assaulted. No less a person than First Lady Eleanor Roosevelt suggested that the U.S. Army be assigned to protect women in the capital. Finally, with the help of the NYPD, a man named Jarvis Catoe was charged with some of the crimes and executed in January 1942.

The failings of the district police led to a shakeup in the department and a congressional investigation. Congress required the department to create a position of captain of detectives, which would be open to experienced investigators from anywhere in the country. The head of the homicide squad in the district only carried the rank of lieutenant, and the department rejected bringing in captains from the outside, so they managed to negate that provision of the congressional act. Although some talented investigators, such as former FBI agents, filled the post, the position did not last long and the police department returned to its usual ways.

The real problem in the department was that it was too open to congressional influence, and every congressman sought to get favors for himself and his friends. The cardinal rule of the department was never to offend a congressman.

In the 1940s the congressional committee responsible for overseeing the district government was chaired by Sen. Theodore "The Man" Bilbo of Mississippi, America's number-one racist. His views were more extreme than Bull Connor's.

In San Francisco, detectives originally fared well in the postwar years. In 1956 the city's leading detective, Frank Ahern, was made chief of police, and he brought with him his partner Tom Cahill to be deputy chief. In 1958 Ahern unexpectedly died, but Cahill succeeded him as chief and remained for twelve years. When he left, Al Nelder, the man who had broken the Moskovitz case, replaced him. San Francisco police inspectors continued to remain prestigious and worked pretty much as they always had. Then the pressures of radical rebellions in the streets changed city politics, and a general anticop feeling altered the police department's standing in the community. Chief Nelder, who had been groomed for the top job for years, resigned after about a year and a half because he realized the climate was no longer friendly to the type of policing he had learned. Chiefs and mayors came and went, while the streets were eventually taken over by criminals and the disorderly.

In Los Angeles, Chief Parker died in 1966 and Thad Brown retired the following year. He was the last of America's famous detective chiefs. From then on, most of them were little known to the public, even in their own towns. In Los Angeles, detectives still stood below intelligence-type squads in importance, and when the department under Parker was confronted with some big cases, such as the death of Marilyn Monroe, it did not look good. The finding that Monroe died of an overdose of drugs was not accepted by many people, who thought it was a murder. Later, in the post-Parker era, the O. J. Simpson case exposed the LAPD to national ridicule.

While the detective mystique began to dissolve in real life, the one place where they continued to be exalted was on TV and in the movies. Thus, vast viewing audiences would not allow governments to reduce detective strength. Most fans did not realize that the detective methods of a Dirty Harry were fictional and any real-life cop who used those tactics would have been fired or indicted. It was the public that, after the 9/11 attack, saved the FBI from being torn apart by Congress and replaced by some British-style civilian security agency. Nothing could make people believe that Jimmy Stewart and Efrem Zimbalist Jr. did not represent real-life G-men. Meanwhile, the detective's prime position in police departments was eroded, particularly by pressure that gave emphasis to patrol strategies. The detective bureau still remained an important component of most police forces but primacy had passed to the men in blue.

14

Reorientation and Restoration

In the modern Western world each century has tended to be quite different than the ones that preceded it, although the differences have not become apparent until fifteen or so years after the new century began. Not until 1815, with the defeat of Napoleon at Waterloo, did the nineteenth century really commence. The twentieth century did not begin until the time of World War I. There are signs now that the twenty-first century is beginning to take shape. The election of 2016 may have opened a new era in American politics. Certainly, it did not resemble the presidential contests that went before it.

In the area of law enforcement, the problems that absorbed policing in the late twentieth century seem to have been supplanted by new developments. Yet most police administrators still wrestle with old issues like community policing, stop and frisk, and broken windows. The broken windows theory held that, just as leaving broken windows in an empty building unrepaired will result in the other windows being broken, ignoring acts of disorder will lead to increased disorder, and in some situations the neighborhood will be taken over by the lawless, including serious criminals. This will result in law-abiding people forgoing use of the streets. In recent years, some scholars have rejected the broken windows theory, while others continue to find merit in it.

The second decade of the twenty-first century witnessed widespread civil disorder and has resulted in a new phenomenon. If a police officer is accused of an improper shooting in one city, it becomes a national issue. Whereas in the past, it was of concern only in the city in which it occurred. So far police administrators have not come to terms with the situation. William Bratton, former police commissioner of New York City and a top leader in American law enforcement, refused to accept the legitimacy of the Black Lives Matter movement. He also spent a great deal of time defending the broken windows theory while pledging to engage in community policing, a concept that he had rejected twenty years back, when he first served as the NYPD commissioner.

As noted in the foregoing chapters, since the inception of modern policing in the mid-nineteenth century, there have been three distinct models of police administration in America. Given current conditions, it is likely that a new model, or a revised version of an old one, will soon be adopted. The first police forces that emerged in America in the nineteenth century were largely patrol forces that had only small investigative components. With the development of a large group of professional criminals who traveled from city to city by rail and of politically protected, violent urban gangs, police patrol was no longer sufficient to control crime. At the end of the nineteenth century, Insp. Thomas Byrnes of the New York City police department brought detectives to parity with the patrol force in his department. By the early twentieth century, detectives were full-fledged partners in American policing, though junior ones. In the post–World War I era, the development of automobiles, which provided greater mobility to the criminal population, and Prohibition, which spawned exceptionally powerful criminal gangs, gave primacy in urban policing to the detective bureau. From then on, detectives were the dominant element in most big-city police departments. The rise of J. Edgar Hoover's FBI produced a detective force that became the leading law enforcement agency in America.

In the post–World War II era, police reformers like O. W. Wilson, a former police chief and dean of the School of Criminology, University of California at Berkeley, began to call for a shift in the balance of policing power back to patrol officers. The reformers pointed out that while police departments depended heavily on the 15 percent of their members who were in investigative jobs, the 65 percent who were in the patrol division were not fully utilized. Wilson sought to install "aggressive, preventive" patrolling in city police departments and to reduce the role of the detective bureau to a supporting function. Reformers did not call for a return to the old-fashioned, much romanticized beat cops but advocated for the mechanization of police departments and the introduction of industrial management methods to get the most out of the force.

As a result, the majority of patrol officers were assigned to cars and directed from a central location. This gave police administrators the ability to know where their officers were at any given moment and to control officers' work by dispatching them to locations where citizens callers reported they were needed. The beat assignments of the cars and their clear markings gave supervisors the ability to control patrol units much more effectively than detectives or foot cops. For example, detectives could disappear for long periods by explaining they were conducting investigations. Wilson even argued that by employing a one-man crew in each car, the number of patrol cars could be doubled, the areas that each covered could be cut in half, and the response time to calls could be reduced by about the same amount. Of course, in the growing depressed and violent areas of inner cities, it was asking a lot for a single police officer to rush into a dangerous situation, and most departments, including major ones like New York, Chicago, and Los Angeles, still retained two-man cars.

What Wilson termed "aggressive, preventive policing" by motorized officers became a central task of the patrol division. Instead of the previous aimless cruising and coffee drinking, cops questioned suspicious persons on the street, stopped automobiles, and gave the occupants the once-over looking for guns, contraband, and stolen goods. Later, such tactics were given the name "stop, question, and frisk." Most of the stops and arrests involved blacks or Hispanics, who were concentrated in the inner-city areas. Wilson and other adherents of vigorous patrol strategies denied that police work was based on racial factors. They argued that enforcement in the inner city was more intense because that was where the crime and disorder rates were the highest.

While detectives might stop and frisk known criminals, there were few complaints because these individuals were not law-abiding citizens. In contrast, ordinary citizens resented being stopped by patrol officers a block from their homes.

There were always some police commanders who maintained the view that there should not be vigorous enforcement of minor laws. They believed that police should walk softly in most communities or they would be constantly at war with the people they were policing. Whether in the blue-collar stronghold of the Chicago stockyards or in the nearby Black Belt, for example, police did not usually interfere with adults who were simply drinking or hanging out on their front porches.

The rise of patrol lessened the importance of detectives. However, investigators continued to command respect from the citizenry based, in part, on the fact that they caught murderers and other serious criminals, a task the public applauded. The strength of detectives' work was in their organization in a powerful bureau. While the foregoing chapters have illustrated many errors and shortcomings of detectives, ultimately the institutional capacity of a big-city detective bureau enabled it to resolve cases successfully, except unusual ones like serial killings, though even this phenomenon was partially mastered toward the end of the twentieth century.

From the 1960s on, when aggressive patrol strategies were the dominant method of fighting crime, the number of offenses across America rose to an all-time high. In New York, for example, murders, which had averaged around 300 per year, increased to 2,245 in 1990.

In the 1960s civil disorder brought forth calls to bring policing closer to the citizenry, and the concept of community policing became popular, though it was never defined beyond generalities. In most places it was more a show operation than an integral part of the local police department. In 1970s New York City, some patrol cars simply painted "community policing team" on their vehicle doors and kept right on working in the old-fashioned way. In some cities, community policing cops worked days and early evenings but were tucked in their beds later at night when crime was raging in the community.

One of the best-planned community policing programs was created in Chicago. Yet it did not stop gang activity, which eventually rose to avalanche proportions, with large numbers of people being gunned down and no seeming way for the police to stop it.

In 1990 New York City decided that the entire police department would operate according to the principles of community policing. However, after a few years, evaluators found that community policing officers were merely a shadow force who spent their time attending meetings while the real police force answered calls and battled crime.

Community policing essentially rested on the myth of the old-time beat cop who supposedly dispensed wise advice, was always around to help people, and won the confidence of the community. This was not an accurate picture. In the old days, no one cop handled a particular beat; rather, because of three different shifts and days off it took several cops to patrol an area over the course of a week, and many did not desire to become a big brother to the citizens. O. W. Wilson himself did not buy the myth of the old-time beat cop. He believed that one reason most officers should be put in cars was to avoid petty corruption, loafing, and drinking on duty.

So enthusiastic were some advocates of community policing that, in certain communities, teams of community policing officers were assigned to carry out detective duties, as a supplement to their other work. One argument was that the team was in a better position to get information. In fact, neighborhood people who were known to "squeal" to the police were sometimes killed by street gangs, and the motto in some areas was "stitches for snitches." Detectives, with long experience in handling criminal informers, knew how to keep such matters confidential. Ultimately, there was no way patrol officers could carry out serious investigations on a part-time basis.

In 1993 the citizens of New York, by electing Rudy Giuliani as mayor, rejected the sort of community policing that had been favored by the previous mayor, David Dinkins, and his police commissioner, Lee Brown. Instead, Bratton was appointed as commissioner, and he instituted proactive police strategies including stop and frisk and order maintenance revolving around the concept of broken windows. New York City under Bratton and his successors saw huge decreases in crime. By the second decade of the twenty-first century, murders in New York were down to the three hundred range annually, and robberies had fallen from one hundred thousand in 1992 to around twenty thousand annually. Large reductions in crime also took place in many other American cities.

Still, Dep. Comm. Jack Maple, who was the principal architect of New York's dramatic crime decreases in the early nineties, was one of those who did not subscribe to the primacy of the broken windows theory. He observed, "Criminals do not leave town because there is less graffiti on the walls." Later, when Maple was in charge of crime-fighting programs in places like New Orleans, he achieved success without relying on broken windows–type enforcement.

In 2013 Bill de Blasio ran for mayor of New York City on a platform specifically attacking vigorous public order (broken windows) tactics and stop-and-frisk policing. When he was elected, however, he named Bratton, once a strong advocate of both programs, as police commissioner. Commissioner Bratton modified some of his previous views. For example, while strongly defending his legacy of following the broken windows theory, in 2016 he acquiesced when the city council reduced offenses such as urinating in public to essentially civil violations. Finally, Bratton announced he would emphasize community policing, which he had dismantled back in the 1990s.

In the second decade of the twenty-first century, even though an African American had been elected president, racial protests began to rise. The death of black citizens at the hands of police in places like Ferguson, Missouri, and Baltimore, Maryland, received huge amounts of attention and resulted in riots (although the federal government exonerated the police officer in Missouri, and a judge threw out the charges against the officers in Baltimore). Hordes of demonstrators now chant slogans that have not been heard since the 1960s, like "burn the pigs." Police have become hesitant to act, especially since amateurs are routinely photographing officers in enforcement situations and showing a portion of the film that makes the police look bad.

In 2015 and 2016 crime began to rise rapidly in some cities. The FBI director at the time, James Comey, argued that the increases were partly the result of police being reluctant to enforce the law. In Chicago, where the mayor, Rahm Emanuel, concurred with Comey's view, there were constant mass killings over large areas, and the city became the poster boy for what could happen in the rest of America.

In June 2016 U.S. Attorney for the Southern District of New York Preet Bharara announced the indictment of three NYPD police officers, including two high-ranking ones, on federal corruption charges. The indicted men were alleged to have taken gifts of cash and jewelry in exchange for performing a number of services for private citizens. In one case, they allegedly closed off a lane in a traffic tunnel. In others, they provided chauffeured rides, sirens screaming, to take certain people to the airport. Two private citizens who were also indicted were both businessmen in the Hasidic community of Brooklyn. The U.S. attorney characterized them as having virtually "a private police force" available to them. In one instance, the indictment noted that a "very high ranking police officer," who was named as a cooperating witness, had appointed one of the indicted officials as commanding officer of the elite Nineteenth Precinct on the Upper East Side of Manhattan based on the recommendation of one of the indicted civilians.

In a related incident, the police firearms licensing section allegedly issued over one hundred gun permits to one of the indicted civilians in return for a payoff. The licenses were then given to members of Hasidic community groups, some of whom were forbidden to own a firearm under any circumstances because of legal restrictions. Eventually several officers were indicted.

Some observers have raised the question of whether this scandal arose, at least in part, from the fact that the NYPD had been stressing community policing, in which commanders are supposed to maintain close relationships with neighborhood leaders. It is possible that the emphasis on doing favors and becoming close to the community led to situations in which police commanders were compensated by "gifts." Apparently, police headquarters was not aware of the situation, because some of the officers who were indicted or under scrutiny had been promoted to their high positions by Commissioner Bratton.

No signs on the horizon suggest that the challenges to police patrols in the inner city are going to lessen; more probably, they are going to increase. Therefore, with patrol strategies no longer effective or likely to be in the future, it is time to reassess the role of detectives and once again move them to the forefront of American policing. Today's detectives have a great many tools they did not have as recently as a generation ago. Now they can use DNA to identify perpetrators in investigations that go back thirty or more years and arrest individuals who thought they had gotten away with the crime. Police once carried crime information in their heads or stored it in desks in their offices. Now they can press a button on a terminal and link fourteen or fifteen databases. Interrogation, which was considered an art that few people were skilled at, has benefited from enhanced training in that subject.

As the first step in police reorganization, a clear line should be drawn between the duties of the patrol force and those of detectives. Patrol officers should maintain order, with due consideration for community feelings, respond to 911 calls, and keep watch for crimes in progress (though rarely is the criminal on the scene when patrol reaches it, and even more rarely do police units see a crime in progress). Patrol cops must also make friends with civilians while at the same time keeping an appropriate distance in order to avoid a scandal like the one that engulfed New York City in 2016. A police officer should help people in a neighborhood, not take orders from a few fixers, nor do favors in return for gifts. Yet such lapses are inevitable when police become too close to people they are policing.

To improve detective operations, it is necessary to put experienced detectives in charge of investigative bureaus and squads. In these units, what is needed is not a management specialist but a strong leader. Police should also publicize investigative operations, as was once done when many detectives were household names. Police administrators do not like having high-profile subordinates because they believe (often rightly) that they become prima donnas. However, that very vanity can permit detectives to rise to even higher levels of performance. Another necessity is to ensure that, in addition to investigating crimes, detectives are returned to their classical role as watchdogs over criminals generally and as the main source of crime information.

There is nothing revolutionary in a proposal to restore detective primacy. It was the norm for fifty years in the middle of the twentieth century, when crime rates were low. In the 1930s and 1940s, many cities recorded a smaller number of annual murders than they would record in a single month at the end of the century. Detective skill, new investigative tools, and the ability to operate below the radar, plus a mystique that fascinates the public, balanced against the problems of patrol strategies, require that detectives lead American policing in the early twenty-first century.

Notes

Citing references to true crime books is not an exact science. Various publications present different versions of the same event. In cases of murder it is common for authors to try to demonstrate that a solution, such as the conviction of Bruno Hauptmann for the murder of the Lindbergh baby, was wrong. In our own time, the majority of the American public does not accept that Lee Harvey Oswald, alone and unaided, killed Pres. John F. Kennedy. Among the many theories that have been advanced to explain the assassination are a Mafia plot, the actions of Cuban Communists or right-wing Americans, or even the accidental discharge of a Secret Service agent's weapon.

The purpose of the present work is not to solve (or unsolve) various cases but to demonstrate how detective bureaus operated in the age when they dominated American policing.

SNAPSHOTS

xi **San Francisco, October 9, 1926**: Mullen, *The Toughest Gang in Town*, 240–47.

xiii **New York City, May 7, 1931**: Reynolds, *Headquarters*, 118–22. Reynolds's 1955 book was essentially a valentine to the NYPD, with no questions asked about why so many cops were unable to end the siege.

xvii **Chicago, March 20, 1953**: Nizer, *The Jury Returns*, 1–62. Nizer presents a view of the case that is at wide variance with the actual crime. He also devotes 137 pages to a sympathetic portrayal of a vicious murderer.

PREFACE

xxi **"The ambitious ones might"**: Murphy and Plate, *Commissioner*, 188.

xxii **The highly regarded management**: Greenwood and Petersilia, *The Criminal Investigation Process*, i–xiv.

xxv **The great French detective chief**: Stead, *The Police of France*, 61.

xxv **He wrote that London detectives**: Summerscale, *The Suspicions of Mr. Whicher*, 52.

xxv **Dickens describes his principal hero**: Summerscale, *The Suspicions of Mr. Whicher*, 53.

I. THE RISE OF AMERICAN DETECTIVES

For the life and times of Allan Pinkerton, see Horan, *The Pinkertons*. On McParland's investigation of the Molly Maguires and the Idaho bombing, see Riffenburgh, *Pinkerton's Great Detective*. The career of Thomas Byrnes is described in Conway, *The Big Policeman*. Accounts of Byrnes by great writers in his own time are contained in Riis, *The Making of an American*, and Steffens, *Autobiography of Lincoln Steffens*. Also see Lardner and Reppetto, *NYPD*, chapter 4. On the career of William Burns, see Caesar, *Incredible Detective*.

5 **The experiences of William Bell**: Lardner and Reppetto, *NYPD*, 35–36.

8 **"The London detective force"**: Conway, *The Big Policeman*, 6.

11 **"to avoid the technicality"**: Burns, *The Masked War*, 147.

12 **"a man of genius"**: "The Bomb Conspirators," editorial, *New York Times*, June 4, 1919.

12 **"American Sherlock Holmes"**: Reppetto, *Battleground New York City*, 106.

13 **"You cannot do detective work"**: Reppetto, *American Police: 1845–1945*, 167.

2. ITALIAN SQUADS

On the career of Joe Petrosino, see Reppetto, *American Mafia*, chapters 2 and 3. On Fiaschetti, see his own *You Gotta Be Rough*. Petrosino and Fiaschetti were great self-publicizers and given to some embellishment.

24 **"a riffraff of desperate scoundrels"**: Reppetto, *American Mafia*, 45.

24 **"The police hire men"**: Flynt, *The World of Graft*, 182–83.

25 **"banded together in a secret"**: Roth, *Infamous Manhattan*, 213–14.

26 **"Let them kill each other"**: Reppetto, *American Mafia*, 24.

28 **"astonished every person"**: Reppetto, *American Mafia*, 14.

28 **"When courts fail"**: Reppetto, *American Mafia*, 15.

28 **"We want the dagos"**: Reppetto, *American Mafia*, 15.

33 **"When murder and blackmail"**: Lardner and Reppetto, *NYPD*, 131.

34 **During the last 13 years**: "Taft and M'Kay at Police Dinner," *New York Times*, February 22, 1914.

37 **"hunt this policeman"**: Reppetto, *American Mafia*, 86.

3. MURDER IN HOLLYWOOD

If there is any place where the truth is less likely to be found, it is Hollywood and the surrounding city of Los Angeles. Lying about simple matters, such as one's age, birthdate, and true name, is routine. Los Angeles journalists traditionally subscribed to the motto "Never let the truth get in the way of a good story."

The Thelma Todd case is examined in Wolf and Mader, *Fallen Angels*, chapter 18. Various individuals are cited as the possible killers.

General information on the Los Angeles police, including men like Capt. "Red" Hynes and Capt. Guy McAfee, as well as the Harry Raymond bombing, is contained in Woods, "The Progressives and the Police," and Domanick, *To Protect and to Serve*.

Various individuals have tried to identify the murderer in the William Desmond Taylor case. Kirkpatrick in *A Cast of Killers* puts the blame on Charlotte Shelby. Giroux in *A Deed of Death* attributes the crime to a gang of assassins working for drug dealers. Higham in *Murder in Hollywood* names Mary Miles Minter as the killer. Mann in *Tinseltown* fingers a minor movie actress named Margaret Gibson. The lead detective, Lt. Eddie King, always believed that Charlotte Shelby was the one who shot Taylor.

41 **"Mr. Taylor's dead"**: Giroux, *A Deed of Death*, 7.

44 **Upon banning her films**: Giroux, *A Deed of Death*, 219.

46 **"I am the ghost"**: Giroux, *A Deed of Death*, 131.

46 **When two Chicago journalists**: Giroux, *A Deed of Death*, 180.

48 **"Dearest Dear"**: Wolf and Mader, *Fallen Angels*, 138.

50 **With his one-year appointment**: Woods, "The Progressives and the Police," 219.

4. THE HALL-MILLS MURDERS

Tomlinson's *Fatal Tryst* provides a full analysis of the Hall-Mills case. Kunstler's *The Hall-Mills Murder Case* is an attempt to place the blame on the Ku Klux Klan, but he lacks any real foundation to do that. Tomlinson points out that a finding of not guilty, which was the eventual verdict in the case, is not the same thing as innocent. The first is a legal judgment that the case was not proven, and the other is a factual one.

On Mayor Frank Hague of Jersey City, see Steinberg, *The Bosses*.

Books on New Jersey police include Coakley's semiofficial *Jersey Troopers*. More information on the New Jersey police, including the troopers, the big-city detectives from Jersey City and Newark, and the FBI, is found in the chapter on the Lindbergh kidnapping and murder.

Among the puff pieces on Ellis Parker is Pratt, *The Cunning Mulatto*.

58 **He became known nationally**: Steinberg, *The Bosses*, 56.

61 **"I suppose only Mohammedans"**: Kunstler, *The Hall-Mills Murder Case*, 151.

63 **After having devoted**: Allen, *Only Yesterday*, 214.

67 **In fact, Parker left**: Coakley, *Jersey Troopers*, 17–18.

68 **"When Adolph S. Ochs"**: Tomlinson, *Fatal Tryst*, 296.

5. THE BIG SQUADS ROLL

Studies of the Chicago police are often more sensational than accurate. The best is former FBI special agent in charge Peterson's *Barbarians in Our Midst* (the title refers to the Chicago Mafia). Peterson headed the crime commission in Chicago for over twenty-five years and was a very careful investigator.

The principal source for information on the Rondout robbery is McPhaul, "'Inside' on the Great Rondout Train Robbery." In the years between the world wars, McPhaul was Chicago's most knowledgeable police reporter. He not only wrote a number of books but ghosted others. If anybody knew where the bodies were buried it was McPhaul.

Much of the information on the Chicago police is based on my personal knowledge and the recollections of older friends and relatives who were involved in law enforcement and crime from around 1914 on.

The Drake Hotel murder was committed in 1944. Less than a decade later, I was working with (mostly under) the men who had investigated the case. In the few times it was mentioned, I never heard any convincing argument as to who the killer was. Most of what has been written on the murder, such as a series of articles in the *Chicago Tribune* by Capt. Tom Harrison of the Chicago police, are simply the opinions of various reporters and detectives. I have speculated that the police relied far too much on polygraph tests.

The Leopold and Loeb case has been the subject of several books and movies. Clarence Darrow, too, has been chronicled many times. I prefer not to recommend any particular account.

72 **"stormy, husky, brawling"**: Sandburg, *The Complete Poems of Carl Sandburg*, 3.

83 **"You can't lose"**: Stone, "The Rondout Train Robbery," Chicago Historic Living Examiner, last modified March 7, 2009, http://www.examiner.com/article/the -rondout-train-robbery (site no longer available).

6. ELIOT NESS PURSUES THE BUTCHER

A recent biography of Ness is Perry, *Eliot Ness*.

The Mad Butcher case has been the subject of many books, such as Nickel, *Torso*. Martin, who in his day was among America's top crime writers, tackled the subject in "Butcher's Dozen." However, he was not able to come to a conclusion about the murderer. Despite lengthy investigations by some competent people, the crimes remain as much of a mystery today as they did then.

The Dr. Sam Sheppard case is covered in Neff, *The Wrong Man*. Though Sheppard was eventually acquitted, many people believe that he was guilty of killing his wife.

The Texarkana murders and the role of Capt. "Lone Wolf" Gonzaullas are covered in Presley, *The Phantom Killer*.

A recent biography of Capt. Frank Hamer is Boessenecker, *Texas Ranger*.

94 **"I've got a bad feeling"**: Nickel, *Torso*, 14.

106 **The *Cleveland Press* ran**: Editorial, *Cleveland Press*, July 21, 1954.

106 **The newspaper ran**: Editorial, *Cleveland Press*, July 30, 1954.

109 **"There is only one riot"**: Boessenecker, *Texas Ranger*, 55.

109 **"I don't want to kill you"**: Presley, *The Phantom Killer*, 3.

7. THE INSPECTORS BUREAU

One of many works on the 1916 San Francisco bombing and the imprisonment of Tom Mooney is Frost, *The Mooney Case*.

The adventures of Captain Dullea and his associates are chronicled in Graysmith's book on San Francisco murders, *The Laughing Gorilla*.

The impact of the 1934 waterfront strike and the corruption investigation that occurred a few years later are analyzed by J. W. Ehrlich, a criminal lawyer and counsel to police organizations, in *A Life in My Hands*.

Long-suppressed information about the V-J Day riots is contained in Fracchia, *City by the Bay*, 26–28, Mullen, *The Toughest Gang in Town*, 259–60; and Carl Nolte, "San Francisco/The Dark Side of V-J Day/The Story of the City's Deadliest Riot Has Been Largely Forgotten," SFGATE, August 15, 2005, http://www.sfgate.com/bayarea/article/SAN-FRANCISCO-The-dark-side-of-V-J-Day-The-2647870.php.

The Moskovitz kidnapping in 1954 was covered by the national press. See. for example, the *New York Times*, January 20 and 21 of that year.

The transition from the old San Francisco to the new San Francisco and the "White Night" riots are discussed by former deputy chief Kevin Mullen in *The Toughest Gang in Town*, 4–10. Mullen was in command of the police efforts on that night. For the recollections of Capt. Dan McKlem, see Virtual Museum of the City of San Francisco, "Chinatown Tong Wars of the 1920s," accessed June 11, 2016, http://www.sfmuseum.org/sfpd/sfpd4.html.

113 **A question that always perplexed**: Ehrlich, *A Life in My Hands*, 87–88.

115 **Years later, Matheson would boast**: Mullen, *The Toughest Gang in Town*, 198.

118 **"That's the bastard"**: Graysmith, *The Laughing Gorilla*, 24, 25.

120 **When Warren's men**: Katcher, *Earl Warren*, 130.

123 **"The unions held everything up"**: Virtual Museum of the City of San Francisco, "The Modern San Francisco Police Department, 1920–1940," accessed June 11, 2016, http://www.sfmuseum.org/sfpd/sfpd5.html.

125 **A prime target**: Graysmith, *The Laughing Gorilla*, 143.

127 **Dullea agreed, but Ahern's request:** San Francisco Police Department, "Chief Thomas J. Cahill: A Life in Review," accessed April 2, 2016, http://sanfranciscopolice .org/chief-thomas-jcahill-life-review.

128 **The note said he was being held:** "Coast Man Saved, 2 Seized in $500,000 Kidnap Case," *New York Times*, January 20, 1954.

129 **From then on, San Francisco:** C. P. Trussell, "FBI Chief Says Reds Incite Youth," *New York Times*, July 18, 1960.

8. NEW YORK MYSTERIES

An account of the Rubel robbery is contained in Alexander's two-part "Annals of Crime: Robbery in Brooklyn."

For a profile of detective Johnny Cordes, see Sayre, "Profiles: With the Meat in Their Mouth," parts 1 and 2

Frank Phillips is the central character in Reynolds's nonfiction work *Headquarters*. As noted, Reynolds viewed all his police subjects in a highly favorable light.

On Judge Crater's disappearance, see Maeder, *Big Town—Big Time*, chapter 9.

On the Schuster murder, see Maeder, *Big Town—Big Time*, chapter 116.

On Willie Sutton's life and times, see his and Linn's *Where the Money Was*.

131 **La Guardia, visibly upset:** Reynolds, *Headquarters*, 175.

145 **"They sent the first team":** Reynolds, *Headquarters*, 156.

146 **"No my name is Gordon":** Maeder, *Big Town—Big Time*, 122.

9. THE REAL CRIME OF THE CENTURY

Many books have been written on the Lindbergh kidnapping. Among the best is Waller, *Kidnap*.

FBI agent Leon Turrou's work is discussed in his autobiography, *Where My Shadow Falls*.

J. Edgar Hoover, once a national hero, now receives mostly negative mention. A balanced biography of Hoover is Powers, *Secrecy and Power*.

148 **Walsh was a special favorite:** Coakley, *Jersey Troopers*, 16.

149 **"Some guy said he was Colonel Lindbergh":** Berg, *Lindbergh*, 240.

159 **Even Hauptmann asked Reilly:** Berg, *Lindbergh*, 328.

160 **"I have the impression that":** Waller, *Kidnap*, 594.

164 **In the early thirties:** Burrough, *Public Enemies*, 368.

165 **Gen. George Marshall:** Brown, *The Last Hero*, 159.

10. AMERICA UNDER ASSAULT

An interesting book on the German bombing campaign in World War I is Blum, *Dark Invasion*. See also Reppetto, *Battleground New York City*, chapter 2.

A well-researched book on the Wall Street bombing is Gage, *The Day Wall Street Exploded*. Note also Watson, *Sacco and Vanzetti*, which, like most recent accounts, places the blame for the explosion on Mike Boda, who was angry over the deportation of the leader of his anarchist band, Luigi Galleani, and the arrest of two of its members, Sacco and Vanzetti.

The 1940 world's fair bombing, in contrast to the Wall Street bombing, has received little attention. There is not even a good suspect. An account of the crime is contained in Esposito and Gerstein, *Bomb Squad*.

A story of Nazi espionage before World War II is found in Ronnie's biography of Germany's agent Col. Fritz Joubert Duqesne, *Counterfeit Hero*.

Concerning the Tresca murder, the definitive account is Gallagher, *All the Right Enemies*.

173 **When the phone rang:** Whalen, *Mr. New York*, 35.

176 **Two days earlier:** Reppetto, *Battleground New York City*, 144.

182 **"God dammit if Vito":** Gallagher, *All the Right Enemies*, 237.

182 **In 1938 Tresca told:** "U.S. Jury Will Sift Poyntz Mystery," *New York Times*, February 9, 1938.

II. THE BLACK DAHLIA MURDER

Wolfe, *The Black Dahlia Files*, contains considerable detail on the crime. Webb, *The Badge*, is more a puff piece for the Los Angeles Police Department.

On Det. John St. John, see Martinez, *Jigsaw John*.

A work that gives the flavor of gangster-era Los Angeles is Lewis's biography of Mickey Cohen, *Hollywood's Celebrity Gangster*.

On Chief Parker's weaknesses, see Gates with Shah, *Chief*.

184 **"Hell, someone's cut this girl":** Wolfe, *The Black Dahlia Files*, 10.

191 **The famous LA detective John St. John:** Reppetto, *American Police:1945–2012*, 217.

194 **As Brown would later observe:** John Dreyfus and Howard Hertel, "Thad Brown: Storybook Success," *Los Angeles Times*, January 21, 1968.

12. THE BRINK'S JOB

Behn's *Big Stick-Up at Brink's* spends more time exploring the work of the Boston Police Department than O'Keefe's *The Men Who Robbed Brink's*, which is almost entirely from the point of view of the FBI. Schorow, *The Crime of the Century*, is a good recent reference for the facts of the case.

Whyte's perceptive comments on the Boston Police Department are found in his *Street Corner Society*, 123–39. A description of the Boston police in the 1930s is found in Harrison, *Police Administration in Boston*.

Boser, *The Gardner Heist*, is an account of the Gardner Museum robbery.

The Bobby Greenlease case in Kansas City is related in Heidenry, *Zero to the Bone*. Relevant newspaper articles are "Hall Is Believed Abduction Slayer; FBI Presses Search for Second Man," *New York Times*, October 9, 1953, and "Woman Is Accused in Kidnapping Tip," *New York Times*, October 26, 1953.

200 **At 7:27 p.m. on January 17, 1950**: Schorow, *The Crime of the Century*, 8.

13. A DEATH IN DALLAS

A history of the Dallas Police Department, with information on Capt. Will Fritz and local criminals, is contained in Stowers, *Partners in Blue*.

Chicago police superintendent O. W. Wilson's career is covered in Bopp's *"O.W."*

221 **"Once you get organized"**: Peterson, *Barbarians in Our Midst*, 294.

Bibliography

Alexander, Jack. "Annals of Crime: Robbery in Brooklyn—I." *New Yorker*, May 13, 1939.

———. "Annals of Crime: Robbery in Brooklyn—II." *New Yorker*, May 20, 1939.

Allen, Frederick Lewis. *Only Yesterday: An Informal History of the Nineteen-Twenties*. New York: Harper, 1931.

Behn, Noel. *Big Stick-Up at Brink's*. New York: C. P. Putnam and Sons, 1977.

Berg, A. Scott. *Lindbergh*. New York: Berkley Books, 1999.

Blum, Howard. *Dark Invasion: 1915: Germany's Secret War and the Hunt for the First Terrorist Cell in America*. New York: Harper, 2014.

Boessenecker, John. *Texas Ranger: The Epic the Life of Frank Hamer, the Man Who Killed Bonnie and Clyde*. New York: St. Martin's, 2016.

Bopp, William J. *"O.W.":O. W. Wilson and the Search for a Police Profession*. Port Washington NY: Kennikat Press, 1977.

Boser, Ulrich. *The Gardner Heist: The True Story of the World's Largest Unsolved Art Theft*. New York: Smithsonian Books/HarperCollins, 2009.

Bratton, William, with Peter Knobler. *Turnaround: How America's Top Cop Reversed the Crime Epidemic*. New York: Random House, 1998.

Brown, Anthony Cave. *The Last Hero: Wild Bill Donovan*. New York: Times Books, 1982.

Bugliosi, Vincent. *Outrage: The Five Reasons Why O.J. Simpson Got Away with Murder*. New York: W. W. Norton, 1996.

Burns, William J. *The Masked War*. New York: George H. Doran, 1913.

Burrough, Bryan. *Public Enemies: America's Greatest Crime Wave and the Birth of the FBI, 1933–34*. New York: Penguin Press, 2004.

Caesar, Gene. *Incredible Detective*. Englewood Cliffs NJ: Prentice-Hall, 1961.

Citizens' Police Committee. *Chicago Police Problems*. Chicago: University of Chicago Press, 1931.

Coakley, Leo J. *Jersey Troopers*. New Brunswick NJ: Rutgers University Press, 1971.

Conway, J. North. *The Big Policeman: The Rise and Fall of America's First, Most Ruthless and Greatest Detective*. Guilford CT: Lyons Press, 2010.

Daley, Robert. *Target Blue: An Insider's View of the NYPD*. New York: Delacorte, 1973.

Doherty, James. "History of the Chicago Crime Commission." *Police Digest*, December 1960.

Domanick, Joe. *To Protect and to Serve: The LAPD's Century of War in the City of Dreams*. New York: Pocket Books, 1994.

Ehrlich, J. W. *A Life in My Hands: An Autobiography*. New York: Putnam, 1965.

Esposito, Richard, and Ted Gerstein. *Bomb Squad: A Year Inside the Nation's Most Exclusive Police Unit*. New York: Hyperion, 2007.

Fiaschetti, Michael. *You Gotta Be Rough: The Adventures of Detective Fiaschetti of the Italian Squad as Told to Prosper Buranelli by Michael Fiaschetti*. Garden City NY: Doubleday, Durand, 1930.

Flynt, Josiah. *The World of Graft*. New York: McClure, Phillips, 1901.

Fogelson, Robert M. *Big-City Police*. Cambridge MA: Harvard University Press, 1977.

Fox, Stephen R. *Blood and Power: Organized Crime in Twentieth-Century America*. New York: W. Morrow, 1989.

Fracchia, Charles A. *City by the Bay: A History of Modern San Francisco, 1945–Present*. Encinitas CA: Heritage Media, 1997.

Frost, Richard H. *The Mooney Case*. Stanford CA: Stanford University Press, 1968.

Gage, Beverly. *The Day Wall Street Exploded: A Story of America in Its First Age of Terror*. New York: Oxford University Press, 2009.

Gallagher, Dorothy. *All the Right Enemies: The Life and Murder of Carlo Tresca*. New Brunswick NJ: Rutgers University Press, 1988.

Gates, Daryl F., with Diane K Shah. *Chief: My Life in the LAPD*. New York: Bantam, 1992.

Giroux, Robert. *A Deed of Death: The Story of the Unsolved Murder of Hollywood Director William Desmond Taylor*. New York: Knopf, 1990.

Graysmith, Robert. *The Laughing Gorilla: The True Story of the Hunt for One of America's First Serial Killers*. New York: Berkley, 2009.

———. *Zodiac Unmasked: The Identity of America's Most Elusive Serial Killer Revealed*. New York: Berkley, 2002.

Greenwood, Peter W., and Joan Petersilia. *The Criminal Investigation Process*. Vol. 1, *Summary and Policy Implications*. Santa Monica CA: RAND, October 1975.

Harrison, Leonard V. *Police Administration in Boston*. Cambridge MA: Harvard University Press, 1934.

Heidenry, John. *Zero at the Bone: The Playboy, the Prostitute, and the Murder of Bobby Greenlease*. New York: St. Martin's, 2009.

Higham, Charles. *Murder in Hollywood: Solving a Silent Screen Mystery*. Madison: University of Wisconsin Press, 2004.

Hodel, Steve. *Black Dahlia Avenger: The True Story*. New York: Arcade Publishing, 2003.

Horan, James David. *The Pinkertons: The Detective Dynasty That Made History*. New York: Crown, 1967.

Independent Commission on the Los Angeles Police Department. *Report of the Independent Commission on the Los Angeles Police Department*. July 1991.

Kantor, MacKinlay. *Signal Thirty-Two*. New York: Random House, 1950.

Katcher, Leo. *Earl Warren: A Political Biography*. New York: McGraw-Hill, 1967.

Kelling, George L., and Catherine M. Coles. *Fixing Broken Windows: Restoring Order and Reducing Crime in Our Communities*. New York: Free Press, 1998.

Kessler, Ronald. *The FBI: Inside the World's Most Powerful Law Enforcement Agency*. New York: Pocket Books, 1993.

———. *The Secrets of the FBI*. New York: Crown Forum, 2011.

Kirkpatrick, Sidney D. *A Cast of Killers: The Sensational True Story of Hollywood's Most Scandalous Murder-Cover Up for Sixty Years and Solved at Last by the Great Film Director King Vidor*. New York: Random House, 1961.

Kunstler, William. *The Hall-Mills Murder Case: The Minister and the Choir Singer*. New Brunswick NJ: Rutgers University Press, 1996.

Kurkjian, Stephen. *Master Thieves: The Boston Gangsters Who Pulled Off the World's Greatest Art Heist*. New York: PublicAffairs, 2016.

Lait, Jack, and Lee Mortimer. *Washington Confidential*. New York: Crown, 1951.

Lardner, James, and Thomas Reppetto. *NYPD: A City and Its Police*. New York: Henry Holt, 2000.

Lehr, Dick, and Gerard O'Neill. *Black Mass: The True Story of the Unholy Alliance between the FBI and the Irish Mob*. New York: HarperCollins, 2000.

Levitt, Leonard. *NYPD Confidential: Power and Corruption in the Country's Greatest Police Force*. New York: Thomas Dunne Books, 2009.

Lewis, Brad. *Hollywood's Celebrity Gangster: The Incredible Life and Times of Mickey Cohen*. New York: Enigma Books, 2008.

Maeder, Jay. *Big Town—Big Time: A New York Epic, 1898–1998*. New York: Sports Publishing, 1998.

Mann, William J. *Tinseltown: Murder, Morphine, and Madness at the Dawn of Hollywood*. New York: Harper, 2014.

Maple, Jack, with Chris Mitchell. *The Crimefighter: Putting the Bad Guys out of Business*. New York: Doubleday, 1999.

Martin, John Bartlow. "Butcher's Dozen: The Cleveland Torso Murders." *Harpers*, November 1949.

Martinez, Al. *Jigsaw John*. Los Angeles: J. P. Tarcher, 1975.

Marx, Gary T. *Undercover: Police Surveillance in America*. Berkeley: University of California Press, 1988.

Mayor's Committee on Management. *The New York City Police Survey (Bruce Smith Report)*. New York: Institute of Public Administration, 1952.

McPhaul, John J. "'Inside' on the Great Rondout Train Robbery." *True Detective Mysteries*, April 1930.

Mullen, Kevin J. *The Toughest Gang in Town: Police Stories from Old San Francisco*. Novato CA: Noir Publications, 2005.

Murphy, Patrick, and Thomas Plate. *Commissioner: A View from the Top of American Law Enforcement*. New York: Simon & Shuster, 1977.

Neff, James. *The Wrong Man: The Final Verdict on the Dr. Sam Sheppard Murder Case*. New York: Random House, 2001.

New York City Police Department. *Policing New York City in the 1990s: The Strategy for Community Policing*. January 1991.

Nickel, Steven. *Torso: Eliot Ness and the Hunt for the Mad Butcher of Kingsbury Run*. New York: Avon Press, 1990.

Nizer, Louis. *The Jury Returns*. Garden City NY: Doubleday, 1966.

O'Keefe, Joseph James. *The Men Who Robbed Brink's: The Inside Story of One of the Most Famous Holdups in the History of Crime, as Told by Specs O'Keefe to Bob Considine, in Cooperation with the FBI*. New York: Random House, 1961.

Perry, Douglas. *Eliot Ness: The Rise and Fall of an American Hero*. New York: Penguin Books, 2014.

Peterson, Virgil. *Barbarians in Our Midst: A History of Chicago Crime and Politics*. Boston: Little, Brown, 1952.

Powers, Richard Gid. *Secrecy and Power: The Life of J. Edgar Hoover*. New York: Free Press, 1987.

Pratt, Fletcher. *The Cunning Mulatto and Other Cases of Ellis Parker American Detective, Told by Fletcher Pratt*. New York: H. Smith and R. Haas, 1935.

President's Commission on Law Enforcement and the Administration of Justice. *Task Force Report: The Police*. Washington DC: GPO, 1967.

Presley, James. *The Phantom Killer: Unlocking the Mystery of the Texarkana Serial Murders: The Story of a Town in Terror*. New York: Pegasus, 2014.

Reppetto, Thomas A. *American Mafia: The History of Its Rise to Power*. New York: Henry Holt, 2004.

——. *American Police: 1845–1945*. New York: Enigma Books, 2010.

——. *American Police: 1945–2012*. New York: Enigma Books, 2012.

——. *Battleground New York City: Countering Spies, Saboteurs, and Terrorists since 1861*. Washington DC: Potomac Books, 2012.

——. *Bringing Down the Mob: The War against the American Mafia*. New York: Henry Holt, 2006.

——. "The Influence of Police Organizational Style on Crime Control Effectiveness." *Journal of Police Science and Administration* 3, no. 3 (September 1975).

Reynolds, Quentin. *Headquarters*. New York: Harper, 1955.

Riffenburgh, Beau. *Pinkerton's Great Detective: The Amazing Life and Times of James McParland*. New York: Viking Press, 2013.

Riis, Jacob. *The Making of an American*. New York: Macmillan, 1901.

Ronnie, Art. *Counterfeit Hero: Fritz Duquesne, Adventurer and Spy*. Annapolis MD: Naval Institute Press, 1995.

Roth, Andrew. *Infamous Manhattan: A Colorful Walking Tour of New York's Most Notorious Crime Sites*. New York: Carroll Publishing Group, 1996.

Sandburg, Carl. *The Complete Poems of Carl Sandburg*. New York: Harcourt Brace Jovanovich, 1970.

Sayre, Joel. "Profiles: Wham! Pow! Zowie!" *New Yorker*, December 26, 1931.

———. "Profiles: With the Meat in Their Mouth—I." *New Yorker*, September 5, 1953.

———. "Profiles: With the Meat in Their Mouth—II." *New Yorker*, September 12, 1953.

Schorow, Stephanie. *The Crime of the Century: How the Brink's Robbers Stole Millions and the Hearts of Boston*. Beverly MA: Commonwealth Editions, 2008.

Shaplen, Robert. "Profiles: Not Like Taking the Waters." *New Yorker*, February, 27, 1954.

Skogan, Wesley G. *Disorder and Decline: Crime and the Spiral of Decay in American Neighborhoods*. New York: Free Press, 1990.

Smith, Bruce, Jr. *Police Systems in the United States*. 2nd rev. ed. New York: Harper, 1960.

Stead, Philip John. *The Police of France*. New York: Macmillan, 1983.

Steffens, Lincoln. *The Autobiography of Lincoln Steffens*. New York: Harcourt Brace, 1958.

Steinberg, Alfred. *The Bosses*. New York: Macmillan, 1972.

Stowers, Carlton. *Partners in Blue: The History of the Dallas Police Department*. Dallas: Taylor Publishing, 1983.

Summerscale, Kate. *The Suspicions of Mr. Wicker: A Shocking Murder and the Undoing of a Great Victorian Detective*. New York: Walker, 2008.

Sutton, Willie, and Edward Linn. *Where the Money Was: The Memoirs of a Bank Robber*. New York: Viking Press, 1976.

Timoney, John F. *Beat Cop to Top Cop: A Tale of Three Cities*. Philadelphia: University of Pennsylvania Press, 2010.

Tomlinson, Gerald. *Fatal Tryst: Who Killed the Minister and the Choir Singer?* Lake Hopatcong NJ: Homerun Press, 1999.

Turner, Ralph F. "Hans Gross: The Model of the Detective." In *Pioneers in Policing*. Montclair NJ: Patterson Smith, 1977.

Turrou, Leon G. *Where My Shadow Falls: Two Decades of Crime Detection*. Garden City NY: Doubleday, 1949.

Waller, George. *Kidnap: The Story of the Lindbergh Case*. New York: Dial Press, 1961.

Watson, Bruce. *Sacco and Vanzetti: The Men, the Murderers, and the Judgment of Mankind*. New York: Viking, 2007.

Webb, Jack. *The Badge*. Englewood Cliffs NJ: Prentice-Hall, 1958.

Webster, William H., and Hubert Williams. *A City in Crisis: A Report by the Special Advisor to the Board of Police Commissioners on Civil Disorders in Los Angeles*. October 21, 1992.

Weeks v. United States. 232 U.S. 383 (1914).

Weiner, Tim. *Enemies: A History of the FBI*. New York: Random House, 2012.

Welch, Neil J., and David W. Marston. *Inside Hoover's FBI: The Top Field Chief Reports*. Garden City NY: Doubleday, 1984.

Whalen, Grover. *Mr. New York: The Autobiography of Grover Whalen*. New York: Putnam, 1955.

Whitehead, Don. *The FBI Story: A Report to the People*. New York: Random House, 1956.

Whyte, William Foote. *Street Corner Society*. 2nd ed. Chicago: University of Chicago Press, 1955.

Wilson, James Q. *The Investigators: Managing FBI and Narcotics Agents*. New York: Basic Books, 1978.

———. *Varieties of Police Behavior: The Management of Law and Order in Eight Communities*. Cambridge MA: Harvard University Press, 1968.

Wilson, James Q., and George Kelling. "Broken Windows: The Police and Neighborhood Safety." *Atlantic Monthly*, March 1982.

Wolf, Marvin J., and Katherine Mader. *Fallen Angels: Chronicles of LA Crime & Mystery*. New York: Ballantine Books/Create Space, 2012.

Wolfe, Donald H. *The Black Dahlia Files: The Mob, the Mogul, and the Murder That Transfixed Los Angeles*. New York: HarperCollins, 2005.

Woods, Joseph G. "The Progressives and the Police: Urban Reform and the Professionalization of the Los Angeles Police." PhD diss., University of California, Los Angeles, 1973.

Index